Similes of the Buddha

Even for what is most subtle and incomprehensible within us, sensory equivalents can be found in nature.

Rainer Maria Rilke, *Werke*, 1955, vol. XI

Similes of the Buddha

An Introduction

by
Hellmuth Hecker

Buddhist Publication Society
P.O. Box 61
54, Sangaraja Mawatha
Kandy, Sri Lanka

First published 2009
Copyright © Buddhist Publication Society.

Cover art and design by Martha Aitchison. The cover illustrates the simile of the mountain that cannot be shaken by the strongest wind, a reference to the Perfection of Resolution.

National Library of Sri Lanka-Cataloguing in Publication Data

---

Hecker, Hellmuth
  Similes of the Buddha: An Introduction/ Hellmuth Hecker; Tr. by Ven. Khantipālo, Piyadhammo; ed. Ven. Nyanatusita.- Kandy: Buddhist Publication Society, 2009.- 216p; 22cm

  ISBN 978-955-24-0336-1   Price:Rs.

  i. 294.3 DDC 21   ii. Title
  iii. Ven. Piyadhammo, Khantipālo-tr.
  iv. Ven. Nyanatusita-ed

  01. Buddhism

ISBN 978-955-24-0336-1

Printed in Sri Lanka by
Creative Printers & Designers,
Bahirawakanda, Kandy.

CONTENTS

Publisher's Note viii
Introduction 1

PART 1: OUR BASIC SITUATION 9

1. The Lost Traveller in the Desert (MN 12.37–42) 9
2. The Man in the Well (Avadāna Sūtra) 13
3. The Escape to the Farther Shore (SN 35:238) 14
4. The Hollow Aggregates (SN 22:95) 17
5. Carried Away by the Current (SN 22:93) 20
6. The Border City and the Coral Tree (SN 35:245) 21
7. The Cow and the Lute (SN 35:246) 23
8. The Six Tied Animals (SN 35:247) 26
9. The Fire (MN 38) 28
10. The Two Oxen (SN 35:232–33) 29
11. The Similes of Nandaka (MN 146) 30
12. Striking a Sappy Tree (SN 35:231) 32
13. The Bait (SN 35:230) 33
14. The Ocean of Saṃsāra (SN 35:228) 34
15. The Tortoise and the Jackal (SN 35:240) 35

PART 2: DEPENDENT ORIGINATION 37

16. The Wheel of Existence 38
17. The Four Nutriments (SN 12:63) 46
18. The Painter and his Painting (SN 12:64) 51
19. Setting Fire to a Dry Grassland (SN 14:12) 54
20. The Deer in the Swamp (MN 19.25) 56
21. The Current to the Lake of Misfortune (It 4:10/109) 57
22. The Great Log in the Ganges (SN 35:241) 61
23. The Nutriments for Fires and Trees (SN 12:52–59) 64
24. The Germs (SN 22:54) 67
25. Rising Tide (SN 12:69) 70

PART 3: THE PATH TO LIBERATION AND ITS FRUITS 72

26. Taming the Horse (MN 65) 72
27. The Paddy Field (AN 8:34) 73
28. Similes for Monks (AN 3:92) 75
29. Making a Boat (AN 4:196) 77

v

30. Destroying the Tree (AN 4:195; SN 12:55–59) 79
31. When it Rains on the Mountain (SN 55:38) 80
32. The Hindrances on the Way (SN 22:84) 82

PART 4: THE NOBLE POWERS 84

33. The Mountain Fortress (AN 7:63) 84
34. The Noble Elephant (AN 6:43; Th 689–704) 87
35. The Royal Elephant (AN 5:140; cf. AN 4:114) 88
36. The Ploughman (SN 7:11 = Sn 76–82 with prose) 90
37. The Divine Chariot (SN 45:4) 93
38. The Non-rattling Chariot (SN 1:46 and commentary) 95
39. The Chariot of the Body (J 544) 96
40. Melting Gold (AN 3:70) 99
41. The Waxing Moon (SN 16:7; AN 10:67–68) 100
42. The Archer (Mil 7.7) 100
43. Similes for the Ten Perfections (Bv 2.117) 102
44. The Cure (MN 105) 103
45. The Chick, Adze and Boat (SN 22:101; AN 7:71) 105
46. The Seven Swimmers (AN 7:15) 107
47. The Riddle of the Termite Mound (MN 23) 110
48. The Glowing Chip of Iron (AN 7:52) 115

PART 5: PURIFICATION OF THE MIND 120

49. Purifying Gold (AN 3:100) 120
50. The Five Impurities (AN 5:23; SN 46:33) 122
51. The Brass Dish (MN 5) 123
52. The Dirty Cloth (MN 7) 125
53. The Five Hindrances (Adaptation of MN 39.14; DN 2) 126
54. The Water Mirror (AN 5:193; SN 46:55) 128
55. The Strangler Trees (SN 46:39) 129
56. The Obstructed Mountain Stream (AN 5:51) 131
57. Similes for Sensual Desire (MN 54, Thī 490–509) 132
58. The Leper (MN 75) 136
59. The Four Herds of Deer (MN 25) 138
60. The Pieces of Wood (MN 36.17–19) 140
61. The Flies (AN 3:126) 142
62. The Foolish Monkey (SN 47:7) 143
63. The Beauty Queen (SN 47:20) 144
64. Seed of the Bitter Gourd (AN 10:104) 146

65. The Hare Imitating the Bathing Elephant (AN 10:99) 147
66. Three Inscriptions (AN 3:130) 148
67. The Sore, Lightning Strike and Diamond (AN 3:25) 149
68. Shedding Old Skin (Sn 1–5) 149
69. Conquering the Citadel (MN 22; AN 5:71–72) 151
70. The Charnel Ground (AN 5:249) 152

PART 6: WHOLESOME SKILLS 154

71. The Divided River (SN 48:43) 154
72. The Mighty Ocean of the Dhamma (Ud 5.5; AN 8:19–20) . 155
73. The Four Noble Truths (SN 56:31–40) 156
74. The Noble Eightfold Path (SN 45:149–160) 159
75. Highest Diligence (SN 45:139–148; AN 10:15; SN 22:102) .. 160
76. The Three Fields and Water Pots (SN 42:7) 161
77. The Sticky Resin and the Dam (AN 4:178) 163
78. The Merchant (AN 3:20) 164
79. The Bamboo Pole Balancing Act (SN 47:19) 166
80. Seven Jewels (SN 46:42) 168
81. Six Causes for Falling Back (AN 6:60) 170
82. The Twelve States of Consciousness (DN 2; MN 77) 172
83. The Cowherd (MN 33; AN 11:18 & 23) 178
84. The Mice (AN 4:107) 183
85. The Palm Stump 184

Index of Similes in the Suttas   190
Abbreviations   207
Select Bibliography   207

Publisher's Note

This book is an introductory guide to the rich, wonderful and profound world of Buddhist similes.

In order to appreciate and make proper use of this book, a basic knowledge of the Buddha's teachings is required. A beginner might find this a hard book, because some of the similes, such as the one on the parents eating their child's flesh, are graphic and uncompromising.

The similes given are retellings or summaries, not literal translations of the originals. Dr. Hecker's explanations of the similes are based on his personal understanding of the suttas and he does not claim that they are definitive.

Bhikkhu Khantipālo and Bhikkhu Piyadhammo translated this book from the German.[1] They submitted their draft translation to the BPS in 2001, but the editor at that time found that it would be too much work to prepare the text for publication. After becoming editor of the BPS, I undertook the revision and editing with the help of others..

Dr. Hecker's writings contain many idioms, wordplays and reflective twists and turns, therefore an overly literal translation would be stilted and difficult to follow. Furthermore, the original book's similes and explanations were based on the German translations of the Buddha's discourses and therefore various adaptations had to be made to conform with the current, popular English translations of the suttas. Thus, this book has been edited in a style similar to Ven. Nyanaponika's and others' work on Dr. Hecker's articles on the Buddha's disciples.

John Bullit's "Index of Similes in the Suttas" (digitally available on the Access to Insight website) has been included as an appendix with permission of the author.

I would like to thank all those who kindly helped with preparing and proofreading this book.

Bhikkhu Nyanatusita

---

1. *Bilder Der Existenz*, Stammbach, 2005.

INTRODUCTION

"What walks on four legs in the morning, on two at noon, and on three in the evening?" This is the question the Sphinx of Thebes asked to passers-by. Those who could not answer the riddle were hurled into an abyss. One day, Oedipus came by and answered, "A person: In infancy, he crawls on all fours; in his prime, he walks on two legs; and in old age, he uses a stick."

Classical Greek literature is rich in such similes:[1] Homer's *Iliad* has one hundred and eighty two, and the *Odyssey* thirty nine.[2] Plato uses them skilfully in his dialogues; the simile of the cave in *The Republic* being the most well known and impressive.[3]

In Chinese literature the simile was also much appreciated, especially in a flowery form. The following anecdote is one of many similes found in Chuang Tzu's *The True Book of the Southern Blossom Land*:

A man once requested his friend to lend him some money because he had gotten into temporary difficulties. The friend, however, replied that he should come back later.

Then the man said, "Yesterday I went for a walk and saw a flatfish in a puddle left from a flood. It asked me for some water so that it wouldn't dry up. I replied, "I will go to the Lord of the West Sea and ask him for some water. Then you will get plenty." The flounder answered, "You may as well put me on a spit right now and sell me as dried fish!"

In Hinduism, there is an abundance of similes in both of its great epics—the *Mahābhārata* and the *Bhagavadgītā*—in the *Purāṇas,* in the *Pañcatantra*, in popular tales, and in the teachings of Rāmakrishna.[4] This is one of them:

---

1. See W. Bedell-Stanford, *Greek Metaphor*, Oxford, 1936.
2. H. Fränkel, *Die homerischen Gleichnisse*, Göttingen 1921
3. P. Louis, *Les metaphores du Platon*, Paris, 1945.
4. See J. Gonda, *Remarks and Similes in Sanskrit Literature*, Leiden, 1941.

A wise man once asked: "If one were to cover all of one's paths with leather in order to walk barefoot without stepping on thorns, glass, and dirt, would that be practical?"

"Of course not," was the reply. "If one puts on leather shoes, one would achieve the same much more easily."

"Similarly," continued the wise man, "if one wants to make the whole outside world smooth, one would never be finished. If, however, one purifies one's mind, one can go safely anywhere."

In Islam, a wide range of colourful, oriental similes is employed to clarify spiritual matters.[5] For example, life in this world is compared to that of a spider: with great effort she spins her web to catch flies—until the housewife comes and, in a twinkling of an eye, sweeps up the spider, the web and the fly. The Persian poet Farid Ud-Din-Attar gives this simile and many others, mostly in allegorical stories, in his famous *Conference of the Birds*.[6]

The New Testament of the Bible also contains many similes. This is one of the many that Jesus told in the four Gospels:

While working in a field, a farm labourer found a treasure, so he sold everything he had to buy the land. Everyone thought he was mad, but he knew what he was doing and he gained the treasure, which was incomparably worth much more than what he had owned before. In the same way, said Jesus, can the bliss of heaven be compared to the treasure in the field. If one has understood its great value, all worldly pleasures are trifling, and in risking everything, one gains everything.[7]

Of Jesus' similes, those of the Good Samaritan, Poor Lazarus and the Foolish Maidens have become proverbial. In the Christian mystical tradition too, there are many similes for the spiritual life. An excellent reason for the necessity of similes for

---

5. T. Sabbagh, *La métaphore dans le Coran*, Paris, 1943.
6. Farid Ud-Din-Attar, *The Conference of The Birds: Mantiq Ut-Tair*, 1177 CE. English transl. C. S. Nott, London, 1954.
7. J. Jeremig, *Die Gleichnisse Jesu*, Berlin 1956. W. Michaelis, *Die Gleichnisse Jesu*, Hamburg 1956. E. Biser, *Die Gleichnisse Jesu, Versuch einer Deutung*, München 1965.

each profound religious exposition can be found in Christian scholasticism. Thus the father of Catholic dogmatism, St. Thomas Aquinas (1225–1274), says in his *Summa Theologica*:

It is befitting Holy Writ to put forward divine and spiritual truths by means of comparisons with material things. For God provides for everything according to the capacity of its nature. Now, it is natural to man to attain to intellectual truths through sensible objects, because all our knowledge originates from the senses. Hence in Holy Writ, spiritual truths are fittingly taught under the likeness of material things. As Dionysius says "We cannot be enlightened by the divine rays except they be hidden within the covering of many sacred veils." It is also befitting Holy Writ that spiritual truths be expounded by means of figures taken from corporeal things, so that even the simple, who are unable by themselves to grasp intellectual things, may be able to understand.[8]

Thomas himself became a mystic through an experience of ecstatic absorption in the last year of his life. A few months before his death he had an unexpected revelation whereupon he stopped his *Summa Theologica* and said; "Whatever I have written appears like straw compared with what I have now experienced."[9]

However, the richest similes in world literature, comprehensively covering all aspects of theory and practice, are those in the discourses of the Buddha. Even before he started to teach, while as Bodhisatta was still striving for enlightenment, the definitive signpost for the way appeared to him in the simile of firewood (MN 36.17–19; see Simile 60). Fifty years later, at the end of his life, he compared his eighty year old body to an old cart which is kept going by being held together with straps (DN 16.2.25, SN 47:9). The whole of the Buddha's message, delivered over a span of forty-five years, is interspersed with similes. At

---

8. *Summa Theologica* Part 1, Article 9: "Whether holy scripture should use metaphors."
9. Joseph Piper, *Thomas von Aquino*, Hamburg 1956, p. 30 ff. Also see Paul Debes, *Meisterung der Existenz durch die Lehre des Buddha*, 1982.

every turn, in almost every discourse, one comes across a simile. In the whole of the Pali canon there are about a thousand of them. Mrs. C.A.F. Rhys Davids counted 568 concepts for which similes are used in the Canon, and mentions, for example, that water is the most used of the four elements, and of animals the elephant is most used:

If we were asked what would be the simile likely to recur with the greatest frequency in a literature, the birthplace of which was said to be the civilized sites of post-Vedic Northern India, it does not call for much imagination to reply 'river, notably the Ganges.' Now, if we group under earth, water, air, fire, all the figures in my index bearing on one of each of these elements, we find the numbers as follows: Earth, etc., 41; air (with clouds and space), 32; fire (*aggi, pāvaka, jātaveda, teja*, etc., with the sun as 'burner,' *ādicca*), 58; water, 114. Of this 114, water in any shape—drops, etc. (*udaka, vāri*)—numbers 31; pool (*rahada*), 14; sea (*samudda, sāgara*, etc., *aṇṇava*), 21; flood (*ogha*), 14; and river (*nadī, saritā, sota*), 35. 'Mountain' might gain, in the question above, a good many votes. And, indeed, under 'earth,' (*pabbata, giri, sela*) recur 18 times. But it should be remembered that, except at the great Buddhist centre of Sāvatthī in Nepal ... the Himalayas ... were but an unseen mythical vision of glory. ... Of animals, the elephant (*kuñjara, gaja, nāga, hatthī*), as might be expected, recurs oftenest; next to him coming that 'chief friend of ours,' the cow. With her appurtenances—bull, calf, herd, and butcher—she occurs some 30 times or more. Horse, snake, deer, and bird (excluding bird species) follow in fairly close succession, approximately 24, 17, 16, and 14 times, the camel, goat, wolf, watchdog, cat, and mouse appearing at the bottom of the list. The lion (*sīha*) makes a fairly good third, while the relative silence respecting the tiger (*vyaggha*) is a feature shared by the oldest Vedic literature. ... Taken together, the facts seem to indicate that the lion, when these books were compiled, was more or less extinct throughout the valley of the Ganges. As we should expect from an old literature, the moon is twice as frequent a simile as the sun. Not surprising, again, is the frequent reference to the tree. Forest, grove, jungle, and creeper all play their part, but tree,

Introduction

as tree unspecified, is used in some 24 varieties of figure. The moderate but interesting role allotted to the lotus (*uppala, kumuda, paduma, puṇḍarīka, pokkhara*) marks a midway position between its non-appearance in the Vedas and its prominence in later poetry. Of human contrivances the most prominent images are the house (24), the way or path (27), the field, seed, and plough (about 30), the ship or boat (13), vehicles and drivers (30), and the snare, trap, and hook (23). Inspection of this sort might be indulged in to any extent. Here let it suffice to odd that the numbers given above are only of the different varieties in each figure e.g., of the clarity, depth, swiftness, etc., of water and not of the times each variety occurs.[10]

This book is intended to draw attention to the similes of the Buddha, and to contribute toward an understanding and appreciation of this wonderful treasure. However, it is not—and cannot be—a first introduction to the Buddha's teachings; a basic knowledge is assumed. It is recommended that one reads the relevant sutta or passage and contemplates it on one's own before reading the explanations given here.

Completeness is not the aim of this book. It just intends to stimulate, to give an impetus to learn from these similes, to create a bridge of understanding, and to provide easier access to the ways and methods of Buddhist similes. Therefore the reader should not expect to find a comprehensive explanation, in the form of a meditative discourse or sermon, such as that given by the German theologian Prof. Thielicke for the similes of Jesus.[11] His work was possible only because the Christian similes and associated concepts permeate our Western cultural understanding, so that the topic could easily be enriched by indicating known facts and

---

10. "Similes in the Nikāyas," *Journal of the Pali Text Society* 1906/7, pp. 52–151. See also the essay "Buddhist Parables and Legends" by the same author which appeared in instalments in 1908 in the American journal *Open Court;* and E.W. Burlingame, *Buddhist Parables*, New Haven 1922. In German, see Paul Dahlke, "Gleichnis-Gleichung," in *Brockensammlung* 1926, pp. 28–48.
11. Helmut Thielicke, *Das Bilderbuch Gottes. Reden über die Gleichnisse Jesu*, Stuttgart 1957.

relationships. All of this is missing with regard to Buddhism, which has been known in Europe for not much longer than hundred years. Buddhism's Indian background is especially evident in similes. Therefore a more simple method of introduction to the Buddhist similes is required.

In order to understand Buddhist similes, one first of all needs a certain sensitivity to spiritual matters in general. The Buddha gives his similes with the intention of making unknown or concealed things easier to understand. Like Jesus, he starts from concrete sense-experience, from the colourful variety of everyday life—that which one has before one's own eyes. The things of everyday life are taken in their deeper sense, so that usually the image chosen contains in itself an illuminative and striking revelation. This gives the listener faith in the penetrative vision and comprehensive experience of the Buddha. Then these images are transferred from daily life to corresponding spiritual, mental, and other-worldly states and conditions. Thus each simile leads from the known to the unknown. This is only possible with such surprising precision because, in the final analysis, the sense-world is just a reflection of the mind, a simile of the psyche. Because of this, it can be noticed easily and with increasing clarity that the whole world is nothing but a symbol of psychological forces. That is why the similes are not just embellishments or interesting folkloristic additions or concessions to human superficiality, but one of the principal means to show the unity of the inner and the outer, of the world and the psyche. Viewed from this perspective, similes turn out to be one of the core teaching elements for the understanding of the mental character of phenomena.

The authenticity of the texts can be measured by the quantity and significance of similes. One of the characteristics of many post-classic Buddhist texts is the total absence of similes. This absence contributes to the dryness and dullness of the Abhidhamma works. Studying these texts, one could get the impression that, in contrast to the discourses (suttas), the authors had had no understanding of the unity of the inner and outer and therefore were unable to create similes..

Introduction

One exception seems to be the *Milindapañhā* ("Questions of King Milinda"), written in about 100 CE, which almost flows over with new similes. These similes, however, are not always of high quality. Sometimes shallow or unclear images are used, obscuring problems that were explained by the Buddha with clear and powerful similes. There are few gold-nuggets, comparable to the original rich similes in the suttas, for example, the Simile of the Archer, which is Simile 42 in this book. Nevertheless, the *Milindapañhā* shows that an abundance of similes is not a guarantee for the profoundness of a later Buddhist text, though the absence of similes is a sure indication for being distant from the Buddha.

In the Buddhist literature of even later times the content of similes is meagre. Where they appear, especially in the colourful, long Mahāyāna texts, they mostly disappoint in comparison with the original canonical texts. They are rather playful and more literary ornaments than guides to the realization of reality. Nevertheless, wherever the knowledge of the simile-like nature of things is taken seriously, substantial similes can be found again here and there, for example in the early Chinese Chan tradition. Later, however, this tradition froze the similes into lifeless koans.

The oldest similes, as found in the Pali canon,[12] are scattered throughout the texts. In the Majjhima-Nikāya, there is a special "Chapter of Similes" (*Opamma-vagga*) (MN 21–30), and in the Saṃyutta-Nikāya, there is a special book called "Connected Discourses with Similes" (*Opamma-saṃyutta*) (SN 20). Yet many of the most profound and imaginative similes are found elsewhere.

Roughly four kinds of similes can be distinguished:

Comprehensive similes: These are the so-called parables, which often are extended into a story such as in the "Chapter with (the Simile of) the Poisonous Snakes" (SN 35, ch. 19). Such

---

12. The canons of other early Buddhist schools are extant in manuscript fragments and in Chinese translations. The suttas and the similes contained in them are quite similar or identical to those of the Pali canon.

extensive similes concern at least one of the Four Noble Truths. In this book, they are represented in the first three chapters.

Specific similes: By far the majority are similes on specific points of the teaching or on particular relationships. Some deal with only one attribute of the teaching; others with several. There is also the occasional parable, but usually they are allegories or simple comparisons. There are a large number of these in the texts. Some particularly profound and striking images are selected in the latter part of this book.

Illustrative similes: There are many situational, illustrative images appearing in the flow of the discourses, illuminating them. Such comparisons are usually self-explanatory and are therefore rarely included in this book.

Concrete similes: The Buddha sometimes created similes by tangible, concrete demonstrations—for example, by turning a vessel upside down (MN 61.2–6), by picking up leaves (SN 56:31), or by taking up a little dust on his fingernail (SN 13:1; SN 20:2; SN 56:51). Sometimes he used what his audience was experiencing at that moment—for example, what they were hearing (a jackal screaming, SN 20:11–12), or seeing (a log of wood carried down the Ganges river, SN 35:241–42; moths flying into the flame of an oil-lamp, Ud 6.9). These comparisons are usually self-explanatory.

Apart from these four types, the Buddha, with his thirty-two "marks of a Great Man," was himself a walking symbol. His body was a picture book of the virtues he had acquired in earlier lives. This physical image puzzle is meticulously solved in the Lakkhaṇa Sutta.[13]

---

13. DN 30. Discussed in length in Hecker H., *Die Merkmale von Staat und Ernte, insbesondere nach der 30. Lehrrede der Längeren Sammlung*, Hamburg 1991.

Part 1

OUR BASIC SITUATION

In the first of the Four Noble Truths, the Truth of Suffering, the Buddha describes the existential inadequacy a person experiences. This is the starting point of all questioning and searching for improvement. Before one can improve anything, one has to make a thorough analysis of the situation and correctly take stock of the facts. Such an existential account of the totality of inadequacy is given by the Buddha when he expounds the five aggregates (*khandha*) of form, feeling, perception, mental activity and consciousness. These five categories designate and comprise all transitory, conditioned phenomena. The condition for their arising, craving (*taṇhā*), is mentioned in the second of the Four Noble Truths.

The five aggregates as such are mentioned only in very few similes; instead, to facilitate understanding, the Buddha usually employed more accessible and concrete illustrations of them. Thus he would often start concretely at the inner six sense-bases—the five senses and the mind—and their inseparable outer counterparts, i.e., what is nowadays called the "subject-object relationship."

The five aggregates, their range of implications, and the six sense-bases are the topic of this part of the book. It is unavoidable that elements of topics treated here also appear in later parts and vice versa; however, the focal point here is comprehension of the basic existential situation.

1. The Lost Traveller in the Desert (MN 12.37–42)

Scorched by the sun, a lost traveller wandering through a desert area is weary, exhausted, trembling, thirsty. He seeks refreshment, a cool drink, a cooling bath and a pleasant shady spot, however, not knowing which direction he should go, he takes a path going straight towards a charcoal pit full of glowing embers, deeper than a man's height and without apparent flame or smoke, and falls into it. Stuck in it, full of terror, he experiences extremely painful, burning and piercing feelings.

Without knowing where it goes, he can also take a path going straight towards a cesspit, deeper than a man's height, full of stinking filth, disgusting and loathsome. He falls into it and is stuck helplessly in the excrement, experiencing extremely painful, burning, piercing feelings.

Or he takes a path going straight towards a rocky spot where a thirsty, almost dried up tree stands, with stunted branches and few leaves and only small patches of shadow. He sits or lies down in the sparse shade of that tree, which protects him only a little from the sun, and still he is filled with many painful feelings.

Or he takes a path going straight towards a tree growing in good soil, having a broad canopy of lush green foliage, and with deep shade. Sitting or lying under the tree, he experiences some well-being. Glad to have escaped from the sun and heat, he enjoys the shade.

Or he takes a path going straight towards a spacious mansion, plastered within and without, with a pleasing balustrade and scented sunscreens in front of the windows. Inside is a couch spread with rugs, blankets, the softest antelope coverlets, and crimson pillows for both head and feet. There he rests in the pleasant coolness on the soft, splendid couch, feeling only bliss.

Or, having been told by an experienced traveller that this is the right path, he takes a path going straight towards a lotus pond with clean, agreeable, refreshing, clear water. The pond has smooth banks and is near a dense, shady forest. Delighted, the exhausted traveller plunges into the water, bathing, then drinking his fill, and when all the distress and fever of exhaustion is stilled, he sits or lies down in the forest grove, desireless, happy, feeling only bliss.

Explanation

Broadly, the *lost traveller* represents the mind or heart. The *desert* is the round of existence, saṃsāra. The *scorching sun* equates to painful feelings. *Thirst* is craving, the desire for well-being, refreshment, and quenching. The *shade* denotes decreasing painful feelings. The *bathing* and *drinking* are the cessation of thirst, of craving. *Taking the path* to the first five places is ignorance.

The *pit of burning embers* is hell where, in addition to the burning sun, hellfire is burning. There are no flames and no smoke to warn one. One does not expect hell; it appears unexpectedly. It is as though one is grabbed and thrown in by two strong men (SN 12:63). Only when one's demeritorious kamma has expired can one get out. In hell there is only all-pervasive, excruciating pain. The Buddha said that it is hard to give a simile for the suffering in hell. The pain of a man who suffered a hundred sword strokes three times a day would, in relation to the suffering in hell, be like a pebble compared to the Himalayas (MN 129).

The *stinking cesspit* is the animal realm with its dumbness and coarseness, where there is nothing higher than feeding and procreation and the constant threat of enemies. One eats or is eaten; all soon become excrement and manure. The animal world is full of pain, with little well-being that must be paid for by diving into the pungent manure to get away from the burning sun. According to the Buddha, it is not easy to express the suffering of the animal realm in words. The likelihood of a blind turtle, rising to the surface of the four great oceans only once every hundred years, and putting its head through a bobbing, wind-tossed, single-holed yoke is greater than that of an animal becoming a human being again (MN 129.24; SN 56:47–48).

The *thirsty, almost dried up tree* represents the realm of hungry and thirsty ghosts, the petas. The tree grows in rocky, poor soil. The soil of merit—the foundation—is very poor. One has done just enough good to avoid being reborn in the animal realm or in hell. Only a little shade can develop under this tree, one still predominantly feels hunger, thirst and pain.

The *tree with lush foliage* is the human realm. To be born as a human, one must have done much good, i.e., one has to have the fertile soil of merit. Some comfort and well-being can develop there, like deep, cooling shade. There one can enjoy the fruits of one's merit, but the heat of the sun is still very close and there is no water. If the sun moves, one also has to move; therefore one is constantly on the move to sustain the well-being. Winter—old age—when the tree will lose its leaves, is looming.

The *beautiful mansion* is the celestial world, heaven, paradise. Since it is artificially erected, the house is not a part of nature but a bulwark, made from good deeds and providing protection from heat and sandstorms. Thick walls maintain a permanent coolness; there is no danger of losing shade provided by foliage. Instead of poor soil, there is a soft couch; one can rest on the laurels of one's merit, one's good conscience. Everything in this divine world is beautiful, pleasing to the eye, and everywhere there is harmony. One is enthralled, experiencing only pleasant feelings. But the situation here is only a substitute for real relief, since even here there is no water.

The *lotus pond* represents desirelessness, release, Nibbāna, freedom from the thirst of craving. The man takes this path after meeting an *experienced traveller*, the Buddha or one of his noble disciples, who tells him that there is a another path that he could not see earlier due to being blinded by the sun (ignorance) and that only this path leads to the quenching of thirst. Having faith in what he is told, the man follows the path and eventually reaches the pond of Nibbāna. Here, and only here, there is finally water. Here he can finally immerse his dehydrated body in water. Here he can quench one's thirst with delicious fresh water—the deliverance from craving. After this no wishes remain, as the traveller, the mind, is desireless and happy. In the lush, evergreen forest, the traveller can rest in the lasting peace of Nibbāna, the highest happiness.

2. The Man in the Well
(*Avadāna Sūtra*[14])

A man lost in a jungle is being chased by a mighty tusker elephant. Full of fear, he tries to escape and sees an old well with a large tree-root dangling into it. Desperately seeking a refuge, he quickly climbs down the tree-root into the well and hangs on to the tree root. As his eyes become accustomed to the darkness in the well, he sees a huge snake, a python, winding itself slowly towards him from the bottom of the well. Looking sideways, he sees that on each of the four sides of the well there is a poisonous viper threatening to bite him. Terrified, he looks up only to see that two mice—one white and one black—are gnawing the tree root he is holding on to. Moreover, a forest fire is burning the tree. The roots will soon be chewed or burned through and he will fall down only to be strangled and crushed by the python. On another root above him there is a wild bees' nest and the bees, angered by his presence, frequently sting him, making him flinch from the pain. At the height of despair, however, five droplets of honey drip onto his face from the hive. Greedily he licks them up, enjoying their sweetness, and entirely forgets his desperate situation.

Explanation

The *jungle wilderness* is saṃsāra, the round of existences. The *lost man* is the ignorant worldling, one who does not know the Buddha's teaching. As the Japanese proverb goes, he is "like the frog in the well which is ignorant of the great sea." The *great elephant* is the destructive power of impermanence. The *well* is worldly existence, life. The *climbing down the tree root* is vain hope and expectation with regard to life. The inevitable strangling and crushing by the *huge snake* is death. The *four vipers* are the four elements, full of danger. The *two mice*: night and day, sun and moon, which gnaw away life. The *forest fire* is sickness and old age that keep charring the *tree* of the body. The *angry bees* are

---

14. No. 217 of the Taishō edition of the Chinese Buddhist Canon.

changing vicissitudes. The *stings* are the constant stings of vicissitude. The *five honey drops*: the five sense pleasures, which are longed for, loved, thrilling, connected with desire, charming. *Licking* is indulging in sense pleasures, and forgetting the precariousness of saṃsāra. Even though the compassionate Buddha has warned of the dangers of the pit of saṃsāra and pointed out that there is an escape, Nibbāna, the worldling takes no heed and continues indulging in sensuality.

* * *

This popular simile is widespread and is found in various versions. It is found in Hinduism (Mahābhārata 11.5–6), in Jainism (with Hemacandra), Indian Buddhism and in Chinese Buddhism. Along with the Buddha biography called *Lalitavistara* (of the Sarvāstivādin school) it came to the Middle East and from there it came to Europe in the Christian "Barlaam and Josaphat legend" (VI.a). It reappeared later again in Tolstoy's *Confession* and Ivan Franko's poem "A Parable about Life." It is not found in the Theravāda tradition.

The version retold here is found in the *Lalitavistara*, as well as in the *Avadāna Sūtra* (or "Parable Sutta"), preserved in Chinese.

3. The Escape to the Farther Shore (SN 35:238)

There are four very venomous vipers that are easily irritated. One day, a man comes along who desires happiness but he is told that he must handle these four vipers from time to time to feed them, bathe them, and put them to sleep. Should one of the vipers become annoyed, it will certainly kill him. Frightened, the man flees, but as he does so, he is told that he is pursued by a gang of five murderous enemies who plan to kill him and are coming closer and closer. As he tries to elude these five, he is told that another murderer, an intimate friend, is pursuing him and threatens to cut off his head. Fleeing from him as well, he comes to an abandoned village where each house he enters is empty. Robbers have looted every house, and he is told that they will return at any time. Trying to get away from the four vipers, the gang of five murderous enemies, his murderous "friend," and from the robbers, he arrives at a very wide river. On the shore he is threatened by all these dangers; on the other shore he would be safe, but neither boat nor bridge can be seen. He decides to make himself a raft, and then paddles with his hands and feet until he arrives at the farther shore.

Explanation

This simile about the realm of the six senses contains not only the factors of suffering but also those of its cessation. Thus it concerns more than just the First Noble Truth; however, it starts with this truth and hence is discussed here in this section.

The person who experiences all these phenomena stands for undistorted perception (*avipallatthā-saññā*) or right view (*sammā-diṭṭhi*). This is what he sees:

The *four vipers* are the four elements. In the same way that the man had to pick up, feed, wash and put those vipers to sleep, one has to make this body rise, and feed, clean, and dress it. Included here are also all other material things comprised of the same four elements; they have to be grabbed and lifted, maintained and improved, safeguarded from damage and being left alone for a while. These four inner and outer elements have to be dealt with continuously or else they will kill the one who takes care of them. If one doesn't look after the body properly, if one doesn't treat the surrounding material world properly, one will die. Thus the elements are dangerous at all times, ever ready to spit their lethal venom. Whether one accidentally ingests arsenic or runs into a speeding car, the result is the same.

The five *murderous enemies* are the five aggregates or *khandhas*. The sixth enemy, the *intimate friend*, is delight and lust (*nandirāga*), which arises within us. Unless one has been informed by the Buddha's teaching, delight and lust appears to be friendly and good, but then they stealthily cut off wisdom, one's head. In SN 22:85 a murderer pretends to be a very helpful and friendly servant, gaining his master's trust only to kill him. Even though the "friend" does not appear to be dangerous to his trusting master, he is actually about to murder him. Just so, the Buddha says, the aggregates deceptively appear as permanent, pleasant, and self to the ignorant person.

The five aggregates exist because of previous grasping, while delight and lust are present grasping. Both are related to activity. By grasping the five aggregates, because one likes to delight in them, one exists—and that is why one is mortal, for one is killed by these very five aggregates.[15] The man is being warned and encouraged to flee by well-wishers: the Buddha and his disciples.

The empty village denotes the six senses, which are empty (*suñña*) because for someone with right view there is no abiding self in them. Further, the six inner and outer bases (*saḷāyatana*) relate to each other like an empty village to its robbers. The *robbers* are the tempting worldly sense pleasures, causing one to overexert the body so that it is plundered: over-straining, over-doing the pleasures of life, and frittering away its life-energy. The six outer bases lure with their objects, pestering continuously, draining, causing to waste energy, and leaving one exhausted.

The man experiences painful feelings whenever he perceives the snakes, murderers and robbers—the whole shore full of insecurity and danger. He who desires happiness and loathes pain finds nothing but suffering on this shore. The *man* is personality (*sakkāya*), the expression of suffering.

The *river* is the stream of consciousness and existence with its four great tidal-waves (*ogha*): sense desire, becoming, views, and ignorance. These four tendency groups are the obstacles in getting from this shore to the other. In perceiving the danger comprehensively, the man (right view) also perceives safety: the overcoming of suffering where all pain ends, that is, *the farther shore*, Nibbāna. The *raft* is the Noble Eightfold Path, which is the way to overcome the fearful waves of habit by changing one's

---

15. The aggregates are "external" murderers in the sense that it is not the aggregates themselves that are grasping (*upādāna*), but the grasping is the internal desire for them (SN 22:82 *yo tattha chandarāgo taṃ tattha upādānaṃ*). This desire is the real "intimate" killer, for it kills wisdom. The aggregates of an arahant will finally break up at his passing away. Since desire and lust have been abandoned, there is no longer an internal killer of wisdom that will cause the taking up of another set of aggregates.

attitude towards them. *Paddling with hands and feet* is the main power on the Eightfold Path, namely, right effort (*sammā vāyāma*). The one who has reached the farther shore is the arahant, the liberated one who knows that he is beyond all danger.
See also the simile of the raft in MN 22.13–14.

4. The Hollow Aggregates (SN 22:95)

While dwelling on the bank of the river Ganges the Buddha said:

> Suppose the Ganges carries along a large lump of foam. Someone investigating it would find it to be hollow and insubstantial. Just so, that lump of foam can be compared to the aggregate of form (*rūpa*), which is hollow and insubstantial.

Appearing so firm and substantial, form or matter in reality is of an entirely different nature, namely, empty space. Modern physics also explains matter as being nothing but empty space and stress. Just like a ball of foam, which is compounded of spray, flotsam, and air—all waste products of the river—so the division in the world of diversity is woven and spun together by the mind. "We are such stuff as dreams are made on," says Shakespeare. The apparent substance is different from what it seems to be, namely, a mere shape, and not at all necessary because there are realms of existence entirely without form. Without a core, without a centre, without anything firm to rely upon, like a lump of foam on the river Ganges, so is form empty, hollow, not the essence, and not an independent, self-contained entity.

The Buddha says further:

> Suppose rain falls in heavy drops and a bubble appears on the surface of the river. Someone investigating the bubble would find it to be hollow and insubstantial. Just so, that bubble can be compared to the aggregate of feeling (*vedanā*), which is hollow and insubstantial.

Just as a bubble cannot exist on its own but is the product of a rain-water falling and splashing into the water of a river or puddle, so, too, is feeling dependent on the contact of the inner and outer sense bases; it has no essence or substance. There is nothing permanent in feeling but change. Splash follows upon splash; bubble upon bubble appears and disappears.

The Buddha says further:

> Suppose a mirage appears at noon in the last, hottest month of summer. Someone investigating the mirage would find it to be hollow and insubstantial. Just so, that mirage can be compared to the aggregate of perception (*saññā*), which is hollow and insubstantial.

Like a mirage shimmering in the heat and projecting an image that does not exist where it appears to be, so the inner heat of the mind's taints generates the distorted perception of seeming permanence, pleasure, substance and beauty (*subha*) in things. In the same manner, the ceasing of distorted perception comes about through developing the undistorted perception of impermanence, suffering, insubstantiality and ugliness (*asubha*) in things. One could take the simile even further. The oasis that appears as a mirage to the wanderer in the desert is in a completely different place; the freedom of Nibbāna that the wanderer in *saṃsāra* desires is the same—it is not within this cycle of existence but outside of it.

These similes for feeling and perception are also found in the Dhammapada:

> As a bubble see this world,
> As a mirage, this universe,
> One who considers thus,
> Won't be seen by Lord Death. (Dhp 170)

The Buddha says further:

> Suppose a man who desires heartwood (the firm, mature core of a tree) goes into the forest with a sharp axe. There he finds a banana-tree, straight, young and tall. He fells it at the root, cuts off the top and peels it open. But peeling it, he would not even find sapwood (the soft, new wood), let alone heartwood. Just so, that banana-tree can be compared to the aggregate of mental activity, which is hollow and insubstantial.

For the first time we encounter the doer here, the person. Form, feeling, perception are purely passive; they come to the

Our Basic Situation

person as the harvest of his past deeds. But now he is becoming active, looking for the core of existence and for permanent spiritual security, yet he is looking wrongly. Though seemingly firm, a banana tree, like an onion, consists only of layered leafy sheaths; there is no wood. In the same way, all things that have come into being are without a core, without a self—one exerts oneself for nothing.

Then the Buddha says:

> Suppose an illusionist or his assistant shows a trick at the junction of four roads. Someone investigating the trick would find it to be hollow and insubstantial. Just so, that illusionist's trick can be compared to the aggregate of consciousness (*viññāṇa*), which is hollow and insubstantial.

The illusionist (*māyākāra*) lets an illusion arise (*māyā*). Likewise, a person comes up with something by himself; that is, by means of consciousness, something seemingly objective and concrete arises. And thus everything is one: just an illusionist and his creation. Everything arises dependent upon consciousness. Reflecting, consciousness projects all of its contents.

Lumps of foam and bubbles on the river, the mirage of water in the desert, the succulent, fleshy banana tree—all these are insubstantial. Everything is just an image projected by consciousness that has no independent, separate content. Likewise, according to the Buddha, a painting is painted by the painter's mind and has no reality apart from that of being a painting (SN 22:100). Everything that the illusion-maker (*māyākāra*) creates is coreless and transient—only something that is inside himself can be reflected and projected. A dreamed "I" in a dreamt world—that is *māyā*. And the being accustomed to taking the dream for real—this is the illusionist who deceives himself about his creation. Therefore *māyā*, illusion, is only the deception of consciousness about itself.

The Buddha concluded the sutta with the following verses:

> Matter is like a lump of froth,
> Feeling's like a water bubble.
> As a mirage is perception,
> Activities are like a banana tree,
> And consciousness like an illusionist's trick:

Thus the Kinsman of the Sun has shown.
However one contemplates it,
And thoroughly examined sees,
Empty, insubstantial this body is
To him who sees it wisely so.
With reference to this body
The One of Broad Wisdom has taught
That when abandoned by three things,
You'll see a form cast aside.

When life, warmth, and consciousness
Have left the body and are gone
Then thrown away in charnel-ground
It lies insentient, food for beasts.

Such is this continuum,
This illusion, beguiler of fools;
It is taught to be a murderer,
Here no substance can be found.

Therefore the monk with energy
Should clearly see the aggregates thus,
Continually, both day and night,
Attentively and clearly aware.

Let him get rid of all fetters,
Make a refuge for himself,
And as though his head's on fire,
Strive toward the imperishable state.[16]

5. Carried Away by the Current (SN 22:93)

A river flowing from far up in the mountains is rapidly carrying downstream everything in its way. On both banks are grass, sawgrass, reeds, creepers, and bushes dangling in the river. If a man who was swept away by the current tried to grab hold of any of these, they would break, and he'd come to misfortune and misery.

---

16. Adapted from Ven. Bodhi's translation in *Connected Discourses of the Buddha*.

Explanation

The *river* coming from afar is again the stream of existence, in which a person swims and in which he is swept along by his desires and habits. It is said that he cannot hold on to those five kinds of plants any better than he can hold on to the five aggregates.

The *grass* simply breaks and that's it: this is form. It breaks because that is its nature. The razor-sharp, brittle *saw-grass* not only breaks but also cuts his hand: this is feeling, which always turns into suffering. The *reed* is likely to be pulled out of its shaft and then break, demonstrating the deceitful aspect of perception. The *creepers*, besides snapping easily, are slippery; they are the activities one cannot get hold of and which do not produce anything one could grasp. And the seemingly firmest of all is the ever-present consciousness, the *bush*. It does not break but rather comes out by the root.

6. The Border City and the Coral Tree (SN 35:245)

On the border of a country, there is a well fortified city. It has six gates and an intelligent, sensible gatekeeper who allows in only those he knows, while sending strangers away. A pair of messengers arrives from the east and they ask the gatekeeper where the lord of the city is staying. He answers them by saying, "In the central square of the city, at the intersection of the four roads." After they have delivered their message correctly to the lord of the city, they return the way they came. Later in the same way, messengers arrive from the north, west and south, deliver their messages and return the way they came.

Explanation

The *city* is the body made of the four elements, built up with materials from the outside world and finally returning to it. Like the conditioned nature of the body, the city is made up of non-living external materials. Nevertheless, in the city there is also life, i.e., consciousness.

The *six gates* are the six inner sense bases. They are the intermediaries between the outer world of form and the inner world of the mind. The six gates are the six doors to the mind by which good and evil enter. The only way to contact and change the mind is via the six sense bases.

The *intelligent, sensible gatekeeper* is mindfulness (*sati*), which can distinguish between right and wrong, and is trained in the Dhamma. His intelligence is the wisdom with which he no longer regards the five aggregates with distorted perception, with ignorance, but wisely. Thus the gatekeeper is a simile for right view, seeing things the way they are. It is up to the gatekeeper to use his discernment to let the teaching in.[17]

The *pair of messengers* are calm and insight (*samatha* and *vipassanā*). These two qualities come as messengers, ask questions, are tested, and are thereby approved. Only by virtue of this approval is it possible that these qualities can enter.

The *lord of the city* is consciousness, the life-force which controls the body (city). It is this consciousness which can pick something up by cognising it through the six sense doors. It is also character, habit, including the longing for liberation. It is this lord that receives the messengers.

He lives at the *central square*, i.e., in the body made of the four elements, where the roads from the six gates intersect, and where the messengers come from the four directions. The six gates become four roads by putting the six senses into the four categories of seeing, hearing, sensing, and thinking, which is sometimes done in the suttas. Therefore, consciousness lives in the centre where all experiences meet, the place toward which they are directed.

The *message*, the truthful word of how everything really is (*yathābhūta vacana*) is Nibbāna, that is, the highest well-being. The messengers, calm and insight, show the way leading to Nibbāna. In this way they aim at a refinement of feelings (through calm) and increasing understanding of feelings (through insight) up to the highest well-being beyond feelings. (See AN 9:34 & 47–51.)

---

17. See also Simile 33 where the gatekeeper also stands for mindfulness.)

The way by which they came and by which they are returning is the Noble Eightfold Path, or, in extension, the Noble Tenfold Path. Why? Calm and insight (steps eight and nine) are harbingers of Nibbāna (step ten). As long as this final step is not completely reached, the messengers always return. The noble practitioner (*sekha*) does not always maintain full calm and insight, but he remains on the Noble Eightfold Path.

The four roads to Nibbāna come from *the four directions,* namely, understanding by way of:

1. the six inner sense bases,
2. the five aggregates,
3. the four elements, and
4. "whatever has the nature to arise, all that has the nature to cease."

Whoever understands Nibbāna through one of these four ways has heard the message of one of the four pairs of messengers. All four are equally good, even though they indicate four different approaches leading to Nibbāna. To elucidate this, the Buddha gives another simile:

The coral tree (*kiṃsuka*) appears completely different at different times of the year so that someone who does not know it would believe he has seen four different trees. At one time it is black, without leaves, looking like a burnt tree stump. Then it blossoms with many red flowers, still without leaves, looking like a piece of meat. Later one can see it with seed-pods, like an acacia tree. Finally, one can see it without blossoms but full of leaves, like a banyan tree.[18]

7. The Cow and the Lute (SN 35:246)

The Voracious Cow

There is a lustful, voracious cow and a negligent watchman. The cow goes into a field with ripe barley, eats her fill and enjoys it

---

18. *Butea frondosa* or *Erythrina variegata*. For more information on this tree, see Bhikkhu Bodhi's footnote to his translation of this sutta (*Connected Discourses of the Buddha* 1427, n. 204); also see Jātaka story 248.

while the watchman is sleeping. However if the watchman is wakeful and takes his work seriously, he will seize the cow by the muzzle and give her a good beating with his staff. If she enters the barley-field again, he beats her again, and in this way, a third and fourth time until she stops.

Explanation

Like the ripe barley are the six outer sense bases (outer form), the fruits of previous kamma, the sensual pleasures. Like the greedy cow is consciousness, which under the influence of greed, hatred, and delusion, is going after sense pleasures. Like the lax watchman, so is lack of mindfulness and wise attention. When a greedy person grasps at sense pleasures just like the cow, his desires are gratified by getting the objects, giving him a feeling of well-being and wholeness.

The monk, however, mindfully and earnestly watching the contact of the senses bases with their objects, does not follow his mind's desire, but finds quietude within. He will therefore take care of his mind with earnestness and make efforts to stop wrong delight should it occasionally arise. He perceives form wisely so he is not taken in by it, with the consequence that, as greed diminishes, his mind becomes calm and unified.

A second simile in the sutta supplements the above simile. This one is not concerned with the outer but with the inner sense bases, and their relationship to the five aggregates:

The Sound of the Lute

A king hears a lute for the first time and the sound of it enraptures, fascinates, and delights him. He asks what makes the sound and is told that it is a lute. The king arranges the instrument to be brought to him, but then, being disappointed with it, asks to be given only its sound. However, he is told that the sound is produced in dependence on the components of the lute, such as the body, sounding board, bridge, neck, strings and plectrum, and the effort of a capable musician. Hearing this, the king breaks and burns the lute, saying that it is a wretched thing that people are mistakenly taken in by. And so it is said to be with the five aggregates.

Explanation

Here the aggregate of *form* is the lute with the sixfold inner sense base: body (seeing), sounding board (hearing), bridge (smelling), neck (tasting), strings (touching) and plectrum (thinking), as explained further below.

Feeling is the pleasantly intoxicating sound of the music.

Perception is the 'I'-perspective mentioned at the end of the discourse.

Activity is the playing of the lute.

Consciousness (*viññāṇa*) is the player. As long as the player (consciousness) plays (activity) on the lute (form) there will be sound (feeling), and this sound will be perceived as existing independently (perception). Only when one clearly sees how the sound is totally lacking in independence, depending entirely on the lute (the sixfold sense base), can one let go of the thoughts concerning it and lose interest in the instrument.

These two similes relate to each other as follows:

Form, like the barley-field is the outer form, the lute the inner form, that is, the outer and inner sense bases.

Feeling is the enjoyment of the cow, corresponding to the lute's intoxicating sound.

Perception is the negligent watchman, corresponding to the perception of the king who thought the sound to be an independent entity, a self.

Mental activities is the eating of the cow, corresponding to the playing of the lute-player.

Consciousness is the habit of the cow's feeding, corresponding to the habit of the lute-player's playing.

Expanding on the second simile, the six inner sense bases are compared to a lute with its six parts corresponding to the six senses. Just as the body of the lute determines its shape, so does the sense of sight limit vision. Just as the sounding board (skin, ribs) is the sounding board of the lute, so is the sense of hearing with the eardrum being the place to register sounds. In the same way that the bridge protrudes, so the nose protrudes with the sense of smell. Like the neck of the lute, the neck of the human body is closely associated with the tongue and the sense of taste. And in the same way that strings are the most sensitive part of the lute—that which is touched and which vibrates—so the body's nervous system with its sense of touch is also palpable and vibrating.

Furthermore, just as the plectrum is a special tool to play the strings, so the mind, as the sense of thinking, is something special compared to the other five senses, though its sole use is only to act upon the body with its five senses. When the mind plays on the nerves, the whole body vibrates and resounds under the control of the mind. Use of the five sense tools begins with the mind's intention to employ them.

A similar simile is found in the mysticism of the Eastern Orthodox Church. In the *Philokalia* by Kallistos[19] it is said that the heart is like a lute, the five senses are like the strings, and the mind is like the player of the lute. Here, the heart is the locus of the tendencies and the five senses are merely the shuttle service by which the heart makes its sensitivity known and makes expression of its sound. However, no distinction is made either between the mind as a sense or its activation by the player.

8. The Six Tied Animals (SN 35:247)

If a man with festering wounds on his limbs were to go into a shrub-jungle, then sharp grass and thorns would scratch his wounded limbs at every step, and consequently he would suffer even more pain and misery. In the same way an impure monk would suffer everywhere from sharp reproach if he did not restrain his senses.

How does he not restrain his senses? If he becomes aware of a pleasant sense object, he follows it, and he abhors an unpleasant one. Faint-hearted, he does not have the body under control and so will never become free. It is just like a man who catches six animals with completely different habits and feeding grounds—a snake, crocodile, bird, dog, jackal and monkey—and ties them all together with a rope, then lets the bundle loose. Each animal pulls towards its own feeding and living place: the snake to the termite mound, the crocodile to the water, the bird into the sky, the dog

---

19. *Gebet des Herzens*, Zürich, 1957, p. 222.

to the village, the jackal towards the charnel ground, and the monkey to the forest. Then, when they have all grown tired, they follow the one who is the strongest and are subjugated to his will.

It is the same with the monk who has not developed mindfulness: each sense pushes and pulls towards the pleasurable and away from the unpleasant, and causes him to be unrestrained. The restrained monk, however, is comparable to a man who tied the animals to a firm post. When they become tired of their struggle, they sit and lie down at the post.

Explanation

The *eye* is bound to pleasant forms, bodies, and colours like the *snake* that moves towards the termite mound. In the tropics, the favourite dwelling places of snakes are termite mounds that have deep tunnels underground. The eye is also constantly looking for dwelling places where it can rest at ease. Just as the clay structures of termite mounds provide shelter, so the eye is primarily looking for forms with which to find ease. Like the snake trying to find shelter, so does the eye strive by looking out for form. Just as the snake feels safe when it finds shelter in a tunnel of a termite mound, so the person feels safe when he can visually lean against familiar forms. This is the objective of the eye when urging towards form.

The *ear* is bound to sounds like the *crocodile* to the water in which it wants to swim. We want to "bathe" ourselves in sounds, want to hear pleasant talk, want to feel assured, want to be approved of, acknowledged. Like the crocodile seeking water, we want to immerse ourselves in the intoxication of encounters and experience ourselves in the echo thereof. We want to immerse ourselves in the acknowledgment "you exist."

The *nose* is bound to smells like the bird to the sky in which it soars. As the bird lifts itself and rises in the air searching for food, so the nose breathes in air searching for pleasant scents.

The *tongue* is bound to tastes (*rasa*; lit. juices), to liquids, to nutrient solutions into which solids are transformed, like the *dog* is bound to the village as its source of food. The sense of taste wants pleasant flavours like the dog wants to be fed with scraps in the village.

The *body* as a general organ of touch is bound to physical sensations, like a *jackal* which heads to the charnel ground where it finds its food. The sense of touch looks for pleasant touches, for closeness to other bodies, feels attracted, particularly to sexual partners. As the jackal looks for a rotting carcass, the sense of touch in sexuality looks for other mortal bodies to rub against. This is how the longing for touch nourishes itself.

Finally, *thinking* as the sixth sense is bound to thoughts, like the *monkey* is to the forest, the wild jungle where it leaps about. The mind is the dimension of the heart[20] with its manifold concerns. In the realm of ideas and associations, one darts about like a monkey in a jungle thicket. Of all the senses, the mind is the most restless, and the mental objects are the most opaque and manifold. Other senses want something in particular, but the sixth sense wants only wilderness, so that it can jump about. Therefore the Buddha (and his disciples) compared the heart or mind again and again to a monkey.[21]

Reflect on how the six senses want to pull us in different directions: the eye wants to see a football game, the ear wants to listen to a concert, the nose wants to smell a fresh sea-breeze, the tongue wants to go to a restaurant, the body wants to loll in the bathtub, and the mind wants to participate in a discussion. So we are pulled here and there until finally we blindly follow the strongest one. Where is there a self? Is it not just a mental knot connecting the six senses?

9. The Fire (MN 38)

Another simile on the realm of the six senses concerns the six outer bases. Although consciousness arises dependent upon both the inner and outer sense bases, it is named after the internal sense bases. On the other hand, consciousness is frequently compared to fire, which is named after its external conditions: The Buddha says:

---

20. "Heart," "spirit" or "soul" (in German *Geist*) is here used as a term for the totality of all tendencies, without connotation of permanence.
21. See SN 12:61; Dhp 334; Sn 791; Th 125 & 1111; J 348.

As by burning of wood there is a wood fire, so by way of form is seeing-consciousness;

As by burning of brushwood there is a brushwood fire, so by way of sounds there is hearing-consciousness;

As by burning of hay there is a hay fire, so by way of odours there is smelling-consciousness;

As by burning of cow-dung there is a dung fire, so by way of tastes there is taste-consciousness;

As by burning of straw there is a straw fire, so by way of tangibles there is touch-consciousness;

And as by burning of rubbish there is a rubbish fire, so by way of thoughts there is thinking-consciousness.

Explanation

Wood, as a prominent type of matter, compares to visible forms.

Brushwood crackles and rustles as it burns, so it is comparable to sounds.

Hay gives off many scents and fumes—especially the smoke from fresh, moist hay—so it can be compared to odours.

Dung is the residue of that which was tasted. In India, cow-dung is dried and used as fuel for cooking fires. Its odour disappears in the drying process so it can be compared to flavour.

Straw burns quickly, vanishing with the flame, and in the same way touch is a straw fire. Touch is that sense which is most lacking in substance—just as is straw.

And *rubbish*, consisting of the sweepings of the five other fuels, are thoughts, the rubbish of the senses so that nothing is in the mind that has not been before in the senses.

10. The Two Oxen (SN 35:232–33)

When a black and a white ox are bound together, the black ox does not hold the white one nor does the white ox hold the black one, but rather the yoke keeps them together. In the same way, the six inner bases do not bind the outer ones, nor the other way around, but rather the fetter is the desire and lust that arises dependent upon both the inner and outer bases. Were the eye to be the bond of form or form the fetter of the eye, no escape from saṃsāra would be possible because they are the foundations of life. But the desire and lust can be abandoned without affecting the existing foundations.

Explanation

It is noteworthy that the six inner bases are described here as dark and the outer ones as light. The six inner bases are dark to us because we usually direct the light of our attention to the six outer objects, which thereby seem light or white to us and which are thoroughly investigated by science, while the inner bases with their spiritual background lie in the dark. Yet the bondage lies exactly here. One must penetrate the darkness of the inner senses in order to see clearly the bondage of the heart.

11. The Similes of Nandaka (MN 146)

Nandaka, the arahant foremost in teaching nuns, explains to them how the six inner bases, the six outer bases and the six consciousnesses arising dependently upon these bases are to be regarded as they truly are with perfect wisdom, that is, as impermanent, painful and not-self. Nandaka gives a sequence of three similes for such contemplation.

The Burning Oil Lamp

The oil, wick and flame of a burning oil lamp are all impermanent; how much more so is the radiance emanating from it. In the same way, suggests Nandaka, because of the impermanence of the six impermanent inner sense bases, the feelings arisen dependent upon them are also impermanent.

Explanation

The *wick* is the body, that is, the six inner sense bases.

The *oil* is the life-force created by the tendencies (*anusaya*), because of which the wick can burn.

The *flame* is the burning consciousness conditioned by life-force and the body (as in MN 38).

The *radiance* is feelings, which are concurrent with these three things present altogether. Only those feelings conditioned by the body are meant here, the purely physical ones (for example, a feeling of energy or toothache), or, in the case of the sixth sense, purely mental ones (for example, good or bad moods).

The Great Tree

The roots, trunk and foliage of a great tree are impermanent. How much more so is the shade conditioned by it. In the same way, suggests Nandaka, because of the impermanence of the six impermanent outer sense bases, the feelings arisen dependent upon them are also impermanent.

Explanation

The *trunk* is the six outer bases, namely the world, objects, so-called matter—the seemingly firm and stable.

The *root* is the underground maturation of the kammic harvest in the realm of becoming. While the trunk is visible, the roots are invisible. The foliage is consciousness. Because of the root and trunk, foliage grows.

The *shade* is those feelings appearing from external stimuli. Just as the canopy of the tree creates shade, so consciousness creates feelings at each contact. Existence of the inner bases is presupposed here, in the same way that a tree can provide shade only when there is sun light.

The Slaughtered Cow

Suppose a skilful butcher slaughters a cow without tearing any of the meat or skin. Then with a sharp knife he separates the muscles, sinews and ligaments between skin and flesh until the hide can be removed in one piece. If he were to put the hide back on the mass of meat, then the cow would look much as before, even though it would be no longer connected to the hide. In the same way, explains Nandaka, the inner mass of meat is the six inner bases; the outer hide stands for the outer bases; the muscles, sinews and ligaments are the delight and lust (*nandirāga*); and the sharp knife is a description for wisdom's cutting of the inner bonds.

Explanation

This simile points out how in worldly, unenlightened people the inside and outside are inseparably connected, interlocked by the defiled mental connections and bonds produced by desires. Due to distorted perception, the inside and outside seems to be one, a single unit, just like a living cow. Only wisdom has the capacity to cut the bonds between inside and outside, the delight and lust, and to free people from bondage. The fetters have grown from the inside to the outside, and that is where they must be cut. In this image, the cow and hide are closely connected and hold each other, but it is also shown here how they can be separated by a skilled butcher. Likewise, if one investigates and sees the inner, mental bonds and skilfully cuts them with right view, then one can will be completely freed from all bondage.

12. Striking a Sappy Tree (SN 35:231)

If there were a tree containing a lot of milk-sap or latex—that is, a banyan or some other kind of Ficus tree—fresh, young and full of sap, and a man were to strike its trunk with a sharp axe, then the more he struck it, the more sap would exude. Why? Because the tree is sappy. In the same way, if somebody is attracted to, repelled by or deluded by forms cognizable by the eye and does not reject his attraction, repulsion or delusion, then even if only a few insignificant forms strike his vision, they will still spoil his mind, not to mention the effect of many significant forms. It is the same for the other five senses. But as an old, dry, sapless tree does not exude sap no matter how hard it is struck with an axe, so it is with somebody who has destroyed the tendencies with regards to the six senses.

Explanation

The mind in the body with its taints or defiling influences (*āsava*) is like the sap in the tree. In a tree, the sap permeates the whole trunk; in the same way, those taints pervade the whole body. If anything pleasant or unpleasant is noticed, then this contact is like the stroke of an axe. Like sap flowing from a tree, the inner taints flow out. That is why the *āsavas* are also called "effluents" or "influences." Whoever tolerates such taints inside him is at the mercy of objects, whether he wants it or not. Things upset and ruin him and create agitation and suffering.

The arahant is like the sapless tree, and is free of taints (*āsava*). Whatever he is subjected to, he remains calm and dispassionate. Of course the simile means an arahant is 'dry' only in respect to this particular aspect under discussion; not 'dry' in the negative sense of barrenness or atrophy. When we say an alcoholic is 'dry,' that too has an exclusively positive aspect. Similarly, dryness here means not being flooded by the taints. In the same spirit, the first verse of the Therīgāthā deals with dried-up greens (greed) in an earthen vessel (body).

Compare also Simile 67 below, where the wrathful heart is compared to a sore exuding pus at every touch. The six senses are the connections between the taints and the outside world. Something similar is also said in SN 35:248 about six sheaves of barley thrashed by six flails until they are completely empty. Similarly, the six senses are thrashed, crushed and plundered by pleasant and unpleasant objects.

13. The Bait (SN 35:230)

A man who wants to catch a fish throws a baited fish-hook into a lake. A fish looking for food sees the bait, swallows it, and is thereby at the mercy of the fisherman, who can now do with it whatever he wants. Because the bait was secured to a fishing line, the man hauls the fish in and kills it.

In the same way, there are six baits in this world, in this ocean with its sharks, sea-monsters, and dangerous waves. These six are the pleasant and desirable sense objects; whoever delights in them is like a fish swallowing bait and thereby is at the mercy of Māra, the Evil One.

Explanation

In the Pali canon the sense objects are often compared to Māra's bait (SN 4:17), with the bait of the deer-hunter (MN 25), with the glue of the monkey-trap (SN 47:7), with a snare (SN 4:4–5; 15), and with a fish-bait, as here (SN 17:2; J 472; Thī 508).

Sense objects provide what the corresponding cravings and desires want; therefore one is constantly attracted to them, enjoys them and then is at the mercy of such impermanent objects.[22] The desires become so strong that one is pained when the objects pass away. The object is considered as part of oneself and one consequently becomes vulnerable. The six senses are treacherous; through the senses, craving pursues objects until death. Māra, as Death, lures people with the six objects. When he catches them, they are subject to him, just as the fish caught by the fisherman.

Greed, hatred and delusion abide within the six senses, while outside are "sharks, sea-monsters, and dangerous waves."

As is said in the Itivuttaka:

> One who has destroyed greed
> Along with hate and ignorance,
> Has crossed this ocean
> With its sharks and monsters,
> Its fearsome waves so hard to cross.
> He has overcome every attachment,
> Free from acquisition, he left Death behind,
> Forsaking suffering and renewal of being.
> Vanished, he cannot be defined, I say—
> He has bewildered the King of Death.[23]

14. The Ocean of Saṃsāra (SN 35:228)

The worldly person speaks of the ocean as just a great body of water. But the real ocean, the real deep sea, is the six inner sense bases—with its surges (*vega*) coming from the outer bases. Whoever can nonetheless withstand the ocean with its surges, whirlpools, sharks, and sea-monsters, stands on the other shore as an arahant.

Explanation

To the worldly person, the ocean is something measurable; it is a calculable, deep ocean, which these days can even be exploited. But the six senses are the really deep ocean with its depth of

---

22. See also MN 75.16 and SN 22:79 on being devoured by sensual pleasures.
23. It 69. Adapted from J. D. Ireland's translation in *Udāna and Itivuttaka*.

consciousness, with its depth of mind. It is because craving abides in the six inner bases that the outer bases can be so influential, and surges (*vega*) can overcome and excite the mind. If forms of the six outer bases come in contact with the six senses, the mind becomes excited, lashed by the storms and great waves. There are eddies and whirlpools spiralling down into the abyss; there are monsters (explained in detail in MN 67 and It 109; see Simile 21); there are things that tempt and repel one. The external impact on the senses creates the choppiness, the disturbance in the mind.

Only the arahant has crossed over the dangerous ocean; the safe shore has been reached. (Cf. SN 1:1 and MN 140.32.) Whatever comes from the outside is no longer a danger. There are no more storms.

As is said in Theragāthā 412:

> Just like a great ocean wave,
> So do birth and old age overcome you,
> Therefore make a strong island of yourself,
> Because there is no other refuge.

15. The Tortoise and the Jackal (SN 35:240)

A tortoise sees a foraging jackal coming from a distance so it pulls its neck and legs in and stays inside its shell quiet and still. But when the jackal sees the tortoise, it thinks, "I will wait. If it sticks out any of its limbs, I will grab it, pull it out and eat it." If the tortoise does not stick out any limb the jackal will get frustrated and leave because it gains no access. Similarly, says the Buddha, Māra is constantly on watch to gain access to the six inner bases; therefore, the monk should restrain his senses.

Explanation

Matching the appendages of the tortoise to the six inner sense bases is challenging. The tortoise has four legs and the neck as a fifth 'limb' according to the sutta (*soṇḍipañcamāni aṅgāni*). In the same way it is said of a baby that it is bound by bonds on all four limbs with its neck as a fifth (MN 80.16). How does this match the six senses? Or is the tortoise's tail the sixth 'limb'? In the simile the tail is not mentioned; it states clearly "limbs with the neck as fifth." Moreover, the jackal would probably have trouble grabbing the tiny tail of a tortoise. So how do the five and the six relate to each other? One could consider the following: the tortoise can pull in the five senses (four legs and neck with head) completely and will then be safe if its endurance is better than the jackal's. Is this a hint? Is the sixth 'limb' the sixth sense of thinking, for if the tortoise thinks that the jackal has got fed up and has left, a wrong view concerning its enemy will have influenced it and it will be eaten as soon as it extends any of its limbs out from the safety of the shell.

Just as the tortoise sticks out its limbs as soon as the mind orders it, just so is the thinking sense the determining principle for human activity. If a man thinks it is not dangerous to follow the five senses, he goes after pleasures with all five. Only when he attends to his thinking can he retract the senses and rest quietly inside himself, that is, attain *samādhi*. Just as it is said, be like the tortoise that it is without zeal and still *(appossukko tuṇhībhuto)*, contented within itself and without clatter of the mind tempting it to go outside. As brought together, the verse at the end of the discourse:

> Just as the tortoise pulls its limbs into its shell,
> So pulls the monk his mind's thoughts in—
> Independent, and going after no one,
> He becomes desireless and griefless.

One has to become self-sufficient, to be able to rest within, to be able to diminish the need for the outside world more and more. Only then can one stand to be on one's own and can pull the senses in, in order to escape death.

Part 2

DEPENDENT ORIGINATION

INTRODUCTION

The second of the Four Noble Truths—the Noble Truth of the origination of suffering—is taught by the Buddha in terms of a multi-faceted interrelation of conditions, which is usually called "dependent origination" or "dependent co-arising" (*paṭiccasamuppāda*). In its detailed, full exposition it connects twelve conditions. The causes and effects of all things are identified in this chain, and therefore it explains the origin and destination of all the phenomena of existence. When this analysis of existence is correctly comprehended, not a single phenomenon will appear as an independent, permanent causal entity, as a "self" uninfluenced by conditions. Existence will be seen as just a causal chain of conditions and phenomena, without a "self" originating, being involved in, or arising out of the process. By means of this chain, the Buddha explains how "I" and the "world" originate and cease, and what are the origins and consequences of deeds. What stands so starkly juxtaposed for us, from the perspective of "here the 'I'" and "there the 'world,'" turns out to be a system of interrelationships which reciprocally conditions and changes itself. This analysis shows how the world, the so-called "outside," influences the "I," which in turn designs the "world." That which we juxtapose as subject and object, and treat as ultimate categories, when examined more deeply turn out to be things that have come into being due to conditions and are continuously worn down and transformed into one another (i.e., the subject or object) in a process of nourishment. This psychological reality, that is, the process of the interaction of subject and object, is the theme of the Second Noble Truth, the truth of the seed and harvest or cause and result relationship (*kamma*). It is the truth of the turning of the wheel of saṃsāra, as the only *perpetuum mobile*, that which winds itself up by itself.

16. The Wheel of Existence

In the Buddhist traditions of the Himalayan countries the twelve factors of dependent origination are arranged pictorially in what is called the "wheel of existence" (*bhava-cakka*) or "wheel of saṃsāra" (*saṃsāra-cakka*). This picture wheel is first mentioned in the *Vinaya-vibhaṅga* and *Divyāvadāna* texts of the early Buddhist school called Mūlasarvāstivāda. According to these scriptures, the Buddha gave detailed instructions on what the wheel should depict and said that it was to be made at the gateways of monasteries for educational purposes. Part of a fifth

Dependent origination

century mural depicting the wheel of existence can still be seen on the porch of a cave at Ajantā in western India. There is a 10th century mural depiction of the wheel in the Yulin cave-temple at the Dunhuang silk-road oasis in the sandy deserts in the far northwest of China. Although all wheel paintings share the same general characteristics, there are variations in the images and in the amount of rebirth realms and rings. Here, the focus will be on the images of one version.[24]

The whole wheel of saṃsāra, is held up by a demon-like figure, the King of Death. Depending upon the version, it consists of three or four or more concentric rings.

The central ring depicts three animals biting each other in the tail: a snake, a pig, and a rooster (or duck). These animals symbolize the roots of unwholesomeness (*akusala-mūla*) that fuel saṃsāra: greed, hatred and delusion. The snake symbolizes hate, the pig greed, and the rooster delusion. The animals pursuing each other, and the biting each other in the tail, symbolises the defilements fuelling each other: delusion giving rise to greed, greed giving rise to fear and anger, anger giving rise to more delusion, and so on.

The next ring, only found in some versions of the wheel, depicts a man walking up and down a circular stairway. This symbolizes the cycle of ascending and descending in saṃsāra through performing good or bad actions. The man descends only wearing a loin cloth, symbolizing poverty and suffering, and ascends well dressed, symbolizing prosperity and happiness. Higher up the stairs the man carries a light, symbolizing the wisdom acquired as a result of performing wholesome deeds. This light of wisdom is needed to escape from the darkness of ignorance. In some versions hell-wardens forcefully drag down the descending man and the ascending man becomes a monk and meets a teacher who points him the way out of the cycle.

---

24. For more information, see Bhikkhu Khantipālo, *The Wheel of Birth and Death*, Wheel Publications 147–149, BPS, Kandy, 1970, and Stephen F. Teiser, *Reinventing the Wheel—Paintings of Rebirth in Medieval Buddhist Temples*, Washington, 2007.

The next ring has six compartments depicting the six different rebirth modes: god, asura, human, ghost, animal, hell-being. In each realm there is a standing Buddha (or Bodhisattva) who teaches the beings.

The outer rim depicts the twelve factors of dependent origination. The majority of the images originate from similes used by the Buddha himself. The twelve image similes are as follows:

1. Ignorance (*avijjā*) is an old blind man with a stick, walking in the direction opposite to that in which he is being directed. There are four points to this picture.

- a) His walking through existence with the aid of a stick, denotes his lack of personal knowledge, forcing him to use the mental crutches of others. In contrast, an instructed person who knows the goal (Nibbāna), gained as his first achievement the knowledge that he is "independent in the Dispensation of the Master (*satthu-sāsana*)" (MN 56.18).
- b) His old age denotes the old and well-worn habit of journeying through saṃsāra. As is said in the Dhammapada: "… Long is the ignorant person's journey through saṃsāra." (Dhp 60).
- c) His blindness denotes not seeing the reality of his situation and not knowing how he can be healed. The darkness of delusion prevents him from seeing the sun of liberation (It 87–88). One who knows liberation, who has been instructed (*sekha*), and who has seen briefly (see AN 3:25 & SN 12:68), gradually accustoms his eyes to the light. It is only the arahant who has fully knowledge and vision.
- d) His inattention to the directions of the Buddha, stubbornly walking in the wrong direction, denotes his persistence in self-centred clinging to that which he is accustomed to. As is said by the Buddha: "Tathāgatas are only showing the Way." (MN 107.14; Dhp 276).

2. Activities (*saṅkhārā*) are depicted by way of a potter engaged in his work. Five vessels are finished and the sixth one is on the wheel.

Dependent origination

a) A potter is depicted, which means the habit of constantly creating. This continuous desire to create and do is rooted in ignorance and is found even in those who doubt whether there is a deeper meaning to activity and existence. Out of ignorance, one takes creation and activity for granted, with the consequence that the "uncreated" (*asaṅkhata*), i.e., Nibbāna, is not seen.

b) The clay vessels—a potter cannot produce anything else—symbolize the fragility and mortality of all things created out of ignorance.

> Just as the clay pots
> crafted by the potter,
> all end up broken,
> just so are mortals' lives. (Sn 577)

c) The hexad of the pots probably points to the six senses: The five sense bases have been created earlier and are ready for use in this life. The pot on the potter's wheel, however, represents mental activity, which is already preparing the future, the next rebirths.

3. Consciousness (*viññāṇa*) is depicted as a monkey in a tree. The monkey, addicted to sense-pleasures, is looking greedily for fruits growing between the leaves and blossoms. Five fruits are still hanging in the tree while the monkey has just grasped the sixth with his right hand. This symbol is the only one on the outside ring of the wheel depicting an animal, and it shows the one most closely related to the human being.

a) Just as with activities, so here also six objects are shown which are again divided in the ratio of five-to-one. The monkey seizes and shakes the five sense-doors (Th 125) because he wants to get to the five sense objects, while he already has thinking firmly in hand. It is the same in the simile with the six animals (SN 35:247; Simile 8), in which the monkey symbolises thinking.

b) The momentum, habituation, inclination, and drive in a human are created by ignorant thinking, and what is thereby driven runs around in constant unrest much like the monkey jumping about in the forest (SN 12:61), hunting for fruits to gorge on (Dhp 334). Unsteadiness is the characteristic to which the monkey is compared (Sn 791; Th 1111).

4. The Mental and Physical, or Name and Form (*nāma-rūpa*) is symbolised by a boat being carried down a river with the current. Inside are four people, three, the passengers, are sitting. Two of these are sitting very close together. The fourth, the helmsman, stands and controls the rudder.

a) The boat is a simile for the body (Dhp 369; Sn 321; AN 7:67). Endowed with the body, we sail through the world with its waves and whirlpools, through the ocean of saṃsāra. Boat and ocean together comprise corporeality (form, image, the physical). As a whole, i.e., the boat together with its helmsman and passengers, it is the called the "conscious body," *saviññāṇaka kāya* (SN 12:19. Cf. SN 18:21 and MN 109.13.)

b) The group of three people in the boat consists of those who give in passively to the situation: contact (*phassa*) from outside (*nāma-rūpa*) and from inside (*viññāṇa*). Out of contact arise feeling, perception, and intention (MN 109.9; SN 35:93). These three things are remembered in the mind for later repetition. The inseparable two, namely, feeling (*vedanā*) and perception (*saññā*), sit close together (MN 43:9).

c) The fourth person, the helmsman, does not allow himself to sit passively but looks ahead and controls the rudder: the journey is in his hands and he steers the boat of the living, conscious body through the ocean (world). This helmsman is attention (*manasikāra*) and he aware of the possibility for a change of course. A boat led by wise attention (*yoniso manasikāra*), going upstream to Nibbāna, is the counterpart of the boat led by unwise attention (*ayoniso manasikāra*) following the current of desires down to lower realms. The Buddha defines mentality (*nāma*) as a pentad of feeling, perception, intention (the three passive persons), contact (passivity) and attention (the helmsman).

Dependent origination

5. The six-fold realm (*saḷāyatana*) is a stately building surrounded by a broken wall. It is a large, towering palace, but completely empty of humans.

   a) The emptiness of the structure points to the simile of the empty village (six inner bases) plundered by robbers (six outer bases) (SN 35:238; see Simile 3).
   b) The wall or fence is broken. It has six entrances: five obvious ones and one difficult to see. This could symbolise the six doors of the senses—one has to watch over them like the gatekeeper watches over a city so that one is not plundered.
   c) The palace probably symbolises a whole city; just as the inner bases are compared to the gates of a city (SN 35:245; see Simile 6.).

6. Contact (*phassa*) is illustrated by showing two lovers sitting on a bench tightly embracing. Just as tight is the conjunction of the inner and outer sense bases. Whoever bases himself on external sense objects coming to him, and is dependent upon them, he remains caught in the duality, the split, and is vulnerable.

7. Feeling (*vedanā*) is portrayed by a man who has been struck in the eye by an arrow: he sinks to the ground, holding his left hand on his heart. The eye exemplifies all of the senses. An extremely painful, alien element is stuck in the sensitive eye, the arrow of craving. Thus struck the man falls to his knees and fearfully holds his heart. Feeling, when not properly seen with wisdom, blinds one with the arrow of craving. For the simile of the person struck by two darts (SN 36:6), see Simile 45.

Ultimately, all feeling—whether pleasant, unpleasant, or neither pleasant-nor-unpleasant—is to be regarded as suffering because the conditions for feeling are impermanent and subject to change (SN 36:11). The highest happiness, the happiness of Nibbāna, however, transcends all feeling (MN 59.16; SN 36:19).

8. Craving or thirst (*taṇhā*) is depicted as a man sitting with his legs folded on a mat while a woman gives him something to drink. His thirst denotes his craving for and dependence on the gratification of his desires. This thirst is his constant companion, leaving him never truly free (SN 35:63). Therefore the Buddha says: "Delight is the root of suffering" (MN 1.171).

The woman, perhaps a prostitute, symbolizes sensual desire (*nandi-rāga*), the companion of craving (*taṇhā*). She gives the man an alcoholic drink that makes him intoxicated. When drunk, he loses his mindfulness and indulges with her in sensuality. The alcoholic drink symbolizes ignorance, which gives rise to more thirst, to more craving, leading to more ignorance, and so on. This reciprocal relationship of ignorance and craving is shown in the combination of ignorance and craving in the suttas: "The beginning of this saṃsāra is inconceivable. A starting-point cannot be discerned of the beings obstructed by ignorance and fettered by craving who are running and coursing around in saṃsāra" (SN 15:1). Ignorance and craving keep beings circling around in the wheel of saṃsāra, going from one existence to the next.

9. **Grasping** (*upādāna*) is depicted as someone who is plucking flowers from a blossoming tree, his basket is already so full it overflows. Grasping, i.e., acquisition, is without limit, just as are the gratification of craving and enjoyment of feelings. Plucking beautiful flowers continues even when there are more than enough in the basket. As is said in the Dhammapada:

> Beings with attached minds,
> only picking the flowers (of pleasure),
> being insatiable in sense pleasures:
> the Ender will make them his vassals. (Dhp 48)

Enjoyment knows no boundary and no stopping; it just wants to collect, acquire, for today and tomorrow. It is insatiable.

> Had a king conquered the world,
> Ruling lands up to the sea,
> Still this limit upsets him:
> He's longing for the further shores. (MN 82.42)

In this way grasping always grabs into what is empty and lacking: sleep, intoxicants, sex—one can never get enough (AN 3:104).

In this image only the grasping of sensual pleasures is depicted, however, there are three other kinds of grasping:

Dependent origination

grasping of views, grasping of virtues and vows, and the grasping of a doctrine asserting a self. These kinds of grasping are all on a mental, spiritual level and are more firmly and deeply grasped than sensual pleasures. Only the Buddha teaches the understanding and abandoning of the fourth kind of grasping, that is, the abandoning of the distorted view that there is a permanent self or personality (*sakkāya-diṭṭhi*; MN 11.14). This grasping is abandoned at stream-entry. As is said in the Suttanipāta,

> Together with the arising of noble vision,
> Three things are abandoned:
> Personality-view, doubt, and
> Whatever (grasping of) virtues and vows,
> One is freed from the four lower realms,
> And can't do the six heinous deeds. (Sn 233)

10. Becoming or **existence** (*bhava*) is depicted as a pregnant woman. That which has grasped insatiably prepares its return. It goes into the latency of time and will return sometime later, just as the infant in the mother's womb is already there but takes a nine-month incubation between conception (grasping) and birth.

In some versions of the wheel the image for *bhava* is of a copulating couple, the man impregnating the woman, making a new being. *Bhava*, as future existence, a new being, is conditioned by present kamma, by present grasping.

There is no permanence or essence in any form of existence. Impermanence will put an end to staying in any station of rebirth and even the highest, longest living gods are bound to move on to a new destination in saṃsāra.

> Those beings in the form realms,
> And those staying in the formless,
> Not knowing (craving's) cessation,
> They will come to a new existence. (Sn 759)

11. Birth (*jāti*) is symbolised by a woman delivering. Her mouth is open and she is screaming. With the birth of a body, the whole harvest of suffering arises out of the latency of becoming. As is said in the Suttanipāta:

> Dependent upon grasping, there is becoming (*bhava*),
> Having become (*bhūto*), one undergoes suffering,
> For one who is born, there is death:
> This is the coming to be (*sambhava*) of suffering. (Sn 747)

12. Dying (*maraṇa*) as the end of aging (*jarā*) is depicted by an angel of death, who carries the deceased to his appropriate place, a new existence, where the ignorant person will begin the cycle anew, thinking it is "he" who was born, lives, and will die.

17. The Four Nutriments (SN 12:63)

The four similes given in this discourse for the four nutriments have as little connection with each other as the images of the wheel of existence, but the subject matter itself is connected and forms an interrelation of conditions. The four similes stand out because they are very graphic and are probably meant to shock, and thus to shake the usually positive connotations associated with the phenomenon of "nutriment." However, a modern person, who has been desensitised by horror movies, etc., may take these images in a noncommittal way, reducing the efficacy of the similes.

The Son's Flesh

Two parents travel with their beloved and only son through a barren desert. Soon their meagre provisions are used up. The parents ponder what should be done. So that all three of them do not have to die, they decide with a heavy heart to slaughter their beloved, only son in order to survive on his flesh. They kill him and make dried meat, which they preserve with pepper. They live on this, but with every bite they mourn and wail for their only beloved child. Finally, they manage to get out of the desert. Certainly, they would not have eaten for the pleasure of feasting, nor for enhancement and beautification—that is, as delight for their taste buds or for a healthy body—but they ate exclusively to stay alive, to escape from the dangerous desert.

Explanation

The *first nutriment* is the material nutriment for the body, which is sustained by solids, liquids, gases, and heat. This nutriment—coarse as food and drink, fine as air and warmth—is purely a circulation within form, wherein the outer form (nutriment) nourishes the inner form (the body).

By comprehending nutriment, one penetrates the greed for the five sense objects. In the Theragāthā (v. 445) contemplating this simile is mentioned as a means to counteract greed for tastes. Through greed for tastes one builds up the body, so as to enjoy sense objects with the body. Just as physical nutriment was a necessary evil for the parents in the simile, so it should also be for the monk. He should just sustain his body with it in order to cross the desert of saṃsāra in this lifetime, just as the parents were able to get out of the desert.

Furthermore, every nourishing of one's body involves the killing of other beings. This happens in the coarsest form when one eats meat, but also when one eats vegetarian food because of the insects and other creatures killed during ploughing and cultivation. Even as one breathes, one accidentally kills microbes and other small creatures. Thus one's life is always at the expense of others. The normal person accepts this and eases his or her conscience with vegetarianism. The simile, however, teaches what a murderous place the coarse sensory world actually is and that one should get out of it. By such contemplation, one can diminish and eventually abolish the desire for tastes as well as greed for all sense objects experienced through the body. Whoever lives in a body, lives at the expense of other beings. If one does not want this, one must strive not to build up another body in the future and eliminate sense desire.

The Flayed Cow

There is a flayed cow; a cow without skin. Its flesh lies open and exposed. Wherever it stands it will be pestered: If it stands at a wall or at a tree, in the water or in the open, hungry insects that live there pester it, sucking its blood, and eating its flesh. If, terrorised, it escapes into the water, fish and small creatures that live there come to eat at it. If it escapes from there into the open air, hungry flying creatures land and suck on it. Wherever the cow is, these pests pounce onto the exposed mass of flesh and eat it, and this would be even more intense in the heat of the tropics. By comprehending sensory contact as nutriment in this way, one also penetrates all three kinds of feelings.

Explanation

The *second nutriment* is contact. The body with its sense organs was formed by the body-forming nutriments and now it can and must be touched by experiences. Through contact with the inner sense bases, the mind is now continually fed by sensory nutriment. Mentally, one is confronted, moved, affected by the constant stream of experiences.

The *cow* represents the living person, that is, the name and form or mind and corporeality (*nāma-rūpa*) occupied by consciousness. The *flayed skin* (being without skin) is the six inner sense bases. The *four places*—the wall, tree, water and open air—are similar to the four elements (*dhātu*), which, as outer bases, confront people in the way of contact (*creatures*). Wherever one may be, the mind with its cravings is constantly touched by external things via the six sense doors. There are constant pressures, strokes of fate and injuries, coarse or fine, in consequence of which three things are nourished: feeling, perception and activity. As is said in MN 109, these three aggregates (*vedanā, saññā, saṅkhārā*) all have their basis in contact, which is the condition and nutriment for them. All are conditioned by the suffering of duality, in which an urge ("I") is touched by something ("the world"). If something confronts me, I am affected. I feel good or bad. My perception introduces the feeling-triggering object, evaluates it and reacts. Thus contact nourishes these three things, all of which are suffering, i.e., hardships which have to be endured.

The Pit of Glowing Embers

There is a deep pit full of glowing embers. A man passes by who wants to live and not to die, who desires happiness and loathes

Dependent origination

pain. However, two strong men seize him by the arms and, although he is struggling and resisting so as to save himself, they drag him to the edge of the pit against his intention. He knows he will die if he falls into the pit. His struggle to get away is at best only causing some delay. Whoever comprehends the nutriment of mental intention, says the Buddha, has also penetrated all three kinds of craving.

Explanation

The *third nutriment* is mental intentions. The two other intentions named in the Canon, i.e., physical action and speech, are included here because underlying and accompanying all physical activity and speech there are mental activities programmed by mental intentions.

Elsewhere in the Canon, the *pit of glowing embers* is an image of hell (MN 12.37); accordingly the *two men* would be demons dragging a person to hell.[25] All the person's striving is directed towards well-being and so consequently he strives to get as far away as possible from the most extreme pain (hell). All the striving of a person—all efforts, all plans, intentions, reflections, and considerations—may perhaps occasionally take him to the finest realms of well-being, but these are impermanent, and nobody can permanently escape downfall into the lower realms unless he has reached stream-entry (*sotāpatti*) or beyond (AN 3:114). This means that all intentions directed towards this world of impermanence, towards saṃsāra, are vain attempts to escape suffering. One can nourish the mind with thoughts and intentions as subtle and wholesome as one might, but none of them will lead him out of saṃsāra. As long as the mind is polluted by greed, hatred, and delusion, mental intention has a natural inclination to go on a downward course in saṃsāra. If saṃsāra is evaluated positively, then consciousness is inclined to worldliness, that is, to saṃsāra, and eventually to

---

25. Perhaps the two men should rather be seen as bodily and verbal kamma. Having mentally intended unskilfully, one acts unskilfully by body and speech, and thus creates the unwholesome kamma dragging one to hell.

the pit of glowing embers, hell. Even though the person wants nothing but happiness, still in the end he creates pain for himself again and again. Hence it is exactly there in his thinking and intending—just where he thinks he is free—that he is coerced and forced into the mechanism of conditionality. The entire intending of the worldly person is a vain struggle away from unsatisfactory situations. As part of the Buddha's path, wholesome intentions are to be developed, not for a pleasant life or a good rebirth, but as a means, as a vehicle to reach Nibbāna. Only those instructed by the Buddha can set up thorough wise attention (*yoniso manasikāra*) as to the impermanent, painful nature of the world, which then leads to the intention to deny and go transcend all intentions, all activity, and all nourishment of the heart-mind (MN 56).

Three Hundred Sword Blows

A robber is brought before the king so that a penalty can be imposed on him. The king sentences him to a hundred blows with a sword in the morning. When at noon the king finds out that the offender is still alive, he orders another hundred blows. When in the evening the king hears that the robber is still alive he orders a further hundred blows. If the robber feels pain and agony from even a single blow, how much more from three hundred! The Buddha says, whoever understands consciousness as a nutriment in this way has also understood name and form (*nāma-rūpa*).

Explanation

The *fourth nutriment* is consciousness itself.

Consciousness is the nutriment for all name and form, both inner and outer. Only through consciousness can the body take in physical nutriment, and thus condition contact and intention. Consciousness mirrors the world. As nourishing habit, it does not cease at death (cf. DN 25). It always nourishes rebirth, descending into a womb, and building a new name and form (*nāma-rūpa*). Just as the robber in the simile did not die despite three hundred strokes, so, despite all the suffering of saṃsāra, consciousness does not die and does not want to. Again and again, it nourishes a mortal form (corporeality). Therewith the inseparably connected mind keeps a diary of the suffering in the morning, at noon, and in the evening. Again and again, consciousness (the robber) is struck by name and form (punishment), but it never has enough; instead it lets itself be punished again and again.

18. The Painter and his Painting (SN 12:64)

There is a painter whose paints are four natural dyes of India, namely scarlet (made from lac, the resinous secretion of arboreal insects); yellow (made from turmeric); indigo (made from the plant of the same name); and red (made from the roots of the Bengal madder). Also, there are three kinds of bases he uses for making a painting: a polished wooden panel, a stone wall and a piece of fine cloth. When the painter likes to paint, he, in accordance to his idea, takes the paint and creates a painting out of contours, creatures, figures, pictures that he paints on the base. The people take form as male and female, with colours that are deceptively similar to the original models, lifelike and realistic, featuring every detail.

It is the same when all four nutriments of existence are present—body-forming nutriment, contact, mental intention and consciousness. One is attracted to them, craves for them and, when grasping them, is satisfied. By grasping, a footing or base is given to consciousness, and it grows. Wherever consciousness becomes established and flourishes, there is the development of name and form (*nāma-rūpa*). Thereby one grasps further activity, thereby one develops further becoming, and thereby the result is birth and death with sorrow, lamentation and despair—in brief, with pain.

Explanation

The *colours* are the same as those mentioned in MN 21.14 with regard to the painting of space, and in AN 5:193 concerning pollution of water (for the first hindrance). The physically pure primary colours (blue, yellow, red, white) form another tetrad (DN 16.2.15; AN 8:46), which is also mentioned as the content of perception (MN 43.8) and of meditation (MN 77.23). Both sets are occasionally mixed to give blue, yellow, red and scarlet (MN

7.2; MN 75.20; MN 99.12).

The quickly fading turmeric is similar to momentary contact; the multipurpose, ambivalent, and changing indigo is similar to mental intention, which can be directed to many things. That the body-forming nutriment is symbolized by blood-red scarlet from dead insects is obvious because people sustain themselves on dead animals and plants; thus nutriment is something dead as well as deadly. And this is, in this simile, the painter's material.

The *bases* are the three possibilities of attraction, namely the three worlds (sensuality, fine-material forms and formlessness). Thus it is said in AN 3:76 that consciousness firmly fixes itself in the three ways of being. Paint adheres to wood the least, not penetrating deeply, and so colour is most impermanent there. The wall on which one paints a fresco accepts paint somewhat better and more deeply, so that frescoes last longer than paintings on wood. The fine cloth, however, lets the colour penetrate most deeply so that it is the most lastingly absorbed. The three worlds are constituted in the same way with regard to their permanence: life is shortest in the sensual world, it lasts incomparably much longer in the fine-material world and lasts longest in the immaterial world.

The *painter* is the grasping self, satisfying its craving by taking colours and actively creating something on the base of the world. Just as the painter is attracted by the blaze of his colours and visualises his painting as an idea, so the craving, thirsty self is fascinated by the four nutriments and throws itself onto them, nourishing itself from them.

The *paintings* are as follows: the painter paints female images (*itthi-rūpa*) and male images (*purisa-rūpa*), that is, form (*rūpa*) as a particular living form (*nāma-rūpa*). By grasping the fourth nutriment—consciousness—name and form (*nāma-rūpa*) grows. Consciousness as the nutriment of nutriments nourishes the appearance of "I and the world," that is, the apparent split between them. When the painter paints on the base, the figures are there; when craving grasps nutriments in the three ways of being, it forms name and form. The habituation of consciousness (subject) and the manifestation of name and form (object) mutually condition each other like two upright bundles of reeds supporting each other (SN 12:67). They stand together or not at all.

However, the nature of ignorance is to see the painting as reality, though it is formed only out of an idea. Just as one takes a painting on the wall to be a real world and sees the painted objects in one's imagination as three-dimensional, so we experience the products of craving, which we regard as external and independently existent, although they stand and fall with the existence of consciousness.

The *further colouring*: where there are forms (objects) for consciousness (subject), the creation process continues. In ever-new brush strokes, the painter confirms the idea of his design and materialises it in ever more pronounced ways. In the same way, the grasping of activity multiplies existence in becoming, birth, old age and death, that is, the last four members of the interrelation of conditions called dependent origination.

The *sequence of suffering*: by believing oneself to be in the painting, by identifying with it, one is subjected, between birth and death, to all the suffering of sorrow over the transitory nature of existence and of despair over the hopelessness.

For *the opposite*, the overcoming of suffering, another simile is given at the end of this discourse:

The Window

A hut consisting of only one room has windows in three directions (north, south and east). When the sun rises, a shaft of its light would fall on the western wall, reflect there and create shadow images. But if there were no wall or if there were another window, the shaft of light would fall only onto the ground. If there were no ground, it would fall onto the water. If there were no water, the light would not find any footing at all. Similarly, if there is no impulse, satisfaction, or craving for the four nutriments, consciousness finds no footing, and then there is no name and form, nor any other suffering.

Explanation

The triad of *wall, earth, and water* could here refer to the "three worlds." Built by humans as a possession, the wall is the coarsest footing (sense world); the natural earth, not claimed as a possession, is comparable to the fine-material world; and the finer substance of the water would be comparable to the formless world.

The *sun* with its radiation is activity (*saṅkhāra*), including thought-habituation, which has come into existence through it. As the sun rises and warms, permitting growth to take place and throwing shadows, so activity creates friction, embellishes the world, and throws the shadow of transitoriness.

Finding no foothold: when the three worlds are fully denied mentally at the stage of arahantship, there is no activity any more which nourishes and multiplies the four nutriments, there is nothing for consciousness to establish itself upon, and all forms—and therewith all states of suffering—collapse. Beyond the three actualities of saṃsāra (the three worlds), is the actuality of Nibbāna, the basic element of desirelessness. There ends the creating of activity (*saṅkhāra*) because perfect well-being has been reached, where there is nothing more to improve.

The simile of the painter is also found in another context, SN 22:100, with regard to the five aggregates instead of the four nutriments.

19. Setting Fire to a Dry Grassland (SN 14:12)

There is a completely dried-up stretch of grassland ready to blaze into flames at the least tinder. A man throws a burning torch of grass onto this dangerous place. The dry grass bursts into flames, burns and kills all the creatures that live in the grass (insects, worms, snakes, etc.). However, this outcome is not inevitable. The man could prevent the fire from spreading by quickly extinguishing the fire with his hands and feet with all his energy.

It is the same with ascetics and priests. If an unwholesome, erroneous perception arises in them and they do not negate, discard, finish or exterminate it immediately, they will be tortured by sorrow, despair and passions in this life, and after death descend into the lower realms.

Explanation

The *dry grassland* is the parched, thirsty mind, full of desires, which reside in the body. Through the senses the mind lurks obsessively for objects with which it can let itself be set aflame. It is empty, dried up and lacking since it does not get what it wants and is occupied by the three kinds of wrong intentions (*saṅkappa*): 1. sense addiction (lusting towards the external objects), 2. hatred, and 3. cruelty. Because it longs for a continuity and great variety of experiences, the mind is averse to obstacles to the fulfilment of desire, and seeks to defend itself against competitors and those who disturb it. These threefold basic elements of lust, hatred, and cruelty stand for the inner potential of the grassland to burst into flames.

The *burning grass torch* thrown onto the grassland is a phenomenon that emerges from 'outside.' It is only because there is an inner sensitivity—flammability (dry grass)—that the touch of the six sense objects from the outside (the grass torch) can affect anything. Many other similes illustrate this same relationship between the inner sensitivity (consciousness) and impingement from the outside through the six sense bases: for example, the image of a stone thrown on a mound of moist clay (MN 119.23), a sappy tree and an axe (SN 35:231/190; see Simile 12), open wounds and irritating insects (SN 12:64; see Simile 17), a festering sore and a blow with a broken shard of pottery (AN 3:25; see 68).

The *blazing grassfire*, the ignition and the conflagration—these are the experiences of perception, following on from the contact between inner sensitivity and external impingement. If we experience what our inner desire longs for, the mental imagination throws itself onto that, and inflamed by the fantasy forgets everything else. Thus is the inner fire of greedy, hateful, and cruel perception conditioned by the respective basic element.

Not to extinguish the fire with hands and feet means not to use the means at one's disposal, with proper regard for the consequences of this fire, to extinguish it, that is, with right thought. One lets pass by the possibility of right, fire-extinguishing contemplation. One doesn't use the power of right judgement. Thus one loses the opportunity to quench the fire. The perception that arises out of an inflamed drive-conditioned basic element is unavoidable and the consequent tendency to mental approval is purely a result. But not to follow the first spark of approval any further, this is the possible chance, the opportunity, to extinguish the conflagration.

The *burning to death of beings* is the harming of one's own concerns. Every drive feels as though it is a self, as though it is a living being. Just as there are a countless insects buzzing about in a place of dry grass, so in the unliberated heart there are countless 'I's, countless desires wanting to experience well-being and loathing to experience pain. Whenever the perception of fire—of greed, hatred and delusion—is approved of, out of that approval instantly arises intention, feverish passion, and pursuit. Out of these come unwholesome actions in thought, word and deed. Craving becomes ever stronger, turns into fever, while outside, one creates painful torches, burning experiences, even unto the hellfire of the underworld. Burning inside and outside, one suffers painful feelings. Because one has not extinguished (*nibbāpeti*) them, one is even farther away from desireless happiness, from Nibbāna (= no-more-burning).

20. The Deer in the Swamp (MN 19.25)

A large herd of deer is grazing in a wooded area on a mountain slope near an expansive, low-lying marsh. A man comes by who is ill-disposed toward the deer, seeking their harm and bondage. He closes off the path that is safe, fit and pleasant and instead opens a false way leading down into the swamp, while at the same time praising it as fit, and encouraging the herd to take it. If the herd take it, its numbers would diminish. Now, suppose another man who has compassion for the herd, wishing it well-being, freedom and security, comes by and reopens the former path that is safe, fit and pleasant, while at the same time blocking the way leading down into the swamp to keep them from taking it, then this large herd of deer would increase, flourish, and prosper.

Explanation

The *wooded area* is existence. The *herd of deer* are beings, collectively, in whatever world, who are not free from desires,

Dependent origination

who seek them over and over again. The *expansive, low-lying marsh* represents the world of sense pleasures (*kāma-loka*). It is a world of dependency on the outside, the only world with hellish pains. Although swamp plants that the animals particularly like grow in the marsh, this is the lowest of the three worlds. Māra, the evil one or Lord of Death, dwells in the sense-world and is here symbolized by *the man who is ill-disposed towards beings*, who wants to control the deer, and keep them in his realm of suffering, like a tyrant entraps his subjects. The *way down* is the wrong eightfold path leading from wrong view to wrong calm, to the spurious calm of being bogged down in the swamp of complacency. This false path follows the impulse for satisfaction, the addiction to enjoying the temporary satisfaction of fulfilling one's desires. Following desires, fulfilling them, one moves deeper and deeper into the swamp. It is ignorance that depicts this way as fit, justifying it as a safe track, and being fascinated by it. Out of ignorance one follows enjoyment; since one believes the way into the marsh is secure, out of ignorance one follows it seeking satisfaction. Or, put differently: where an apparently fit pasture lures, one ends up in a bog out of ignorance. Thus, *the compassionate man* (the Buddha) must first come to open the right Noble Eightfold Path and to block the way leading down.

Since one only knows things from the perspective of the marsh of desires, and since, when there is no Buddha, Māra prevents knowledge of the way out, therefore one cannot distinguish between the right path and the way leading down. One walks down the wrong way by enjoying sense pleasures. Thus, one strays further and further away from the right way leading out of the marsh and forest up to true security and safety, to well-being and liberation, to the lofty states of insight and calm praised so much at the end of this discourse.

21. The Current to the Lake of Misfortune (It 4:10/109)

Seeing a swimmer carried along by the apparently pleasant and attractive current of a river, a sharp-sighted man shouts from the bank, "Listen! You'll be carried into danger by that seemingly pleasant and attractive current of the river! Downstream is a lake with large waves, whirlpools, crocodiles and demons. If you reach it, you will die or suffer deadly pain." As soon as the swimmer hears the warning voice, he paddles vigorously with hands and feet against the current.

Explanation

The *current of the river* is the current of tendencies and desires expressing themselves in craving, which is perceived as a lack of gratification and a sense that something is missing. We all swim in this current of craving and are so accustomed to it that we do not notice and take it for granted. It appears pleasant and attractive because objects temporarily satisfy the desires that reside in the sixfold realm of the inner sense bases.

This is the reason why the six inner sense bases are called 'the pleasant pretence.' "Yesterday that object satisfied me, so I want it again today!" says craving, driven by well-being. And so I follow that craving and satisfy myself over and over again, swimming as I do in the currents of the sixfold realm of the inner sense bases, of contact, feeling, craving and grasping.

This is the present situation. However, the consequence is symbolized by the dangerous lake to which the swimmer is being carried. The *lake* is the world of sensuality to which the swimmer is bound with five lower fetters (*saṃyojana*): personality-belief, doubt, clinging to virtues and observances, sense desire, and hatred. In the lake are *the strong waves* of anger and rage (hatred) and *the whirlpools* of entanglement in the world and sexuality (sense desire). Through these two fetters one remains bound to the world of sensuality and does not rise up to the state of non-returning where only the five higher fetters exist (see Simile 46).

The *sharp-sighted man standing on the bank* is the Buddha. If the *swimmer*, the person instructed by the Buddha, understands what is ahead of him—having to satisfy the desires over and over again without any lasting result—he begins to swim against the current. This is renunciation, turning away from sensual pleasures.

Paddling with hands and feet is the energy arising from the confident resolution to renounce.

The sutta closes with this verse:

> Desiring future security from bondage
> One should abandon sensual desire
> However painful this may be.
> Rightly comprehending with wisdom,
> Possessing a mind that is well released,
> One may reach freedom step by step.
> One who is a master of knowledge,
> Who has lived the holy life,
> Is called one gone to the world's end,
> One who has reached the further shore.[26]

This simile of swimming against the current to escape its dangers is found repeatedly in the Canon with several variations (e.g. see MN 67.14 = AN 4:122; It 69; SN 35:228–229/187–189; and, without the images for danger, AN 4:5). Another simile (Simile 5) depicts the swimmer who cannot find safety by grabbing hold of the five aggregates (SN 22:93). The simile of seven swimmers diving in the water (AN 7:15) will be discussed in Simile 46. Further similes are concerned with crossing a river in order to get safely to the other shore (SN 35:238/197; DN 13; MN 34; MN 22.13; SN 1:1; MN 64.8; AN 4:196). In all cases water is the dangerous element in which the person cannot survive if he doesn't make effort. Either he sinks or he is carried off (SN 1:1). The goal is to achieve a firm stand, to reach the safe shore where there is no more flowing (MN 140.32). Thus this simile presents a teaching which recurs many times in the Canon and stands here in lieu of many other statements.

In the similes the recurring images are of strong waves, whirlpools, crocodiles and demons that denote the perils that lie ahead for the unwary.

1. *Waves and surges*, the first evil, are compared to anger and despair. In MN 67.16, this danger for the swimmer is

---

26. Translation by J. D. Ireland, *The Udāna and the Itivuttaka*, pp. 188–89.

compared to one who is resisting the commands and regulations of the monks' community, i.e., as a protest. One reacts to unpleasant situations with anger and rage. These inner surges well up as forms of hatred. In other places as well the Buddha uses the image of surges (It 69; AN 4:122; SN 35:228–229/187–189).

2. *Whirlpools and eddies*, the second evil, are compared to the five sense pleasures (see also MN 67; SN 35:241/200). In MN 67, the danger of the whirlpool (*āvatta-bhaya*) is illustrated as follows. A monk sees a householder using sense objects and bustling around with them to his heart's content. He remembers how he used to live in a house in the same way, and comes to think that it would be sufficient to do good deeds, and thus once more enjoy sense pleasures, instead of restraining from them as an ascetic. So he gives up asceticism and returns (*āvattati*) to lay life. He does not see nor think anymore about the struggles and sorrows of the household life; he only sees the household life in a sentimental, distorted, deluded way.[27] Blinded by delusion, he is pulled again into the whirlpool of the senses and spins around in endless circles like a piece of wood in a vortex (SN 35:241). The five outer sense bases catch us, bind us, and pull us down into their vortices.

3. and 4. As the third and fourth evils, *Crocodiles and demons*, "demons and ogres" (*gaha* and *rakkhasa*; also It 69; SN 35:228–229) are compared to gluttony and lust for the opposite sex. The expression "demon" (*gaha* literally means "seizer") is a term for crocodiles, which snap at and seize the swimmer, drag him down and eat him. *Rakkhasa* is a kind of water-ogre or ogress. In western mythology, they would be called mermaids, who lure swimmers down into their realm.

Waves and eddies are dangers associated with the nature of water and can be avoided by the swimmer staying away from the

---

27. Compare the Chinese proverb "Memory has a golden paintbrush," and the Italian proverb "Time makes the bitterest tears taste sweet."

places where they exist. However animals and beings living in the water that can pursue and kill the swimmer are the more perilous danger. This is matched to the monk's situation. In MN 67, crocodiles and sharks (*kumbhīla* and *susuka*) are defined as gluttony and sexual desire. Just as the gluttonous crocodile opens its huge jaws to pull down and devour its food—the swimmer—so the monk is pulled down and devoured by his greed for tasty food that lures him return to the world. Just as the hungry shark pulls down and devours the swimmer, so the monk is pulled down and devoured by sexual desire and leaves the holy life. Thus the lust for internal flesh (i.e., for eating meat) and the lust for external flesh (i.e., the carnal desire for touching attractive flesh) are closely connected.

22. The Great Log in the Ganges (SN 35:241)

If a great log of wood in the Ganges does not becomes stuck on this or the other shore, if it does not sink in the middle of the river or become stranded on a sandbar, if it is not taken by humans or nonhumans, if it isn't drawn into a whirlpool or become rotten, then it will incline, bend, and tend toward the sea. Why is this? Because the Ganges inclines, bends, and tends toward the sea. In the same way, if one does not have these eight hindrances, one will incline, bend and tend toward the extinction of the taints (*āsava*). Why? Because right view causes inclining, bending, and tending toward the extinction of taints.

Explanation

The *great log of wood* is the conscious body, the person. The *Ganges*, India's holy river, stands for the deepest and most intrinsic striving of beings toward final liberation, from which, however, almost all are distracted. Were the eight hindrances not there, or were they overcome, one would reach Nibbāna as the Ganges reaches the sea. In contrast to most other similes, where the current leads to danger and a misfortune, here the current leads to the ultimate well-being. The current of the river is here the informed, mindful current of right view—something that can be induced only by a Buddha.

The *eight hindrances* divide themselves into two groups of four each.

Becoming stuck on this shore denotes attachment to the six inner bases. One identifies oneself with the body and its six senses, and so one becomes stuck with the six sense bases, which gradually decay and die. One blindly sticks to the mortal "self" instead of following the current to the Deathless.

Becoming stuck on the other shore concerns the six outer bases. One throws oneself onto possession, onto the "mine," onto a world one takes to be real, be it even the finest Brahmā world. One entangles oneself in transitory things and thereby gets drawn away from the wholesome.

To sink in the middle of the river is to be swamped by delight and lust (*nandi-rāga*). The piece of wood is gradually saturated with water and becomes heavier and heavier, until the stream finally can no longer carry it. Similarly, the hedonist soaks and immerses himself in desires that weigh him down more and more through pleasure-approval until he finally loses all energy. He also sinks down—in saṃsāra. In the simile of the seven swimmers (AN 7:15), the first three people drown because they only ask for gratification of feeling without regard for the consequences.

Becoming stranded on a sandbar is to be snared by the "I am" conceit (*asmi-māna*). Conceit or pride (*māna*) always elevates itself above any situation so that it feels it is the master. Whether it be the primitive pride of success in the sense world or the fine conceit attributing mental successes to the self (see MN 113), one is literally stranded, though believing oneself to be secure. If one rests on one's own laurels, one does not strive. Conceit is always a self-pleasing self-mirroring. One has such a high opinion of oneself that eventually one compares oneself to others and looks down on them.[28]

---

28. Although pride is the most common form of conceit, the suttas mention three types of "I-am conceit" (*asmi-māna*): "I am better," "I am equal," "I am inferior." See, e.g., D III 216, Sn III 48, and Sn IV 87. Thoughts that one is equal or inferior are forms of conceit (*māna*) since they affirm the "I."

Dependent origination

These four images name the immediately visible possibilities for the piece of wood to become stuck in the four directions of right and left, above and below. The second tetrad describes how the piece of wood comes out of the current through being taken by humans or gods, or by being caught in eddies, or by decomposition through rotting.

To be taken by humans is to become stuck in socialising. One is enjoying the company of family and friends. Forgetting one's aim, the safe shore, one is completely out of the current, caught by the laity. This is said of the monk who forgets his monkhood in the company of householders, rejoicing when they are happy, being sad when they are sad, and gets involved in their affairs.

To be taken by nonhumans, (i.e., superhuman beings or gods), is to become stuck by aspiring for celestial rebirth. The extrovert lets himself be taken in by socialising, while the introvert is taken in by possibilities for self-development. He wants to become a god, to realise paradise. The aim of his endeavours in virtue and in meditation is self-preservation. However, such a one is disinclined, as it is said in MN 16, to make efforts in self-penetration. This is also true of mystics who aspire to a pure existence so as to enjoy it eternally. While this is the finest possibility if one were to come out of the wholesome current, nonetheless one will miss indestructible well-being.

To be taken by an eddy or whirlpool is to be caught up in the endless variety of sense pleasures. Just as the piece of wood is swirled around and around and goes nowhere, so the sensualist is swirled around and around in the sense world and remains there drifting in circles. He takes each day as it comes, and in the end he is no further forward. Once again he stands there empty-handed. He may think he has achieved something—raised children, lived a full life, all respectable and reasonable—yet in the end the cravings and desires clutch only air. He has to wander on in saṃsāra, leaving his beloved things behind. This is the eddy of the realm of contact. Apparitions pass by and vanish again.

What is it *to become rotten inside*? The Buddha defines it as follows. It is a monk who is without virtue, who is full of evil, impure, of suspicious behaviour and secretive. Although he is not an ascetic, he pretends to be one; although he is not living the life of a celibate, he pretends to be celibate—he is flooded inside with foulness (see AN 4:241; AN 7:68; AN 7:19/20 = Ud 5.5.). Although all five faults are listed with respect to the monk, the last fault—being secretive—deals with a specifically monastic situation. Here is a monk who is no longer truly a monk but only pretends outwardly to be one. He secretly transgresses the laws of true monkhood, but nevertheless tries to retain monastic status, enjoying its reputation and the donations given by householders out of faith in the Sangha (the monastic order). Instead of admitting his limitations and weaknesses, and openly and honestly choosing to resign from the Sangha (which is always possible), he keeps up the pretence. This is to rot inside. Such a sham monk contradicts himself, he tears himself apart inside, destroying every wholesome possibility within. Just as a rotten piece of wood eventually disintegrates, so such a monk loses substance. This is the reason the Buddha says that it is better to swallow a red-hot iron ball and die than to be a sham monk and pave the way to the lower realms of existence (AN 7:68). Lacking substance, he is completely out of the current. There is nothing that can be carried by the current.

While the monk who cannot resist sensual pleasures (the eddies) and leaves the Sangha to enjoy life as a householder again can always return to the Sangha, it is not so with the monk who has committed one of the offences entailing defeat (*pārājika*), that is, engaging in sexual intercourse, theft, killing a human, and making false claims of having superhuman powers. He is thereby excluded from re-entry into the Sangha for life. He is as non-existent as the rotten piece of wood when it decomposes and disintegrates.

23. The Nutriments for Fires and Trees (SN 12:52–59)

The eight suttas that will now be discussed deal with the origination and cessation of suffering. Here we will only deal with the origination parts of these suttas. The cessation, which makes up the other half of these suttas, is discussed in Simile 30.

Dependent origination

Suttas 12:52 through to 12:57 begin with:

Whoever dwells seeing satisfaction in things that can be grasped ... that can cause bondage, increases craving. Conditioned by craving, is grasping, ... becoming, ... birth, ... conditioned by birth, are old age and death, sorrow-lamentation-pain-grief-and-despair—that is, the whole mass of suffering.

In Suttas 12:58–59, the sequence is taken back before craving to name and form in Sutta 12:58 and to consciousness in 12:59—that is, to the phenomena on which craving and grasping are based. Suttas 12:52, 55 and 56 concern graspable things, while 12:53, 54 and 57–59 deal with binding things. Crucial, however, are the four similes given in these discourses, two concerning fire and two concerning a tree.

1. If there were a huge bonfire burning from ten to forty heaps of wood (*mahā-aggikkhandha*), and from time to time a man were to throw on dry grass, dry wood and dry cow dung, then nourished by that fuel and grasping it, the fire would continue to burn for a long time (12:52).

2. If there were an oil lamp burning because of the oil and the wick, and from time to time a man were to refill the oil and add more wick, then nourished by that and grasping it, the lamp would burn for a long time (12:53-54).

3. If there were a mighty Banyan tree fed by roots going downward and laterally, then nourished by that and grasping it, it would feed sap to its crown and would exist for a long time (12:55-56, 58-59)

4. If there were a sapling and from time to time a man were to come and clear the area around the roots and add water and humus to it, then nourished by that and grasping it, it would come to growth, fruition and fullness (12:57).

Explanation

Initially, let us examine the three steps in the relationship between satisfaction and craving.

The first is the seeing of satisfaction or gratification: life is the source of satisfaction for the person and the tree, in the same way as burning is for the fire. This is the tacit assumption underlying all these similes.

Secondly, out of ignorance, there is acceptance, welcoming and pulling in of this satisfaction by the person, the tree, and the fire. Each of them takes satisfaction to be real, lasting satisfaction and takes this to be a positive, pleasant thing. The human does this by thinking, by mental activity, which also leads him to act by body and speech. In similar ways, the tree and fire also grasp their nutriment and suck it in. Activity, the positive evaluation of that which appears as pleasant, is what is alluded to here. The tree does this naturally, instinctively; the fire naturally, mechanically, so that it appears as grasping only to external observer.

Third is the consequence: the person continues to exist endlessly as a being subject to craving and suffering, the fire burns for a long time, the lamp shines for a long time, the tree lives for a long time, and the sapling matures.

This triad—that of satisfaction, activity, and consequence—is expressed in the first three factors of dependent origination. Deluded and distorted perception, which always has satisfaction as its aim, is ignorance (*avijjā*). Accepting satisfaction leads to activity (*saṅkhāra*), the central act of creation. And the consequence, according to Sutta 12:59, is consciousness (*viññāṇa*), and all further factors conditioned by it—name and form, the sixfold realm of the sense bases, contact, feeling, craving, grasping, becoming, birth, etc., through to suffering—of which only the sequence of factors from craving to suffering is mentioned in suttas 52 to 57. This latter sequence can be regarded as representing the initial sequence of conditions in an explicit way since these latter factors are experienced even by one who doesn't know about their underlying causes and consequences.

The nourishing factor of grasping occurs in two of the four similes as a trio (throwing hay, dung, or wood on the fire; clearing the weeds around the roots, adding humus and water to the sapling), in the other two as a duo (replenishing the oil and wick; the roots sucking water from below as well as laterally). Is this meaningful? Perhaps one could consider it in the following way.

In the last mentioned duo, the oil supply and the underground roots are the more hidden and deeper components, while the lateral roots in the surrounding earth and the wick are the more obvious aspects in the foreground. In the same way, one has to discriminate between the three ways of action, namely, mental activity (thinking) on the one hand and the bodily activities (talking and doing) on the other. Thinking is hidden, invisible, deep (like the subterranean roots or the oil supply), while talking and acting are obvious, visible, superficial (lateral roots, wick).

For the triads in the two similes first mentioned, one could consider the following.

Dry grass (hay) burns fastest; it blazes up and turns immediately to ash. Cow dung (a common fuel in India) lasts somewhat longer. Wood, however, lasts longest and is therefore the best fuel for fires. In a similar way, clearing the soil has relatively the smallest effect, the adding of humus is somewhat more effective, but watering is the most important for the continued existence of the sapling. Perhaps one can see here again an image for the so-called three great activities (physical, verbal and mental). Relatively least important for existence and its future are physical activities because they mostly pass away quickly (throwing hay on the fire, clearing the soil). Then come the verbal activities (throwing dung on the fire, adding humus). However, the most fundamental activities are mental activities (adding wood, watering) which, by appreciative or depreciative thinking, affect the continuation of consciousness and craving (see MN 56).

24. The Germs (SN 22:54)

There are five kinds of germs: root-germs, trunk-germs, top-germs, joint-germs, and seed-germs. If these five kinds of germs are not broken, rotten or destroyed by wind and sun, if they are fresh and well stored, and if there is enough earth and water, they will come to growth, development and maturity.

Explanation

In Pali as well as Sanskrit the term used for 'seed,' *bīja*, has a wider sense than in English. *Bīja* encompasses any kind of generating element or source of life. That is why any part of a plant, such as a bulb, rhizome or sucker, that causes a new plant can be called a *bīja*, a germ or seed.

The *five kinds of germs* represent the five aggregates. Consciousness finds its nourishment and basis, its *earth*, in the four stations of consciousness (*viññāṇaṭṭhiti*), i.e., the aggregates of form, feeling, perception, and mental activities, or, more concisely, in name and form (see DN 15 and SN 12:65). *Water* represents delight and lust. When there is delight in the four other aggregates, consciousness takes them as its foundation, and establishes itself. By seeking satisfaction, it will come to *growth, development, and maturity*. However, if the desire for name and form is overcome, then the basis is cut off and there is no longer the establishment of consciousness. This consciousness then develops no further; it no longer creates; it is liberated; it stands content, unshakable.

Consciousness nourished by the other four aggregates. Within them, it stands like a plant in the earth. How the five kinds of germs relate to the five aggregates may be left open here. Evidence is lacking whether, for example, plants out of roots (the first) or those out of seeds (the last) stand for consciousness; perhaps even both are possible.

However, the growth of the plants occurs only if there are five qualities favourable and positive for consciousness and saṃsāra but definitely unfavourable and negative for liberation, for Nibbāna; they are worldly faith, complacency, heedlessness, lack of concentration, and lack of wisdom. The greedy, untamed consciousness aiming at gratification and satisfaction is nourished by these five qualities and relies on the fact that no wholesome qualities influence it, that is, that it does not come under the influence of the five powers (reasoned faith, energy, mindfulness, unification of mind, and wisdom). Accordingly, the unbroken germ of the untamed consciousness represents a wrong, worldly faith, which has not been broken by right faith (*saddhā*). The germs that are not rotten, that are hard and strong, and not softened by *samādhi* are the unappeased addiction to action. Germs that are not damaged by the sun and wind and waiting for their time to sprout represent complacency, unaffected by the warmth of energy and effort (*viriya*). Young and fresh seeds from the most recent harvest represent mindless intoxication and the unrestrained heedlessness of the young, whereas the fully ripened seed would be mindfulness, distanced from the exuberant energy-fount of youth. Lastly, well-stored seeds are those kept away from too much moisture or too much heat, in a good environment where there is no breaking, rotting or drying up. Everything serves for their preservation, just as ignorance serves the preservation of lustful desires by all possible means. On the other hand, wisdom serves the storage of the seed under the influence of the Buddha, whereby the power of lustful desires are reduced and penetrated by all possible means.

When worldly faith, complacency, heedlessness, lack of concentration and non-wisdom are the qualities and habit of consciousness, then greed has not been overcome and it flourishes in the fertile soil. But when right faith, energy, mindfulness, calm, and wisdom break the unwholesome force, greed is overcome, the four stands or bases are no longer sustained, and consciousness ceases.

Elsewhere in the Canon similar similes involving seeds/germs are found: In AN 3:76 it is said that kamma is the field, consciousness is the seed, and craving the moisture for future becoming (*punabbhava*). In SN 5:9 the seed/soil/water simile is also found and the result are the aggregates, elements, and sense-bases. A similar seed simile is given in AN 3:33 where it depicts the origination of kamma due to greed, hatred and delusion, leading to rebirth; and the destruction of kamma through non-greed, non-hatred and non-delusion, leading to the end of rebirth. A man, representing wise attention, *yoniso manasikāra*, reduces the (unspecified) seeds to ashes (the earth-element), by burning them in a fire (the fire-element), letting the ashes blow away in gust of wind (the wind-element), or throwing them in a river or stream (the water element). Thus this destroying of the seeds denotes the development of insight through the contemplation of the body by way of the elements. If the body is fully seen as it is, as just a mass of elements, the seeds of consciousness can not sprout in a new birth. As is said about the arahant in the Ratanasutta:

> The old is destroyed, there is no coming to be of the new—
> Those who are dispassionate towards future existence,
> who have destroyed the seeds and have no desire sprouting,
> Those wise ones will extinguish just like this lamp. (Sn 235)

25. Rising Tide (SN 12:69)

If the great ocean surges, it makes the great rivers surge; if these surge, the smaller streams surge; if these surge, they fill the great valleys; if these are filled, they fill the smaller valleys. In the same way, if ignorance surges, formations surge; if these surge, they make consciousness surge; if that surges, it makes name and form surge; if that surges, it makes the six sense-bases surge; if those surge, they make contact surge; if contact surges, feeling surges; if that surges, it makes craving surge; if that surges, it makes grasping surge; if that surges, it makes becoming surge; if that surges it makes birth surge; and if birth surges, it makes old age and death surge as well.

Explanation

Take the city of Hamburg for example. When there is a storm tide in the North Sea, the Elbe river surges; if the Elbe river surges, the Alster canals surge; if the Alster canals surge, the Alster watershed fills; if the Alster watershed fills, the water further up in the Alster valley surges.

This is easy to see in nature, but how is the simile to be understood when five sequential events in nature are put in relation to twelve mental phenomena? The discourse does not give the slightest indication for resolving this question. The solution can emerge only out of the subject matter itself. It is like a koan over which one can brood. One has to contemplate the twelve factors until they themselves formulate the solution.

The Buddha often mentions "the tide of ignorance" (*avijjogha*, DN 33.4, SN 35:197) surging in the *great ocean* of saṃsāra. When distorted ignorant perception surges, when the person is so flooded by it that he believes he exists in an objective world, then his activities necessarily have to increase, he has to create more, to sustain himself.

The *great river*, the mighty current, is thought-activity, mental creativity. Streams of thought urged by ignorance, the "flows of conceiving" (*maññanassavā*, MN 140.30), flow powerfully, immediately causing the stream of consciousness (*viññāṇa-sota*) to flow, both being like a single flow of impulse and energy. On the stream of consciousness, name and form float, along with the six sense-bases—that is, the living, conscious body, described in SN 22:95 (see Simile 4) as a lump of foam on the river, or in the wheel of existence as a boat (see Simile 16). When the water rises, the foam and the boat would also rise with it. Thus these four mental phenomena—formations, consciousness, name and form, and the six sense-bases—are all included in the image of the great river.

The *smaller streams*, the tributaries of the great river, flowing into the river and flowing towards it, are a simile for contact (*phassa*) with its three consequences: feeling, perception (here, craving) and activity (here, grasping). Craving is often compared to a river and its current (see Simile 21), just as consciousness, whose outflow it is.

The *great valley filled with water*, the large lake, is becoming (*bhava*), the infinity of time, the latent content of consciousness, the reservoir feeding all rivers. The great lake is the "primordial source" of becoming, the seeming source of events, although it also depends on the surging of the tide, which turns valleys into lakes. It is a stretch of standing water, a state of affairs, while all the aforementioned things were flowing. The state of becoming is the base of all movement and change, just as the faithful imagine God to be the primordial source of all creation.

With the *small valleys* being flooded, the ponds and pools, birth and death, are the last outflow of the storm tide arising in the great ocean. These are as limited and concrete as becoming is unlimited and abstract. As far away as the ocean's tide is from the pond, just as far is the real cause of birth and death for us, namely the distorted, ignorant conception that there is an "I" who is involved in this whole process.

Part 3

THE PATH TO LIBERATION AND ITS FRUITS

While the first two truths of the Buddha concern suffering, the misery of *saṃsāra*, comprising the truth of suffering and how it arises, the last two truths concern the liberation of Nibbāna, firstly as the truth of the dissolution of suffering, secondly as the means to achieve this, (i.e., the truth of the respective path). The Third Noble Truth shows the goal and the Fourth Noble Truth shows the way to achieve it. Since only a goal makes a path to it possible, therefore the truth of the goal is mentioned before the truth of the path leading to the fruit of realization of the goal.

These two truths are usually treated together in similes so that it is impossible to separate them. In this third section, similes for the overall path to liberation (the Fourth Noble Truth) and its fruits (the Third Noble Truth) are presented. In the two sections following, similes for the two main elements of the path are treated: that is, the tendencies of craving and their diminution, which are the only concern of purification in Part 4; and similes for individual abilities which are developed during and for purification in Part 5.

In this part the similes are sometimes not presented separately but are incorporated within the explanations.

26. Taming the Horse (MN 65)

A skilful horse-tamer receives a beautiful, noble horse. That is, a skilful mind finds a heart longing for liberation.

First, the horse has to be trained at the bit. That is, a bit is placed in its mouth so that it can be trained. A connection is thus created whereby there can be commitment. Because the horse (heart) has never before experienced a bit (i.e., it has never had undeluded right view), it shows all kinds of moods and temperaments and it kicks. These are mental jerks and agitations. Gradually, however, the steed quietens down and becomes contented; the heart becomes habituated and it attains right view.

Secondly, a saddle is put on the horse so that it can carry a rider. Once again the horse refuses at first because this training to a saddle is similarly unfamiliar to it, and only step by step does it become accustomed to it. This is the right attitude of mind that must overcome the former wrong attitude of mind, until it becomes trained.

Then the horse must learn to walk, trot and gallop. Right speech is still the easiest gait under the rider; right action demands more effort and the heart is put into a trot; the fastest pace is the gallop, which is right conduct in life, bringing the greatest gain in virtue.

When the horse has mastered these three gaits it can be taken beyond the training ground to learn the skills of running, of going in unknown territory, in the wilderness. This is right effort by which one—so to speak—overtakes or excels oneself.

Afterwards it is taught to jump over obstacles, fences and drains and to train for steeple-chases. This is right mindfulness transcending the obstacles, dissociating from the ground of the five hindrances.

Then, with further training, it accomplishes the royal demeanour, becoming the fastest, fleetest and most reliable of steeds. This is *samādhi*: that is, royal exercise (*rāja-yoga*), the training goal of the horse and the heart, now reaching *samādhi*, according to wish and will in full measure and width.

When the steed becomes contented with that, it receives the last stage of training: rubbing down and grooming, the last grace and evenness. These are the two fruits of the Noble Eightfold Path—insight (lightness, beauty, grace) and liberation (evenness/ equanimity, and disappearance of the last vestige of self-will).

27. The Paddy Field (AN 8:34)

A rice field must have eight qualities so that seeds sown into it grow into tall rice-plants that bear nutritious and abundant grain. Monks walking on the Noble Eightfold Path are like the rice field with eight qualities and the gifts to these monks are like the seeds that bring good results. So, how must the field be prepared for the seeds?

First of all, the ground for the rice field must be cleared of all elevations and depressions, that is, it is levelled off and made even. Similarly, right view levels all extremes, that are wrong views and practices, such as eternalism and externalism, hedonism and self-mortification.

Secondly, rocks and stones must be removed from the field because they will be hindrances for growing the rice. Such obstructing stones compare with wrong attitude of mind, and their clearing away, with the right attitude.

The ground should contain no salt so that the plants will not be burned or killed by it. In the same way, right speech contains no sharp and salty words, and is meek and pleasant.

The field must have a good inflow for the furrows, leading the water to the right place. This is right conduct in life which, by proper treatment of humans and objects, brings an influx of good with it.

Thus prepared, the field must also have an outlet through which the water can run off after use. This is right effort, causing the old, bad habits to run off and make way for a fresh influx of good.

Between the inlet and outlet, where water flows, there must be a slope or descent so that the water reaches the rice plants. Right mindfulness similarly must let the teaching flow, and be vigorous and reliable in its application.

Finally, the field needs a bund, a wall, a boundary so that water stays inside and the owner knows his territory. In the same way, calm of mind creates an independent area, where nothing can enter from outside and disturb its tranquillity.

Donations to such tested and reliable humans (field of merit) yield kammically great fruit (rice) of good feeling (delicious taste, sweet refreshment) and value (abundance of the harvest).

28. Similes for Monks (AN 3:92)

The Emblems of Ascetics

Just as other ascetics distinguish themselves from the multitude by the distinct clothing they wear—being dressed in rags, remnants, furs, woven grasses, fibres, hair, owls' wings, even so monks distinguish themselves from the masses by their virtue, secluded from and disowning non-virtue. They dress in the jewellery of good habits, the self-made treasure of wholesome demeanour. Having abandoned the dress of non-virtue, they don the dress of gentleness.

Ascetics secluded from the multitude distinguish themselves through their choice of food by taking only what grows wild as nourishment, that is, wild herbs, grasses, roots, berries, fruits, bark, leavings from grain thrashing, even cow dung. Even so, monks distinguish themselves from the multitude by right view, and are secluded from wrong view by rejecting and transcending it. They nourish themselves with right view; their mental nutriment is seeing things according to reality (*yathābhūta-ñāṇadassana*), which they constantly have present in mind and which they attend to, nurture, and develop.

Just as other ascetics secluded from the multitude distinguish themselves through their choice of residence, residing only in the forest, in graveyards, on hills and in forest clearings, on piles of straw or in barns, even so monks distinguish themselves from the multitude by ending the taints or influences (*āsava*), dwelling secluded from the influence of the desires and defilements.

Thus is a monk secluded in three ways, that is, in body (virtue), in mind (right view) and heart (freedom from the taints); he has reached the highest and is firmly established in the real, the true, the core.

The Rice Harvest

The monk is similar in the following ways to the rice farmer harvesting his crop.

The farmer first cuts the crop: the monk first harvests right view.

The farmer piles the crop up in sheaves: the monk accumulates the right attitude of mind.

The farmer lets the crop be taken from the field to the threshing floor: the monk lets only right speech leave his mouth.

The farmer heaps up the crop on the threshing floor: the monk accumulates good deeds by his actions.

The farmer threshes the rice: the monk takes up right conduct, threshing out all that is bad by observing the rules of discipline and confessing all violations.

The farmer removes the straw: the monk removes the straw of wrong thoughts by right effort.

The farmer picks out the chaff: the monk discriminates between the wholesome and the unwholesome by right mindfulness.

The farmer cleans the remaining grain from the dust of the threshing process: the monk cleans his mind from the dust of the world by means of calm, *samatha*.

The farmer takes the grain from the threshing floor to another place: by penetrative wisdom the monk attains another dimension, another view, that is, of Nibbāna.

The farmer beats the grain from the husks: the monk in right liberation frees the core from the shell.

The farmer, after removing the husks, has reached his goal: the monk knows in the clear knowledge of liberation that he has completely won the exquisite Nibbāna, the highest goal.

The Shining Sun

Just as the autumn sun at the end of the rainy season shines and glows and blazes in the cloudless blue sky and lightens everything, so too, the noble disciple when the stainless eye of Truth arises in him, is freed of the three fetters: personality view, doubt and adhering to virtues and observances. If he would pass away after having attained and maintained the first jhāna, the noble disciple becomes a non-returner, i.e., is freed from all the five lower fetters,.

29. Making a Boat (AN 4:196)

A man who wants to cross a river takes a sharp axe and goes into the forest where he sees a large tree, straight, young and solid. He fells it at the root, cuts the top off, and clears it completely of branches and twigs with his axe and a knife. He then uses a chisel to hollow out the trunk, then planes it and smoothes it with sandstone. He equips his new boat with a paddle and rudder and launches it into the river. Will he now be able to cross the river? Yes. And why? The tree trunk has been worked well on the outside and is completely cleaned out on the inside. The boat is ready and equipped with paddle and rudder. One expects that it will not sink and that the man will reach the other shore safely.

In the same way, those ascetics and priests who do not see the core of practice in the extremes of self-mortification and hedonism, and who don't attach to these practices, they are well able to cross the river; they are able to achieve clarity of knowledge and awakening. Conversely, those ascetics and priests who teach atonement due to revulsion (*tapo-jigucchā-vādā*, i.e., the extreme of self-mortification), and those ascetics and priests who practise impure conduct by body, speech and mind, and are of impure livelihood (i.e., the extreme of hedonism) are not able to cross the river.

Explanation

The boat building and crossing of the river described here is a description of the Tenfold Path, that is, the Eightfold Path and its two fruits—right knowledge and right release.

Right view fells the deeply-rooted tree of "I"-view, cutting it off at the root. This is the first necessity for building a boat. If one wants to compare the tree to the body, it has to be loosened out of its soil at the roots (*saṃsāra*) and the link to the roots needs to be cut. Right view does this by radically cutting away wrong reference-points, wrong views, and precluding rebirth in subhuman realms.

Right attitude of mind cuts off the top of the tree—the direction of preceding growth and striving. The former factor, right view, went into the past, the root soil, while the right attitude of mind goes into the future. Both have to change. From then on, everything is in the present.

Right speech removes the twigs, the rustling of leaves.

With the axe, *right action* removes the branches that entangle themselves in the world.

With the knife, *right conduct* removes the outside bark, while *right effort* removes the inside core with a chisel, hollowing out the trunk so that it can accommodate a passenger. While the three steps of virtue (right speech, action and conduct) smooth the tree outside, it is by *right effort* that the tree is changed into a boat able to cross the river; this is the core activity. Because the ascetics who saw the essence of practice in self mortification did not train in this core of asceticism—right effort—their boat did not float, says the discourse.

Right mindfulness is working with the carpenter's plane, removing all unevenness. It levels off the conceit "I am."

Right concentration is the sandstone polishing the wood so completely that everything rough is gone and a smooth, uniformly-even surface appears.

The boat is now finished, and the Noble Eightfold Path brought to an end. Installation of a paddle and rudder represents *right knowledge*, the ninth step—i.e., the means to navigate the boat correctly in the new element.

Right liberation consists of the boat now crossing the river easily and the man safely reaching the other shore.

For the last three factors, the Buddha gives another string of similes relating to liberation through wisdom.

Just as a warrior who knows a number of tricks in archery—particularly mastery of the choice of position, (i.e., virtue, as AN 4:181 adds here)—becomes worthy of serving the king and suitable to work as a bodyguard by just three skills, so it is also with the noble disciple.

Just as a warrior can shoot from afar, so the monk perceives in the highest *samādhi* that all five aggregates are essenceless and not-self. Even though he is still within the five aggregates and to that extent still far from Nibbāna, he can even at that distance engage the whole of saṃsāra with right view.

Just as a warrior can shoot like lightning, so the monk recognises in the highest knowledge the four Noble Truths. As the lightning flash illuminates the night, so his right knowledge rapidly penetrates the darkness and illuminates the Dhamma.

Just as a warrior can pierce large objects, so the disciple possesses the highest liberation when he has penetrated the enormous mass of ignorance.

30. Destroying the Tree (AN 4:195; SN 12:55–59)

Conditioned by a tree, there is a shadow. A man fells this tree at the root. After it is felled, he digs up the root, also pulling out all the finer roots. He then cuts the tree into pieces, splitting them and making them into chips. He dries these chips in the wind and sun, burns them and turns them into ash, which he then scatters to the winds or throws them into a river where they are carried away by the rapid current. Thereby the shadow of the tree, conditioned by the tree, would be destroyed at its very base, just as a palm tree torn from the earth is destroyed and not able to regrow. Similarly, if a monk whose heart is completely liberated by destroying the taints (*āsavas*) has attained six constant abidings: If he experiences something through any of the six senses, he becomes neither happy nor sad but abides composed, mindful and clearly aware.

Explanation

This simile is the second half, the corollary of the ones discussed at Simile 23 which dealt with the origination. This simile is also the opposite of the previous one. There the tree used for making the boat was a positive part of the simile, by which one reached liberation safely. Here the tree is something negative, preventing liberation. The tree is often mentioned in the texts as something to be pulled out, and its roots and trunk used as metaphors for the taints (MN 36), sometimes for greed, hatred and delusion (MN 43), sometimes for the five lower fetters (MN 22), and sometimes, for example in the simile above, as attachment binding one to things (SN 12:55–59) (see Simile 23). The path to the eradication of the desires and defilements is the Noble Eightfold Path, though here this is only implied.

Right view fells the tree at its root, as in the foregoing simile. This time, however, the point is to remove also all the finer roots from which it might grow again, that is, to uproot the whole of the tree hidden beneath the earth. This is the work of the *right attitude* of mind, which totally reprograms the person.

Sawing up, splitting and cutting the tree into chips is virtue. *Right speech* provides distinct separate pieces, while *right action* reduces them in size and *right livelihood*, as subdivision of action, is a further refinement of the splitting process where the rules of virtue to be observed become more and more subtle, as in the Vinaya, which regulates particularly the conduct of life.

The drying of the chips is *right effort*. Here the tendencies of desire (moisture) are dried up, just like the piece of wood that has been taken ashore to dry in Simile 60.

Right mindfulness is similar to burning of the chips. Likewise, the conceit "I am" is burnt by the four pillars of mindfulness in the fire of the perceptions of impermanence, suffering and not-self.

Right concentration then is similar to the ashes. The taints (*āsava*) are merely a most refined waft, a residue.

Right knowledge is similar to the scattering of the ashes by wind or water. Likewise, insight becomes universal in every direction, and the limitation of desires and defilements disappears entirely, does not exist anymore.

Right liberation thus consists in the vanishing even of the slightest shadow of being; the perception of time and objects disappears in the attainment of the fruit (*phala-samāpatti*). If the ash is scattered, the last hold which could cast a shadow is gone; the last desire is removed forever, the palm tree destroyed.

31. When it Rains on the Mountain (SN 55:38)

When it rains high up in the mountains, when it falls in thick drops, the water flows downhill. First, it fills troughs, then clefts, and then gullies. When it has filled all these, then it fills small ponds, then bigger ones, then small rivers, then the bigger rivers, and finally the ocean itself is filled. In the same way, a disciple endowed with the four factors of stream entry reaches extinction of the taints (*āsava*).

The Path to Liberation and its Fruits

Explanation

This simile appears frequently in other discourses and is explained in different ways—for example:

—as representing the hearing of the Teaching, discussing it, following its training in calm and insight, all at the right time, leading to the destruction of the taints (*āsava*) (AN 4:147);
—as representing the gaining of faith through the understanding of conditioned origination and by that means (*upanisā*) attaining calm, knowledge and liberation (SN 12:23); and
—as representing the acquisition of calm through developing communal harmony and mutual rejoicing (AN 3:93).

In an abbreviated way, it is also said that just as the *nāgas* reach the ocean by the streams, etc, coming down from the Himalayas, so the disciple supported by virtue develops the seven awakenings (*bojjhaṅga*), the Eightfold Path, or the four bases of power (*iddhipāda*) (SN 46:1; SN 45:151; SN 49:25).

The starting point in these similes is mountains in general, or the Himalayas in particular. The mountains stands for the origin of faith, the highest level which gives the correct gradient. The origin of faith is formulated differently in these discourses but it is always faith in the lawfulness of existence as well as the practice of virtue.

The *rain* is the ever recurring *right view*, which only the mind endowed with faith possesses. Faith continuously waters and refreshes the mind with the aim of liberation.

The *inclination to flow downhill* is the *right attitude of mind* directing all intentions towards calm and concentration, keeping away unnecessary distractions.

The *filling of the cracks, hollows and gullies* of the mountains is the filling up, the fulfilment of virtue by right *speech, right action and right conduct*. The better the speech, the more one flows into action—a rivulet accumulates.

Rivulets filling the *small ponds* and then the *bigger ponds*—that is, the preceding factors feeding the pools of right effort and the mountain lakes of right mindfulness.

The small rivers meandering downhill are the *right concentration* of the mind, with the water's level already coming close to that of the ocean. And the great rivers that form as the water comes together in the broad valleys of wisdom are comparable with *right knowledge*.

The ocean is the extinction of the taints (*āsava*), the tenth step, *right liberation*.

32. The Hindrances on the Way (SN 22:84)

One who does not know the way asks one who does know the right way. He answers: "This is the right way. Walk along it for a while and you will come to a fork in the road. Avoid the left fork and take the right way. Walk along it for a while and you will see a dense forest. Go through the forest for a while, then you will see a huge, miry swamp. Go through the swamp for a while and you will see a steep slope. Go down the slope for a while and you will see a charming area of level ground."

Explanation

The one who does not know the way is the worldling. *The one who knows the way* is the Accomplished One, the Fully-Awakened One. *The way* is the mundane Eightfold Path, the path of the worldling who is aspiring to become a Noble person. This Path is subject to the taints (*āsava*); see MN 117.

Walking on the way is walking the mundane Eightfold Path with mundane right view. *The fork in the road* is doubt, the second of the ten fetters, becoming now more and more manifest in consciousness, leading to a crisis.

The left way is the wrong path which lures so comfortably, which is so widely inviting. *The right way* is the undeluded, undefiled, supramundane Noble Eightfold Path, the inconspicuous way to liberation which does not immediately promise great sights, which is why doubt is nourished. *Walking on the right way* is the progress of the stream enterer who has abolished the first three fetters.

The dense forest is ignorance which becomes visible only when supramundane right view is firmly established and cannot be lost any more. Only then does one realise how enormous ignorance is, how little one knows oneself and one's mind. To know that one knows nothing—that is the ignorance mentioned here. One has to pass through this dark, dense jungle of ignorance; one has to clear one's trail with right view.

The huge, miry swamp is the entirety of sensuality, of the world and worldly pleasures. Here one must tread carefully, seeking out solid ground at each step, taking care not to sink into the swamp. The less one entangles oneself in the world and the more one avoids sensual adventures, the closer one comes to those insights which destroy ignorance.

The steep slope is anger and despair. This instinctive anguish and rejection comes last for the Venerable Tissa, the monk to whom this talk is addressed, because he was immersed in sloth and torpor. He would discover his aggression only after he had walked the path for a long time. Even the most indolent person becomes angry if he is not permitted to follow his slothful inclination. However, the Buddha's teaching demands that one conquers oneself completely, that one relinquishes one's conceit. To traverse the slope of anger and despair requires humility and patience. Impatience, becoming excited, despair over slow progress, anger over duties in the Sangha, anger over reproach from the other monks—to successfully deal with these one has to humble oneself.

The charming area of level ground is Nibbāna, the perfected peace of mind where greed (swamp), hatred (slope) and delusion (forest) are left far behind.

Part 4

THE NOBLE POWERS

33. The Mountain Fortress (AN 7:63)

In an Indian border area, close to the barbarians, there is a fortified town serving as a fortress. For the protection of its inhabitants and as a defence against strangers, it possesses seven kinds of equipment, with food supplies as the eighth. So too, the noble disciple, who is equipped with seven qualities, plus the jhānas as the eighth, is invincible to Māra, the evil one.

Just as a fortress has an unshakeable tower bedded deep into the ground, so the noble disciple has unshakeable confidence in the Accomplished One and therefore abandons unwholesome states and develops wholesome ones. This tower is the centre of the fortress, the solid core which, fixed in the depths, rises up over everything. Just so is confidence (*saddhā*); it is the basis for trust, faith, self-confidence, conviction of liberation and the possibility of realizing it. Confidence is the first and foremost quality reaching into the depth of the soul and including at the same time the highest goal of the mind. In most of the similes of the path which follow, confidence is included, and never under another name. Confidence is indispensable for developing the path.

Just as a fortress has a deep and wide trench and a high and strong rampart, so has the disciple shame and a conscience towards wrong-doing. Where there is a deep sense of shame, a deep humility with respect to one's own failings, there is also a strong sense of what is right and wrong, and high reverence and reserved admiration of the good of others. Since one is ashamed of evil and has high reverence for good, one abstains from evil actions, speech and thoughts. Thus shame and conscience go together as do a trench and the rampart made from the soil dug up for making the trench. The more one digs up evil within oneself, the more one develops a sense of right and wrong and respects goodness in others.

Just as a fortress has a stockpile of many weapons such as arrows and spears, so the disciple possesses experiential learning (*bāhusacca*) in spiritual things, and integrates the Teaching into his life. Thus in his mind he has the weapons as aids to deal with all situations, to respond to challenges in a wholesome way.

Just as a fortress is equipped with a four-fold army consisting of elephant troops, cavalry, chariot troops and a range of infantry (the four components of the traditional Indian army), so the disciple is equipped with the four great exertions that form the core of energy needed to overcome unwholesome things and to acquire the wholesome. The elephants which are like a wall and bounce off everything are comparable with sense restraint—the first exertion. The cavalry with its fast steeds is comparable with the speedy mind by which one overcomes evil thoughts and rides them down—the second exertion. Chariots and supply troops are comparable with the development of wholesomeness, bringing up good things—the third exertion. And the whole of the infantry occupying the enemy territory is comparable with preservation of the good—the fourth exertion. This is the power of energy by which one removes evil and acquires what is good.

Just as a fortress has an intelligent, experienced gatekeeper who rejects strangers and admits only those known to him, in the same way the disciple is mindful, having the power to remember even things that happened a long time ago. Actual mindfulness—with its already mentioned constituents of shame, conscience and experience—is the ability to distinguish between wholesome and unwholesome things. One judges with foresight, remembering the bad consequences that previous inattentiveness brought about, and the wholesome consequences that attentiveness brought about. So like the gatekeeper, one lets in wholesome states and keeps out unwholesome ones.

Just as a fortress has a wall that is high and strong and well-plastered, so the disciple is wise with regard to the arising and passing away of things, i.e., he possesses the wisdom to destroy suffering. Wisdom, like a wall, must be without gaps. If there is a hole in the wall, the enemy can get in, bypassing the gatekeeper. If there is a gap in mindfulness regarding the arising and passing away of things, regarding dependent origination (*paṭicca samuppāda*), one may be surprised by an unknown factor and suffer the painful strokes of circumstances.

Finally, just as a fortress has provisions of straw, wood, water, rice, barley, vegetables and other ingredients such as butter, oil, honey, sugar and salt for the use of the inhabitants to help pacify their fear and for their well-being and independence from the outside, so the disciple possesses peace of mind and the four jhānas for his personal pleasure, pacification, well-being, and help him reach Nibbāna. The jhānas render one self-sufficient, independent of saṃsāra, and thus reflect certain aspects of Nibbāna. In AN 9:48 the Buddha says that in a way (or figuratively; *pariyāya*) the jhānas are Nibbāna, however only the full destruction of the taints literally (*nippariyāya*) is Nibbāna.

Elaborating this image, the first jhāna gives only fuel for cooking; the second contains the basic nutriment; the third the vitamins; and the fourth the aroma. So too, the four jhānas become even more refined from the coarse straw and wood, through rice and vegetables, to the fine seasonings.

With the first seven qualities, says the discourse, the disciple overcomes the unwholesome and develops the wholesome, overcoming that which is blameworthy and developing the blameless while protecting his mind in purity—the jhānas being purity itself.

In this simile mindfulness is mentioned before energy, and wisdom before calm, and thus differs from the structure of the Noble Eightfold path. This is done only in order to fit the structure of the simile.

There is a similar simile involving a fortress and gatekeeper in AN 10:95. Here the wise gatekeeper walks around the fortress to check for gaps and holes. Having done so, he knows that whatever large beings enter the city, they can only do so by the gate, and there is no necessity to know how many enter and leave. Just so the Tathāgata has no inclination to know exactly how many beings depart from saṃsāra, and have attained Nibbāna. However, he has the inferential knowledge that whoever leaves the world does so by abandoning the hindrances and the defilements that weaken the mind, and by developing the foundations of mindfulness and the factors of awakening.

There is also another, less complete simile of a town at Milindapañhā 332.

34. The Noble Elephant (AN 6:43; Th 689–704)

Once, as the white elephant of King Pasenadi of Kosala returned from its bath, the people praised its beauty. On this occasion, the Venerable Udāyi asked the Buddha whether the people praised only such a beautiful elephant as noble or other things as well. The Buddha replied that humans also call other great animals or people "nāga" (something special, unusual, noble), but whoever in this world commits no more evil in action, word or thought would truly be a nāga. Delighted, Udāyi responded with verses in which an elephant is compared to an arahant as the supreme nāga. (As in MN 23; see Simile 47.) These verses have also been included in the Theragāthā as those of Udāyi Thera.

The sequence of the qualities is according to the structure of the body. For the sake of clarity, they are arranged here in a pertinent sequence.

What the *trunk* is for the elephant is faith for the monk. The trunk is the organ of smell by which the elephant first, and most precisely, perceives something. With the tip of its trunk it also feels things and explores them. Likewise, faith is the most refined and immediate relation of a person to truth; it is a feeling and intuition that precedes all conscious reflection. At Theragāthā 1090, the hand of a person, which is also the finest organ of touch, replaces the tip of the elephant's trunk. Opposite to the front part of the elephant which corresponds to faith in liberation is the rear end and tail which corresponds to seclusion from misfortune. Whenever the elephant goes towards something with its trunk, it moves away from something else at its rear end. Thus the ability to live secluded is simply like the tail or rear-end; it follows as a corollary, as a consequence of faith.

The hind feet of the elephant are compared to austerity (*tapas*) and celibacy of the ascetic (*brahmacariyā*).[29] These are two forms of effort by which one supports oneself, by which one strives ahead, as with one's feet. With austerity and celibacy, the monk walks away from evil things.

The neck of the elephant is mindfulness, just like the neck of the Buddha at Theragāthā 1090. Its flexibility allows us to turn our head to look to objects. It is the ability to choose perceptions.

Just as the breathing of the elephant goes lightly, gently and pleasantly—peaceful everywhere and resting in itself—so is the concentration of the monk who possesses *jhāna* and abides in the calmness of mind. In addition, his forefeet are also two kinds of calmness: forgiveness and non-violence.

The elephant's head means wisdom, as does the head of the Buddha at Theragāthā 1090. Just as the head is the highest part of the body overlooking and directing everything, so is wisdom the central control of all powers. It manifests itself in the feeling of equanimity, which is compared to the white tusks of the elephant, which shine purely without colouration.

Furthermore, one additional quality of the elephant is mentioned, which is obscure because of variant readings in the Pali text. I understand the verse line *"vimaṃsā dhamma-cintanā dhamma-kucchi samāvāsa"* to mean: "the investigation (*vimaṃsā*) of the elephant is the complete balance between thoughts (*cintanā*) and the abdomen/body (*kucchi*)," referring to the arahant. In the arahant all desires are gone; there is no more battle between flesh (abdomen) and spirit. He can investigate all things without being disturbed by his desires. Only this is the final victory of the "head" over the "abdomen."[30]

35. The Royal Elephant (AN 5:140; cf. AN 4:114)

If endowed with five qualities, the king's elephant is worthy of the king, suitable for royal service and may be counted as the

---

29. In the verses of the Theragāthā, the two hind feet are associated with mindfulness and clear comprehension, even though mindfulness is also said to be at the neck. This must be a mistake that happened during the transmission of the verses.

king's personal elephant. What are these five qualities?

He is a listener. In every exercise that the elephant tamer has him perform, whether he has done it before or not, he is attentive and diligent. He listens attentively and clearly comprehends what he hears.

He is a fighter. In battle, he attacks and destroys elephants and horses and their riders, chariots and their drivers, and infantry as well.

He protects himself. In battle, he protects his front and back, fore feet, hind feet, head, tusks, trunk and tail, and he protects his rider.

He is patient. In battle, he patiently endures lance thrusts, arrows, sword strokes, blows of the axe, as well as the racket and noise of kettle drums and horns.

He is one who goes. Wherever the elephant-tamer sends him, whether he previously walked there or not, he goes there quickly.

In the same way, a monk with five qualities is worthy of alms, donations, gifts and respect—being the best field in the world for making merit.

He is a listener. When the Teaching and Discipline of the Buddha is being taught, he is attentive, eagerly listening and absorbing it into his mind.

He is a fighter. When thoughts of desire, hatred or violence arise, he doesn't let them find a footing but overcomes them, drives them out, exterminates them and makes them cease.

He protects himself. If he cognises anything with the six senses, he does not grasp the attractive aspects and details of what is cognised, so that no evil unwholesome states, no attraction or repulsion can arise and disturb his mind. He continuously guards the sense doors and remains equanimous.

---

30. K. R. Norman in *Elder's Verses I*, (Oxford, 1995) reading *samātapo* (fireplace) instead of *samāvāso* (balance), translates Th 695 as follows: "His neck is mindfulness, his head is wisdom, investigation (with his trunk) is reflection on the doctrine, his belly is the fire-place of the doctrine, his tail is seclusion." This could be explained as ardent investigation of the Teaching by way of the mindfulness of the body (the abdomen) with the trunk of faith.

He is patient. He endures hunger and thirst, heat and cold, flies, mosquitoes, pestering animals, unfriendly and unwelcome speech, physical pain and strong, piercing, bitter, undesirable or unpleasant things; he endures everything patiently.

He is one who goes. That place which he has not yet gone to during his long travels, the place where there is the pacification of all activity, the letting go of all attachments, the extinction of craving, disenchantment, dissolution, Nibbāna—he goes there in a short time.

These qualities are also the five fighting powers (*bala*): listening attentively is *mindfulness*; fighting and protecting oneself are *energy*; patience is *peace of mind*; going is the *wisdom* of the Noble Eightfold Path; and the *confidence* he shows as an arahant acts as a reliable example for others, for reverence as well as emulation.

36. The Ploughman
(SN 7:11 = Sn 76–82 with prose)

When the Buddha approached a ploughing Brahmin farmer while going on alms-round, the proud farmer reproached him saying that he the Buddha should also only eat after ploughing, sowing, and harvesting. The Buddha replied that he did. The puzzled Brahmin remarked that he could see neither yoke nor plough, neither steel nor pole nor draught animals. Then the Buddha answered him in verse:

> Faith is the seed, austerity the rain,
> Wisdom my yoke and plough;
> Shame is the pole, mind the yoke-tie,
> Mindfulness my ploughshare and goad.
> Guarded in body, guarded in speech,
> Controlled in my appetite for food,
> I use truth as my weeding-hook,
> And gentleness as my unyoking.
> Energy is my beast of burden,
> Carrying me to security from bondage.
> It goes ahead without stopping

To where, having gone, one does not sorrow.
In such a way this ploughing is done
Which has the Deathless as its fruit.
Having finished this work of ploughing,
One is released from all suffering.[31]

Explanation

Faith is the seed. The ability to believe is the seed out of which all wholesome things develop; this is the first prerequisite for the harvest of arahantship. Just as the farmer brings seeds along and sows them in the field trusting that they will sprout and bear fruit, so the monk sows the seeds of wholesomeness trusting that they will sprout into serenity and insight and will eventually bear the fruit of Nibbāna.

Austerity the rain. Just as rain, dew and water moisten the seed and stimulate its growth, so sense-restraint, as well as striving and austere practices, stimulate the faith and confidence of the monk.

The *yoke and the plough* are wisdom. Just as the yoke connects the draught animals with the ploughshare, so wisdom is the supportive condition and spearhead of other wholesome states. Just as the yoke is the supportive condition for the pole, goes in front of it, is fastened to it, is the support for the yoke-tie, and makes the beast of burden go into one direction, so wisdom is the supportive condition for all wholesome states. Wisdom as plough is the insight-wisdom which conjoined with the ploughshare of mindfulness uproots and destroys the defilements.

Energy is compared to the two draught animals that pull the plough. Energy is the tractive power, the power to achieve wholesome endeavours.

The *pole* is shame (*hiri*): shame, as a form of mindfulness, directs conscience. By guarding against unwholesome states, and supporting wholesome states, shame holds up the plough of wisdom.

The *yoke-tie* is mind, that is, calm of mind (*samādhi*). Calm of mind combines the other faculties—faith, energy, mindfulness,

---

31. Bhikkhu Bodhi's translation, *Connected Discourses of the Buddha*.

and wisdom—and makes them work smoothly together as a strong team. The yoke-tie is threefold: the bond between the pole and the plough, the bond between the two beasts of burden, and the bond between the beasts of burden and the driver. Just as the Brahmin fastens and combines the pole, plough and beasts of burden and then engages in his work, so the monk's calm of mind fastens and combines the faculties of faith, mindfulness, wisdom, and energy onto one object, not allowing any disturbance, and thus enables him to engage in his work of developing the path to Nibbāna.

His *ploughshare* and the *goad* stand for mindfulness. With the ploughshare of right mindfulness or non-forgetfulness at the front, the monk prepares the soil for the plough of wisdom: the monk turns over his mind, bringing to the top what was beneath, and enables the plough of wisdom to uproot the unwholesome roots of greed, hatred and delusion, and to destroy even the finest roots of the conceit "I-am." Mindfulness as the goad urges the draught animals of energy to move on. Here mindfulness sees to it that there is no relaxation of effort, that the mind always applies itself to the object of meditation, and does not wander off the right path towards sense pleasures.

The *unyoking* of the draught animals stands for gentleness. Just as the farmer lets the oxen rest and graze, so gentleness as a form of equanimity lets other wholesome states do what they want and does not interfere, leaving them tolerantly alone. This is mentioned here as skill in gaining calm of mind.

Truth is the weeding hook which removes and uproots the weeds of wrong views and distorted perceptions. By seeing things as they are, in accordance with the four Noble Truths, the monk removes the weeds of wrong views (such as eternalism and annihilationism), uproots personality view (*sakkāya-diṭṭhi*) and enters the Noble Path. He then continues to weed away the subtle distorted perceptions of perceiving what is impermanent as permanent, suffering as happiness, what is not-self as self, until they are totally removed.

After the exertion of ploughing and weeding the heart, the harvest is security *(yogakkhema)*— freedom from birth, old age, sickness and death.

37. The Divine Chariot (SN 45:4)

Once the Brahmin Jāṇussoṇi departed from Sāvatthī in a splendid all-white chariot drawn by white mares. People thought that it was really a divine chariot. Venerable Ānanda saw this and reported it to the Buddha, asking whether it would be possible in the teaching to show a divine chariot as well. It would well be possible, the Buddha replied. The Noble Eightfold Path would be such a divine chariot, unsurpassed in victory in battle. If one were to cultivate the eight noble steps, one would put an end to the enemies of greed, hatred and delusion. Then the Buddha described the Path in terms of the analogy in the following verses.

> Its qualities of faith and wisdom
> Are always yoked evenly together.
> Shame is its shaft, mind its yoke-tie,
> Mindfulness, the watchful charioteer.
> The chariot's ornament is virtue,
> Its axle jhāna, energy its wheels;
> Equanimity keeps the burden balanced,
> Desirelessness serves as upholstery.
> Good will, harmlessness, and seclusion:
> These are the chariot's weaponry,
> Forbearance its armour and shield,
> As it rolls towards security from bondage.
> This divine vehicle unsurpassed
> Originates from within oneself.
> The wise depart from the world in it,
> Inevitably winning the victory.[32]

Explanation

Faith is the first horse, which keeps step with the second (wisdom).

Wisdom is the second horse, keeping in step with the first (faith). At times one horse is leading, at times the other.

---

32. Transl. by Bhikkhu Bodhi, *Connected Discourses of the Buddha*.

Shame is the shaft or pole connecting the horses of faith and wisdom to the chariot while upholding it.

Mind, that is, calm of mind, is the yoke-tie firmly joining the horses of faith and wisdom to the shaft of shame.

Mindfulness is the wakeful driver, the charioteer of the chariot who keeps it on to the right track and saves it in time from obstacles and dangers.

Virtue is the external ornament of the chariot. So too, virtue embellishes us with wholesome states and a good reputation, and protects us from coarse unwholesome states.

Jhāna is the axle, that is, the centre of calm absorption in the world of changing phenomena. Everything moves around the absorbed one; he alone does not move. The strong, stable axle of jhāna enables the wheels of energy to move the chariot.

The wheels of the chariot are *energy* or effort. Energy makes us progress; it makes us leave the bad and reach for the good; it creates movement and changes our position.

The chassis, the superstructure that keeps the chariot balanced and together (*dhura-samādhi*), is *equanimity (upekkhā)*, which keeps the mind balanced and centred. Equanimity avoids the extremes of overexertion giving rise to agitation as well as lack of exertion giving rise to sleepiness.

Good will, harmlessness and solitude are the weapons of the chariot, just as they are of the monk. With good will the monk fights hatred. With the weapon of harmlessness, he conquers harmfulness or non-compassion. Solitude is threefold: With physical solitude he conquers desire for company. With mental solitude, or jhāna, he conquers the defilements and purifies his mind. With solitude from mental acquisitions (*upadhi*), he conquers all activities leading to rebirth; destroying greed, hatred and delusion, he attains Nibbāna.

Forbearance, protecting the mind's peace, is compared to the armour of the chariot.

Security from bondage is the chariot's goal.

The chariot *originates from within oneself* by energetically developing the Noble Eightfold Path. With this supreme, matchless vehicle of the eightfold path the wise depart from saṃsāra. Having become stream-enterers, they can not fall off the chariot of the path and will inevitably win the full victory against the defilements—Nibbāna.

38. The Non-rattling Chariot (SN 1:46 and commentary)

An overzealous monk suddenly dies in the middle of his ascetic endeavours and finds himself in heaven where he is greeted with music by gorgeous celestial nymphs who regard him as their master and will fulfil any of his wishes. But, not being aware he had passed away from the human realm, the deva thought he was still a monk and rejected the amorous advances of the nymphs. When the nymphs finally convinced him that he is a deva, he is quite disappointed with the result of his asceticism. Keeping his virtue intact, he went to the Buddha to ask in verse how he could escape from his "grove of delusion."

> Resounding with a host of nymphs,
> Haunted by a host of demons!
> This grove is to be called 'Deluding':
> How does one escape from it?

The Buddha answered him likewise in verse with a simile of a chariot.

> 'The straight way' that path is called,
> And 'fearless' is its destination.
> The chariot is called 'unrattling,'
> Fitted with wheels of wholesome states.
> The sense of shame is its leaning board,
> Mindfulness its upholstery;
> I call the Dhamma the charioteer,
> With right view running out in front.
> One who has such a vehicle—
> Whether a woman or a man—
> Has, by means of this vehicle,
> Drawn close to Nibbāna.

Explanation

Straight is the way of the chariot. The Noble Eightfold Path, the Middle Way, does not deviate to extreme views and practices. Wisdom envisages the goal of the straight path to liberation and strives toward the safe, fearless place—Nibbāna.

The one who runs in front is right view. Just as the king's servants will clear the way before the king comes out of the palace in his chariot, so right view clears the way for the noble path factors (the chariot) by contemplating the aggregates, sense-spheres and elements as impermanent, suffering and not self.

The *wheels of wholesome states* are bodily and mental effort, which arise after hearing and contemplating the Dhamma. The Teaching is like the charioteer urging the horses, which in the preceding simile are said to be faith and wisdom.

Mindfulness is the *upholstery*, the protection; shame is the *leaning board*. Mindfulness protects the monk from dangers, and shame makes sure he does not fall out, keeping him safe.

The name of the chariot is *"non-rattling"* or *"non-creaking"* (*a-kujana*). This means that the chariot, the Noble Eightfold Path, runs smoothly, gently, peacefully. This means the chariot's axle, *jhāna*, is well lubricated. Despite being boarded by many people, the Noble Eightfold Path does not make any unseemly noise because it has no defects and functions perfectly.

The chariot's *destination* is fearlessness. Nibbāna, the highest form of peace of mind, is free from fear.

39. The Chariot of the Body (J 544)

The body take to be a chariot,
The mind its easy charioteer,
Non-violence the axle is,
Generosity, the covering.
A restrained way of walking is the rims,
The spokes, restrained hands;
A restrained belly, that is the hub,
Restrained speech is non-rattling.
Truthful speech is its completeness,

Non-slander—connectedness;
Friendly words is running smooth,
Measured speech, its belt.
Well decorated with faith and absence of greed;
Humble greeting is its carriage-pole;
Mildness, the shaft that doesn't bend,
Virtuous restraint, its harness.
Non anger is its not-unfastening,
The Teaching—the white umbrella;
Experience is its leaning board;
Its bolster, a steady mind.
Knowing the right time—that is its core;
Confidence is its three-way stick.
Humble demeanour the yoke tie is;
Non-arrogance, the lightweight yoke.
A non-slothful heart its floorboard is;
Following the wise is staying free from dust.
The Sage's goad is mindfulness,
His reins, courage and commitment.
The tamed mind, staying on the path;
With horses that are well tamed too.
Restraint is the straight path,
Longing, obsession, the wrong path.
And if the horses are rushing
To forms, sounds, tastes and smells,
Wisdom is the whip at such a time
And oneself is the charioteer.
If one goes by this chariot,
Of calmness and firm courage,
It will fulfil your every wish
And you surely will not go to hell.

Explanation

Here the divine *chariot* is said to be the body and its *charioteer,* the mind.

Faith and greedlessness are the ornaments of the chariot. It is the nature of faith that it does not trust in low, unwholesome things, but in wholesome, higher things. This creates the lightness, the shining colour, the decoration of the chariot.

The Teaching, the Dhamma, is the *white umbrella* of the chariot protecting the passengers from the heat of unwholesome actions, of defilements, and of saṃsāra. That the Teaching is here to be understood as liberation from saṃsāra accords with another small simile of a chariot in SN 41:5 where the white awning stands explicitly for liberation.

Most of the other qualities cited here belong to effort, although the term itself does not appear. Generosity is the *body-covering* of the chariot; generosity makes for a good reputation, and so the covering makes the chariot look good. Virtuous restraint is the *harness*; courage and commitment are the *reins*; and to be without a slothful mind is the *floorboard*. Regarding the wheels, which in the previous simile stood for effort, four things are said: the rims are the restraint of the feet; the spokes are the restraint of the hands; the hubs are the restraint of the belly (eating), and its sound is restraint of speech. As the rim is outside, so are the feet mostly outside. The spokes are somewhat more inside, and so are the hands. The hub of the wheel is like the belly, the centre of the body.

Five things are also said about good speech. Speaking the truth instead of lying is the completeness of the parts of the chariot; non-slandering keeps the parts together; restrained speech is non-rattling or driving without fault; speaking sensibly instead of chatting is the belt, and the yoke-tie is humble demeanour.

Mindfulness is the steering stick the wise man uses to direct the horses (in SN 41:5 mindfulness is "one spoke"). Learning, or experience, here is called the leaning board, which was shame in the previous simile. Greeting others humbly is the carriage pole, gentleness the non-bending shaft, non-defiance the lightweight yoke. All these are forms of appearance of mindfulness.

The bolster of the chariot is the calm and self-reliant mind. Non-anger is the fastening, because when there is loving kindness, the mind is not upset by the defilement of anger. Following the wise (the Buddha) is not to let oneself get dirty from the dust of the world but to direct one's attention to what is essential and to listen to the Buddha.

To know the right time is to always know what is appropriate and necessary for oneself and others. This is the core of the chariot, the heartwood of which the chariot is made. Self-confident maturity, the freedom from embarrassment or self-consciousness is compared to the three-way manoeuvrability of the stick of the chariot: It points to the three directions of activity through deeds, words and thoughts. In these, the mature one is confident. And wisdom itself is compared to the whip, which one uses to restrain movement towards sensual allurements. Attraction to sensual objects is the crooked, wrong way; the straight and right way is restraint.

40. Melting Gold (AN 3:70)

This is one of the very few similes referring each of the five powers in turn. Here, it is said that by contemplation of the devas the mind would thereby become pure, like gold does in the melting process. Just as one thinks about the qualities of faith (*saddhā*), virtue (*sīla*), learning (*suta*), relinquishment (*cāga*) and wisdom (*paññā*) that these gods possess and that one also possesses, so does gold become purified when furnace, salt, chalk, blow pipe and tongs are employed.

Just as the furnace is fired and offers heat to melt gold in order to start the process of purification, so faith stands at the beginning of the path of purification of the mind; it is the fire and warmth that gets us going.

Just as detergent salt is put onto the gold to drive out or wash out the impurities, even so is virtue the catalyst which enters into the mind with detergent power, forcing it to discriminate and restrain.

Just as the chalk joins itself to the gold, gently penetrating it and washing it out, so also learning integrates the teaching into one's life. Thereby learning understands life, penetrating into and purifying it.

Just as the melting process is regulated with the blow pipe—blowing air on it to increase the temperature or dripping water on it to cool it—so relinquishment acts to regulate or calm the mind because problems cool down if one watches them dispassionately, renouncing agitation.

And as the tongs hold the gold so that it can be effectively treated at all times, so wisdom acts as a tong by which one grasps, holds fast and comprehends problems.

Another simile on purifying gold that concerns the stages of the path will be treated below (Simile 49, AN 3:100).

41. The Waxing Moon (SN 16:7; AN 10:67–68)

Whoever possesses faith, shame, conscience, effort and wisdom with respect to wholesome things, may expect progress in the good, by day and by night, and no degeneration, whereas the opposite is true when these qualities are lacking. So too, the moon waxes in the light half of the month continuously in beauty, roundness, gleaming, growth, and perimeter while it decreases in these qualities in the dark half of the month.

In the same way as the moon waxes in beauty, so waxes faith in the wholesome, making one brighter and more serene, illuminating and transfiguring everything through one's confidence in the good.

In the same way as the moon waxes in roundness, in circularity, so acts shame. When one observes one's mistakes or faults in the beam of mindfulness, one wins a comprehensive knowledge of oneself and cannot escape that searchlight anymore.

In the same way as the moon waxes in gleam and brightness so is conscience or respectful shyness. Likewise the admiration for role-models who appear as shining examples and to whom one looks up, towards whom one abandons all rebellion and restrains oneself with timidity.

In the same way as the moon waxes in size, steadily growing larger, so grows effort, through which one steadily grows in goodness.

In the same way as the moon waxes in perimeter, so wisdom spreads over everything unknown and enlarges the horizon so that it knows everything wholesome.

42. The Archer (Mil 7.7)

An archer who shoots an arrow at a target is compared to a yogi, one who mentally exerts himself, who tries to reach his goal.

As the archer plants both his feet on the ground, keeps his knees straight, places his quiver against his waist, holds his body erect, raises his hands to the grip, presses his hand on it, leaves no opening between the fingers, holds up his neck, closes his mouth and eyes, takes a straight aim at the target, and smiles, thinking "I will pierce"; just so the yogi should plant his feet of energy on the ground of virtue, keep straight his (knees of) patience and gentleness, establish his mind in restraint, bring his body under control and restraint, press against longings and infatuations, leave no opening in his mind but remain thoroughly attentive (*yoniso manasikāra*), hold up (his neck) of energy, shut the six sense doors, raise up mindfulness and arouse a joyful smile, thinking "I will pierce all defilements with the shaft of knowledge."

Explanation

The feet of energy find a firm grip on the ground of virtue. There can be no right effort if there is no firm foundation of virtuous conduct. Virtue is the basis for developing calm of mind and wisdom. Patience and gentleness are compared to firm knees (probably the left is patience, and the right gentleness). Just as the archer stands with knees firm, so the yogi remains firm in positive gentleness and lets all negativity patiently pass over him.

Keeping his quiver firmly at his body is compared to the firmly established mind. Calm of mind does not act restlessly toward the outside world, but rests stably within. Effort is compared to the yogi keeping up his head and neck—just as we say to someone who is depressed, "Chin up!" The closing of his mouth and the closing of one eye is sense restraint, keeping the target internally in mind and not distracted by the outside world. Along with holding up his head, the archer keeps his body erect, which is general restraint and self-control. Not allowing a gap between his two grasping fingers is the unbroken, thorough awareness of the yogi.

Just as the archer presses his hand on the bow, both arms of the bow bend, so the yogi presses against, bends and overpowers longing and infatuation, or greed and delusion. This is wisdom, as are the tongs in AN 3:70.

Mindfulness is compared to taking a straight aim at the target. It is concentrating on attaining something specific. In the same way as the archer smilingly and confidently trusts that he will penetrate the target, although both his eyes are closed, so the meditator trusts smilingly that he will eventually defeat all desires. Although he can't see the target with his eyes, the external senses, internally he has the target, Nibbāna, firmly in his mind's eye. This is the confidence of the mature one.

43. Similes for the Ten Perfections (Bv 2.117)

1. Just as a water pot turned upside down lets all the liquid run out and takes none of it back, so the perfection of generosity is not having the slightest thought of remorse over what has been given away, even when one sacrifices absolutely everything.

2. Just as a yak whose tail is caught somewhere will rather die than to tear it off, so the perfection of virtue consists in being always careful about keeping precepts and virtues and not breaking them in any circumstance, even if threatened with death.

3. Just as one imprisoned in jail does not desire anything more intensely than to get out of there, so the perfection of renunciation consists in the longing to get out of the prison of transitory existence and having only the one wish to spit out the impermanent, to be rid of it.

4. Just as a mountain stands immobile and firm even in strong winds and is incapable of being thrown over, so the perfection of resolution consists in remaining unshakeable in one's wholesome determinations and not being distracted by anything.

5. Just as a star never strays from its predetermined course in the sky in spite of the seasons of the year, so the perfection of truthfulness consists in not lying under any circumstances. It means not moving even an inch from the truth for any advantage whatsoever.

6. Just as water refreshes and cleanses both just and unjust persons without discrimination, so the perfection of love is including friends and foes alike and doesn't make distinctions in loving.

7. Just as the great earth remains unmoved and equanimous, avoiding like and dislike whether one throws impure or pure things onto it, so the perfection of equanimity consists in always staying tranquil without repulsion or attraction in pain and pleasure, in strong conflicts as well as in the greatest fortunes.

8. Just as the great earth accepts even the most disgusting things thrown onto it, so the perfection of patience consists in accepting slander and every dishonour without resistance, enduring while letting them pass. (See MN 21.12 & AN 9:11)

9. Just as a lion marshals his strength evenly in all four postures, so the perfection of effort consists in maintaining and winning the battle against one's own desires and desires in every situation.

10. Just as a monk on alms-round neglects no house but goes to all families without exception, so the perfection of wisdom consists in leaving no gaps, leaving nothing out, and of being ready to learn from all wise people and those more advanced, however young they may be.

44. The Cure (MN 105)

A man has been struck by an arrow thickly smeared with poison and now, broken off, is stuck deep in the wound. A surgeon is called, who cuts the wound further open with a knife, and then probes for the arrow-tip with a probe. He extracts it and removes the poison, be it with or without residue, and gives instructions to the patient which he has to carry out himself so that the wound heals.

Explanation

Craving is the arrow and ignorance the poison.[33] The arrow comes from the outside, the six external sense bases, and enters

---

33. As the fundamental causes of continuing in saṃsāra, ignorance and craving are paired in the frequent phrase "beings hindered by ignorance and fettered by craving" e.g. MN 43.16; SN 12: 19; 15:1–20; AN 3:77–78; It 1:14–15.

the body through the six inner sense bases. The six inner bases are the means by which one is wounded; they are the cause of one's vulnerability. Painful physical and mental feelings arise from the wound. Elsewhere, in SN 36:6, the Buddha compares the reaction of the worldling to a man hit by one arrow and immediately afterwards by a second arrow so that he would feel feelings caused by two arrows. When contacted by painful physical feeling the worldling reacts with aversion towards it and thus is hit by the second arrow. Not knowing the impermanent, dependently arisen nature of painful feelings, and not knowing any other escape due to ignorance, he craves for the pleasant feelings that arise from sensual gratification. Distorted perceptions falsely promise fulfilment and cause further suffering, the second arrow. If there were no craving for pleasant sense objects—by seeing their transient, painful and coreless nature—he will not be hit by the second arrow of mental pain. The poison of ignorance can't be spread further by desire and hatred; it is countered by the ointment of calm and insight. Therefore, one ought to understand and penetrate objects with mindfulness and wisdom to find the cause, to find the poisoned arrow.

The surgeon is the Buddha, the symbol of confidence, the cure for all vulnerability. The first thing the surgeon does after arrival is to cut open the wound with a sharp knife. This is wisdom. It hurts to the extent that there is identification with the wound, that is, to the extent one is attached to the internal sense spheres, the body and mind. It hurts to the extent that the tendencies of desire and hatred that tear the wound open are encouraged and allowed to spread the poison of ignorance.

The second thing the surgeon does is to look for the arrow-tip with the probe. The probe represents mindfulness, which curbs all desire. As is said in the Sutta Nipāta: "Whatever streams [of craving] there are in the world, mindfulness curbs them" (Sn 1041).

The third thing the surgeon does is to extract the tip of the arrow and wash the poison from the wound, whereupon the pain is gone and the patient is relieved and feels better immediately. This is the beginning of calm of mind (*samādhi*), when craving is reduced and temporarily quietened.

The fourth thing the surgeon does is to give instructions which the patient, the monk, must follow so that the wound heals. The removal of the arrow is not yet the healing of the wound. The toxin has already penetrated the flesh around the wound. This residue of ignorance can be removed only slowly; hence the patient, although he feels healed, must be careful and continue the treatment so that the wound does not become infected. If the patient neglects the advice of the surgeon and delights in perceiving unsuitable sense objects, lust invades his mind and causes death or deadly suffering, that is, the monk would disrobe or commit a grave offence. Therefore, for complete healing, effort is necessary, and here the surgeon offers four pieces of advice (the four exertions). The patient should not go outdoors in wind and rain so that dust and dirt do not get into the wound: this is the first exertion—sense restraint—in which one protects oneself against the dust of defilements in the world. He should wash the wound so that anything harmful in it is rinsed out: this is the second exertion—the abandoning of unwholesome thoughts. He should apply ointment on the wound to aid its healing: this is the third exertion—the development of the wholesome, the balm of calm and insight. Lastly he should not eat anything unhealthy, that is, not expose himself to deleterious mental nutriment to rob himself of the good; rather he should nourish and maintain the good by right nutriment: this, then, is the fourth exertion.

When the patient properly carries out the instructions of the surgeon, the wound heals and the skin closes completely. Likewise when the monk properly practices restraint regarding the six sense doors, understanding that acquisition is the root of suffering, his mind is cured from all suffering and has no attraction towards sense pleasures.

45. The Chick, Adze and Boat (SN 22:101; AN 7:71)

When a monk has strongly developed the aids for liberation (*bodhipakkhiyā dhammā*), then, whether he makes a wish to be liberated or not, he soon arrives at the extinction of the taints (*āsava*). But if he does not develop these aids, no wish will help him. It is the same with a hen and her eggs. If she sits on the nest until they hatch, the chicks will break through the shell with their claws and beaks, whether or not the hen expressly wishes them to do so. Yet if the eggs are not hatched, all her wishing would be useless.

Hatching stands for the development or and training in wholesome things. When wholesome things are developed, the five powers grow. Just as hatching awakens and perfects the powers of the chicks, so development awakens the five powers, which are the essence of the aids for liberation. One can compare the beak of the chick—the strongest power by which it breaks through its shell—to wisdom, and the other four powers to the claws of the two feet whereby confidence and mindfulness form one pair, and effort and calm the other. This same simile is used in MN 53 for the path to liberation, with the seven right qualities and the *jhānas*, and in MN 16 for the one trained in fifteen ways. In MN 16 the cited qualities can also be traced back to the five powers. In AN 8:11, the Buddha says that he himself can be compared to the chick that first broke through the shell of ignorance with claws and beak.

During this development, the trainee is unable to state the amount of taints (*āsava*) or defilements were eliminated today, yesterday or the day before yesterday, and yet he knows that they are eliminated. This is like a carpenter who would also be unable to state the amount of the wooden handle of his adze has been daily worn away by the gripping of his thumb and fingers, and yet he knows that the diameter of the handle is gradually wearing down.

What affects the defilements are the five powers, in the development of which the monk trains daily. Here again, wisdom stands out like a thumb, while the other powers are the four fingers. Even the four fingers can be compared to individual powers. The index finger is mindfulness which points toward something or is directed towards something; the middle finger, the largest, would be energy; the ring finger, bearer of the most precious (ring), would be calm; and the minimum finger would be faith.

During this development, the fetters become weak and loosen with little effort. This is like the rattan fastening of a seaworthy boat. When at sea for half a year, the rattan's bonds and the joints of the hull are worn away in the water, then when it is pulled ashore for the cold season its bonds are exposed to wind, sun and rain and rot away further. Here the boat is the body. As it is said in Dhp 369,

> Bail this boat, bhikkhu,
> Bailed it will go lightly,
> Having cut lust and anger,
> You will reach Nibbāna.

In the sea of life, the boat is the body on the waves. Here, the boat is held together by bonds, as the body itself is held together and bound by the desires generated by craving. To let these stout rattan bonds rot away fibre by fibre, a usage of the forces of nature is necessary. The bonds of the boat rot first of all by being used at sea where, for the first half of the year, tension and salt water and act on the bonds and weakens them gradually. These two can be compared to faith (tension) and energy (salt water) which comprise half of the training path of the monk, namely the time that he still swims in the domain of desire (the sea). The boat is pulled ashore by the boater in the second half of the year because that is not the season to catch fish or to travel. The boat lies ashore; there the winds blow, the sun burns and monsoon rains pour down. The sun dries out the cane fibres, the wind pulls at them and the rain softens them. By these changing elements, the bonds—already loosened—become thoroughly brittle and rotten. Thus the forces of nature act, as do the three remaining fighting powers (mindfulness, calm and wisdom). Here the wind is mindfulness, the sun wisdom and rain is calm. (Cf. SN 45:158 for this simile in relation to the Noble Eightfold Path.)

46. The Seven Swimmers (AN 7:15)

There are seven kinds of persons with respect to swimming in water.

One swimmer dives in the water, sinks down and remains down. This is a human with very evil and unwholesome qualities. He has a wrong understanding (*micchā-diṭṭhi*), and so everything he does is wrong. He is very unvirtuous and antisocial. He sinks deeper and deeper through the weight of his immoral acts and after death goes to the lower realms, where he remains for a long time. This is going down, sinking in, dropping off, descent into darkness and danger.

The next swimmer is one who dives and rises above the surface for a short time but then goes down again. He thinks that it is good to have faith in the five wholesome things, to develop shame, conscience, effort and wisdom. For some time he makes efforts to acquire these five good qualities, but then he slacks off and forgets about the good; his resolve becomes weaker and weaker and eventually disappears entirely. Although at first they rise up above the surface because of a stroke of circumstances or a teaching, and temporarily become more serious, thinking and endeavouring for the good, they do not anchor or embed it deeply enough. When they feel good again, they forget everything, becoming superficial and gradually sink down again. For them the outflow is stronger than the influx: they take wisdom in but let it run out again.

Then there is the swimmer who rises above the surface and stays where he is. He agrees with and appreciates the five good qualities of faith, shame, conscience, effort and wisdom, but he takes them altogether as an end in itself, not thinking beyond death, or only in the form of a safe, divine realm in which he will be all right. So these qualities do not exactly decrease, yet at the same time they do not become stronger either; they remain sufficient to keep him afloat. He does not consider that swimming itself is already a dangerous situation, he is content with avoiding sinking, and hence he merely dabbles in acts of virtue. At some time, however, in the next rebirth or in another future life, he could give up swimming and sink down.

The fourth swimmer has also risen above the surface through developing the five good qualities. Looking around and penetrating the situation, he strives for firm ground. He sees it is still far in the distance, but it is his goal, and so he swims towards it. This is stream-entry. At this stage, he has shed the three lower fetters that bind the previous three swimmers and lead them sooner or later into the lower realms. Thus while the first three swimmers will sink, the fourth one, the stream-winner, can no longer sink. The stream-winner, although he is still bound to the lower, coarse fetters of sensual desire and anger, they can't pull him down into the depths. Being in the water, he still encounters the dangerous waves, whirlpools, crocodiles and sharks (see Simile 21), but because the powers he has gained he can brave the waves and whirlpools and can fight off the crocodiles and sharks. Even if he does not make much effort, he can only be reborn seven times at the most before putting an end to rebirth, and he can only be reborn in the human realm or in heaven realms (see Sn 230–31).

The fifth swimmer has progressed one part of the way to the shoreline; he makes headway as he swims forward into the vicinity of the firm ground. This is the once-returner. While the stream-enterer has only just penetrated the situation and has just begun to strike out towards his goal, the once-returner has made far greater spiritual progress and has greatly weakened the fetters of sensual desire and anger. The once-returner has more power and experience and is going ahead more easily towards the goal. The waves, whirlpools, crocodiles and sharks only rarely affect him.

The sixth swimmer is the first one to get solid ground under his feet. He is so close to the shore that he need not swim any more, he can wade. He has left behind the dangers of the water and the need to struggle. This is the non-returner who never has to return to the world of sensuality (*kāma-loka*). He has overcome the fetters of sensual desire and hatred entirely and has hence escaped the ups and downs, the surges, of the sensual world.

Finally, the seventh swimmer has left the water completely behind, standing ashore on solid ground. This is the arahant. By means of the five good qualities that everyone who rises possesses, he has extinguished the desires and taints in their totality and completed the Path. He is delivered; he has reached the goal.

47. The Riddle of the Termite Mound (MN 23)

A certain termite mound fumes at night and flames in the day. The Brahmin said, "Dig it up, wise man, with the knife." The wise man did so and found a bolt. The Brahmin said, "Throw it out and dig, wise man, with the knife." The wise man did so and found a toad, a fork, a sieve, a tortoise, a butcher's knife and block, and a piece of meat. Each time the Brahmin said, "Throw it out and dig, wise man, with the knife." Then the wise man found a nāga-serpent. "A nāga-serpent, lord!" he said. The Brahmin said, "Stop! Leave the nāga. Do not harm the nāga. Honour the nāga."

The Buddha gave the following solution to this riddle:

The termite mound is this body made from the four elements, generated by parents, maintained by food and drink, impermanent, subject to decline, wearing out, breakdown and destruction.

Fuming at night is pondering about one's daily chores in the night time.

Flaming by day is doing according to what one has pondered about at night, in actions, words and thoughts. *The Brahmin*: the Accomplished One, the Arahant, the Completely Awakened One. *The wise man*: the struggling monk. *The knife*: noble wisdom. *Digging up*: exerting energy. *The bolt*: ignorance. *The toad*: anger and despair. *The fork*: doubt. *The sieve*: the five hindrances. *The tortoise*: the five phenomena of grasping. *The butcher's knife and block*: the five strands of sensuality. *The piece of meat*: delight and lust (*nandi-rāga*). *The nāga-serpent*: the monk with craving extinguished.

Explanation

This simile is a description of the path from the ordinary being to the holiness of arahantship. The ordinary person identifies himself with his body of flesh, lives and weaves (his existence) in it, and thinks this to be the whole of the person. This body—compounded of the four elements, between conception and decay—is comparable to a termite mound.

What is referred to here is the Indian termite mound, a tower-like mound consisting of chimneys made of brown clay. It often has a structure resembling a body. Usually it is free-standing; occasionally it is built against a rock or tree. Because it sometimes looks like a human torso and is made of the earth element, and also because it is hollow inside, it is often compared to a human body. The body stands like a brown termite mound, but one can see little of the inside of the termite mound with its deep holes from which a snake or some other unexpected creature might suddenly dart. Likewise, the body in reality hides spiritual and mental phenomena which the ordinary person does not know about at all. His mind is caught up in the body of flesh and is helplessly exposed to it. He does not know himself: he does not know what he consists of. He sees only the tower-like building of the body.

It is about this body and its well-being that he thinks at night. In the evening hours humans tend to think about the work of the next day, planning and pondering how to operate, considering what is possible, what obstacles might arise, etc. In AN 4:200, it is asked: How does a monk fume? If there is the thought "I am," there also arise the thoughts "I am that; I am different; I am just like that; I am existing; I am not existing; I may well be, either so or different; oh, that I shall be, either so or different." This is what is called fuming; these foggy thoughts are the wafts of smoke,. Just as one cannot see smoke at night, so humans are unmindful of their thoughts. They think about themselves from the perspective of the body.

During the day, he executes what he has pondered at night. He acts, talks and thinks how to implement the plans of the night under particular circumstances. The flaming during the day is self-consumption; he uses his physical energy in his activities, often over-exerting himself and wearing the body out. In AN 4:200, this type of burning is compared to wrong reflection of a monk. If the monk thinks "I am for this reason," then all the other aforementioned kinds of thoughts arise too, as they now have a basis and object from which to start. Though not knowing it, by night and by day he thinks from the wrong perspective of his desires. Moreover, he doesn't realize that he only increases and strengthens his desires through this kind of thinking.

Thus the normal person knows only a tiny part of reality. Of form, he knows only the outside of his body; he doesn't know the fine-material or divine body, and he pays no attention to the repulsive side of the body, nor has he any idea of rebirth. Of activity, he knows only planning thoughts towards external events. He does not understand their origin; therefore he is unwise in one respect, and powerless in the other.

Noble knowledge can come only from outside, from the Brahmin, namely from the voice of the Buddha. The highest Brahmin is the Buddha who shows the path to overcome obstacles. By his guidance, the person who doesn't know about the noble training becomes a trainee (*sekha*), who in turn desires to become one who is beyond training (*asekha*), an arahant. Through the impetus of the Buddha, he gains the noble knowledge (*ariyañāṇa*) regarding the four Noble Truths, that is, the faculty or power of wisdom (*paññā*). Consequent to the establishment of noble knowledge, the four other faculties or powers are firmly established: faith in the Buddha and the Teaching; the energy to overcome the obstacles and tread the path; mindfulness—the ability to remember well and the ability to practice the four foundations of mindfulness; and the power to develop deep calm through the relinquishment of sense-pleasures and the jhānas. With these powers, he is on the first level of the trainee; he has become a faith-follower (*saddhānusārī*) or a Dhamma-follower (*dhammānusārī*).[34] However, the powers he has are quite undeveloped and need to be perfected. (See SN 48:52) He still has much before him. His insight tells him to dig

---

34. These are the first two noble persons. They have ceased to be worldlings and are equipped with the five faculties and powers, but are not yet fully stream-enterers. They are practicing the path (*magga*) of stream-entry and are bound to attain the fruit of stream-entry before death. In the faith-follower the faculty of faith is predominant and he practices by placing faith in Buddha's teachings on impermanence, etc. In the Dhamma-follower the wisdom faculty is predominant and he accepts the teachings only after pondering on them with wisdom. See SN 48:13–18 and 25:1–10.

up the termite mound of his body in order to get out of everything that covers and obstructs his holiness, that which lives deep down in the burrow as a nāga. Obstructions of mind are what live in the body, what create it and what perpetuate its existence, namely habits, desires and tendencies.

There are seven things to discover, to be removed and to overcome. They are:

1. *The door-bolt* of ignorance. The door-bolt obstructs the vision of all the things within by keeping the door firmly closed. When the door-bolt is removed and the door opened, all other things become visible and knowable. That is why ignorance is the first and foremost obstruction to liberation. The remedy for ignorance is to gain noble knowledge regarding what hitherto has been unknown, the four Noble Truths. Ignorance is not knowing about the true nature of existence. It is only abandoned when its opposite, knowledge, arises. Only when the darkness of ignorance is dispelled by opening the door, and for the first time one sees that saṃsāra is devoid of any self or real being, and that there is an escape, namely Nibbāna. Only then does the path really begin. Since only an arahant has completely removed ignorance, ignorance always plays a particularly important role, such as in this simile. The door-bolt of ignorance falls, so to speak, into its hole in the door jamb again and again and has to be taken out again and again by using the five powers. Each time, however, it becomes easier to remove.

2. *The ugly toad* of anger and despair. In anger and despair the ugly toad swells up, much as the ugly anger-eating yakkha-spirit on the throne of the king swells up when abused in the simile in SN 11:22. Anger and despair are self-created obstacles, yet the ego perceives their cause as external to itself. When these obstacles get in the way of the ego, it inflates and protests against them, and despairs over its inability to satisfy its urge to know and see the causes of those obstacles. In AN 3:25 (see Simile 67) anger and despair are compared to a sore that oozes when touched. Both anger and despair are agitations, the opposite of quietude of mind. When anger and despair disappear, the toad deflates, just like the anger-eating yakkha disappears when praised by the king. By damming anger and despair, one wins the first form of calm in the mind.

3. *The fork in the road.* With the five fighting powers of faith, effort, wisdom, mindfulness, and calm, one is now equipped to clear the last doubts about the correctness of the goal (Nibbāna) and thus win the fruit of stream-entry. One chooses the correct path at the fork of two ways (saṃsāra and Nibbāna). From now on, one knows only one right way. The three fetters (personality view, doubt and attachment to precepts and observances) have ceased forever. Thus the faith follower and Dhamma follower have become stream-enterer. The fork in the road is left behind.[35]

4. *The sieve* of the hindrances. The five hindrances are discovered and understood only at this stage even though one had at times unconsciously abolished or neutralised them before this. When the stream-enterer matures to become a once-returner, the hindrances come more and more into focus especially while the sieve or network of tangles with the world continue to obstruct one's achievement of absorption. The fifth hindrance is no longer the fetter of doubt about the correctness of the teaching but rather an acute doubt about tactics of training and obstacles on the way. The doubt about the right strategy was the fork.

5. *The tortoise* of the five aggregates of grasping. In SN 35:240, a tortoise with its five extremities is used as a symbol of the five senses. Here, however, it is used for the five aggregates. Only when the five hindrances are largely removed and the eighth step (*samādhi*) is reached can one progress to the ninth step and arrive at that knowledge which penetrates and unmasks the five aggregates. This is the step leading from the stage of once-returning to the path of non-returning.

6. *The butcher's knife and cutting block* represent the five strands of sensual desire. The five sense objects are the murderous butcher's knife. They are fixed in the circle of mortality. Because of them, one has to be born and die. The five desires lead to the sense world; they bind to it. Although one can often neutralize sense desire and may not even be able to notice it, e.g. like a Christian mystic, nonetheless until one reaches this

---

35. The same simile is used in SN 22:84 at the beginning of the path. Cf. SN 22:90 on the doubts of Channa.

stage the five desires are not yet abolished from latency. This happens only here and is the fruit of non-returning to the sense-world.

7. *The piece of meat* is satisfaction and allurement. The non-returner still enjoys pleasant feelings from form and formlessness. They are still meat for him—nutriment—but now he notices that they cannot satisfy, and so he lets go, as the last thing, the grasping of such.

8. *The nāga.* Herewith, by discovering the nāga serpent that lives at the bottom of the hole, the seeker has become a arahant; he has in fact become a nāga himself. The arahant is called "the nāga" in AN 4:43. Thus has the trainee (*sekha*) become one-gone-beyond-training (*asekha*), one who has nothing else to extract from the termite mound of the body.

48. The Glowing Chip of Iron (AN 7:52)

An iron bowl has been heated the whole day long and is glowing red-hot. Someone hits it so hard that a chip of it is knocked off. Now there are seven possibilities: (1) The chip might cool down immediately after it is knocked off. Or (2) it flies up a little bit through the air after it is knocked of and then cools down. Or (3) it flies through the air and cools just before contacting the ground or (4) when it contacts the ground. Or (5) instead, the chip flies onto a small pile of straw or wood and sets it on fire, and cools off only when the fuel is consumed. Or (6) the same thing happens with a large pile of combustible material. Or, finally, (7) in case of the large pile, after consuming it the fire might spread to bushes or a forest, burning them and only becoming extinct from lack of nutriment when encountering a wet field, sandy ground, a rock, a stretch of water or agricultural land.

Explanation

The *whole day* signifies a noble disciple who is already able to attain the equanimity of the sphere of neither-perception-nor-non-perception (see MN 106.11), but who has not completely overcome the last five fetters—conceit, greed for existence in form or formlessness, agitation and ignorance.

The *iron bowl* is the body. *Glowing* is the craving of the mind which occupies the body. The *hitting* is being struck by death.

The *knocking off* of a piece of the bowl is the catapulting of the non-returner's rebirth-seeking mental body out of his flesh-body. The glowing red, broken-off piece is his mental body. The seven kinds of rebirth are the seven ways a non-returner may progress in the pure abodes, the home of the non-returner. The standard division of five abodes for non-returners is expanded into seven here through an expansion of the destination of the first non-returner, the one who extinguishes immediately, into three.

1. Shortly after arriving at the gods of the pure abodes, even before reaching the zenith of that lifespan, that non-returner reaches the extinction of ignorance, the cooling of the last, finest defilements, and lives as an arahant on this plane of existence till the end of his life.

2. The piece that flies through the air and cools down denotes the mind that reaches arahantship on the zenith of that life span in the pure abodes.

3. The piece that cools down only shortly before contact with the ground is the mind that flies around even longer, and only as that lifespan comes near its end does the last desire or defilement become extinct.

4. The piece cools down upon contacting the ground of a new existence. The mind completes the full cycle of that existence, and the death of the mental body and the mind's liberation from the last fetters coincide.

5. A small pile of fuel is ignited. It burns (lives) and smokes (thinks), but the fire quickly goes out. The mind does not only fly to the end of that cycle but also ignites a second form of existence. The non-returner returns to the pure abodes for a second time. However, because his desires or defilements are not strong, they are extinguished without any conscious act of will (*asaṅkhāra-parinibbāyi*).

6. The same is true for a large pile. The one concerned needs a conscious, wilful effort to bring the last desires or defilements to extinction. They are blazing brightly, i.e., he still has strong attachment to that existence.

The Noble Powers

7. The fire ignites the environment of the large pile and comes to extinction only when everything combustible is consumed. The mind is still not liberated at the end of the second existence in the pure abodes. It becomes reborn there a third time and is extinguished only then.
8. Who, instead goes beyond the highest possible refinement of perception, the sphere of neither perception nor non-perception (see MN 106.10–12) in this life and becomes an arahant in this world, for him there is no rebirth. Only his body of flesh can still die, his mind cannot die again, because it has realized Nibbāna. As the Buddha said:

> Just as the bourn is not known
> Of the gradual fading glow
> 1Given off by the furnace-heated iron
> As it is struck with the smith's hammer,
> So is there no pointing to the bourn
> Of those perfectly released,
> Who have crossed this flood
> Of bondage to sense desires
> And attained unshakeable bliss. (Ud 8.10)

* * *

The above explanation is in accordance with the orthodox, commentarial Theravāda interpretation, however there is another, heterodox interpretation of the three *anantarā-parinibbāyī* non-returners. According to *antarā-parinibbāyi* means "one who attains parinibbāna in the intermediate (existence)." This interpretation supports the existence of an intermediate existence (*antarābhava*) between two rebirths, which is rejected in the Theravādin Abhidhamma text called Kathāvatthu (Ch. 8). The first simile is interpreted as the non-returner's attainment of Nibbāna without residue (*anupādisesa-nibbāna/parinibbāna*) immediately after death and as soon as he arises (*nibbattitvā*) in the *antarābhava*, i.e., he immediately passes away after becoming an arahant. The second simile means that the non-returner remains for a while in the intermediate existence and passes away as soon as he attains arahantship. The third simile means that he becomes an arahant and passes away in the intermediate existence just before taking up a new existence. In this state, and in the pure abodes too, there is immediate passing away upon the elimination of all fetters because there is no more coarse physical body made of the four elements to make the arahant continue in these realms.

Further support for this interpretation is found in AN 4:131 where four persons are mentioned. The first person, the once-returner, has not abandoned the five coarse fetters and has not abandoned the fetters that obtain a rearising (*upapatti-paṭilābha*) and the ones that obtain existence (*bhava*). The second person, the *uddhaṃsota* or *akaniṭṭhagāmī* non-returner, has abandoned the five coarse fetters but has not abandoned the fetters leading to rearising (*upapatti*) and the fetters leading to existence. The third person, the *antarāparibbāyī*, has abandoned the five coarse fetters and has abandoned the fetters leading to rearising (*upapatti*) but has not abandoned the ones obtaining existence (*bhava*). The fourth, the arahant, has abandoned all fetters and does not rearise or obtain a new existence.

The *antarāparibbāyi* non-returner is like the chip that flies but does not strike the ground, he will not rearise in a new birth, but still has fetters leading to existence in the *antarābhava*.

In SN 44:9, the Buddha states that on the occasion that one puts down this body, and the being (*satta*) has not rearisen in another body, that that being (in the *antarābhava*) is fuelled by craving. Elsewhere, in DN 25, "someone" (*ekacca*), that is, a being, is said to descend mindfully into the womb.[36] In MN 39.20 the seeing of the passing away and rearising of beings by means of the divine eye is compared to a man standing between two houses seeing beings entering the houses and coming out and passing to and fro. In DN 2 the man stands on a tower in the middle of a crossroad and sees some people entering and leaving a house, some going by chariots and some sitting down at the crossroad. These similes suggest that there is a state between existences where beings can stay for some time.

The word *ubhayamantarena*, "in between both" (Ud 8.4 and SN 34:87) has also been in interpreted as a state in between this

---

36. For more on this topic, see Peter Harvey, *The Selfless Mind*, pp. 98–108.

world and the world beyond. See the discussion in Ud-a 92–3, where the *antarāparinibbāyī* is said to mean *sambhavesi*, "(a being) seeking to be" or "(a being) about to be," which is used in the Ratanasutta (Sn 144) in apposition to *bhūtā*, "come into being."

Part 5

PURIFICATION OF THE MIND

49. Purifying Gold (AN 3:100)

The goldsmith's apprentice must watch out for three kinds of impurities or imperfections (*upakkilesa*) within the gold ore—coarse impurities such as rocks and detritus, medium impurities such as gravel and coarse sand, and fine impurities such as dust and mica. What remains after these are removed is granular gold, the gold dust. The goldsmith takes the gold dust from his apprentice and puts it into a melting pot where the grains of gold gradually melt together. The gold is then smelted but its slag is not yet entirely removed for it is not yet malleable and pliable, not bright, and not yet good to work with.

Gold which is melted together has to be made glowing red at some time, sprinkled with water at another time, and from time to time it must be scrutinised. Otherwise, if the gold were left only glowing red, it would eventually vaporise. If the smith only sprinkled it with water, it would cool off and become cold. If he only scrutinised it, it would never be finished.

When the goldsmith has followed all these steps properly and the slag has been fully removed, then the gold is malleable, workable, and bright. It can properly be used for whatever gold jewellery one wishes to make from it—a girdle, earring, necklace, chain, etc.

Explanation

The *gold-smith's apprentice* is one who trains to gain a calm and pure mind (*adhicitta*), but has not yet reached the deeper stages of calm and insight.

The *gold ore* is the mind, which has the potential to become pure and peaceful.

Purification of the Mind

The *impurities* are the mental defilements which trouble and agitate the mind.

Coarse impurities (rocks and detritus) are unwholesome actions (*kamma*) in body, speech or mind. The first five steps of the Noble Eightfold Path are directed against bad action.

Medium impurities (gravel and sand): the three unwholesome considerations of desire, hatred and violence, against which the second great exertion (the elimination of arisen unwholesome states) on the Noble Eightfold Path's sixth step, right effort, is directed.

Dust and mica: subtler thoughts concerning people close to oneself, thoughts about the household life, and thoughts about not wanting to be despised by others.

Gold as granular dust: elevated thoughts of the Dhamma and of one's own experience and understanding of it. One still needs assuring thoughts because inner independence has not yet been gained.

Goldsmith: the noble trainee (*sekha*) who has reached advanced stages of calm and insight.

Melting together: the various jhāna factors and awakening factors are made to work together to produce a pure, calm mind. However, at this stage the mind still has certain subtle defilements, *the slag*, and is not yet capable of developing the higher knowledges. The calm (*samādhi*) one has gained can be sustained only by strenuous suppression of the hindrances; there is not yet the calm, stable equanimity of the fourth jhāna. In the Upakkilesasutta (MN 128), the subtle defilements blocking calm and insight are described: doubt, inattention, sloth and torpor, fear, elation, inertia, overexertion, lack of exertion, longing, perception of diversity, excessive meditation upon forms.

Glowing red: further exertion to reach the deeper states of absorption. *Sprinkling with water*: resting in the respective state of calm (*samādhi*). *Scrutinising*: the equanimity in which one can distinguish what has been achieved and what is still lacking. *Vaporising*: if all one ever does is struggle, one tires and wastes one's energy, and becomes restless and agitated and falls away from the states of absorption. *Cooling off*: if one wants to enjoy only stillness, one becomes slack. *Never becoming finished*: if one wants only to scrutinise, then one does not reach the completion of calm (*samādhi*).

The *slag having been fully removed*: the fine defilements have all been removed. The coarser jhāna factors, such as thought, happiness and joy, have been removed and replaced by the fine jhāna factors of equanimity and mindfulness.

The *gold being malleable and workable, bright*: the mind is at its purest stage of calm and brightness in the fourth jhāna and can be directed to developing the higher knowledges such as the divine eye, and, more importantly, can fully destroy the mental taints and reach the highest state of purity of wisdom, arahantship (cf. MN 140.20).

Like a *girdle*, so are the first three levels of higher knowledge (*abhiññā*), which are concerning this world. As *earrings* form a circle, so remembrance of past lives discerns the cycle of existence, the round of rebirth. Like a *necklace*, so is the knowledge of the arising and passing away; death grips everybody by the neck. As *golden chain*, by far the best, so is the third knowledge worth its weight in gold, representing liberation because one has discerned the chain of dependent origination and the Four Noble Truths.

50. The Five Impurities (AN 5:23; SN 46:33)

Five pollutions or impurities can be found in gold which make it neither malleable nor shining, so that it cannot really be used for gold jewellery. What five? Iron, copper, tin, lead and silver. But if it is freed of these, the gold is malleable, workable and bright. It can properly be used for whatever gold jewellery one wishes to make from it.

Similarly, there are five impurities, *upakkilesa*, of the mind by which it is not malleable, workable, or shining, and cannot come to the necessary one-pointedness to destroy the taints of wilful desire or sensuality, hateful anger or ill-will, sloth and torpor, restlessness and impatience, and obsessive doubt. These are also called the hindrances. Were the mind freed from these five impurities, it could reach the six breakthroughs to wisdom.

Explanation

The *gold* is the mind that shines in the deepest state of calm, and is malleable and workable (AN 3:100).

The *five metals* are added impurities.

Like common, hard and heavy *iron*, so is longing—normal, sensual, wilful desire. Just as iron is not only the most prevalent metal, but also the one easiest to disintegrate by rust, so sense desire is the fundamental hindrance.

Like *copper* which generates a toxic rust, so is hatred or aversion, which poisons one's relations with the world. (Alternatively, the analogy might be that, because of wrath, one becomes red like copper.)

Like dull, brittle *tin*, so is sloth and torpor. There is no gleam, only dull, dozing monotony, and even that is brittle.

Heavy and oppressive like *lead* are restlessness and impatience: the 'I'-pressure, the pressure upon oneself to do well.

Like *silver*, which is close in value to gold and the most difficult to melt out, is obsessive doubt. It appears as a questioner of truth, but in actuality it just wants to think without commitment.

51. The Brass Dish (MN 5)

The mind compares to a brass dish bought from a shop in one of these four states:

1. The first dish is full of dust and rust stains. Its purchaser neither uses nor cleans it but only puts it away in a dusty corner. Thus, after some time, it becomes even dustier and more stained. In the same way, someone's mind may be full of dust and stains, that is, full of worldly desires and defilements. Such a person does not evaluate his state of mind as bad or unwholesome. He doesn't clean the dish of his mind, that is, he doesn't meditate, doesn't exert his willpower and doesn't fight the defilements. He criticises others for their blemishes. He lets his mind remain in darkness; he doesn't care about its purification, just as a dusty dish thrown into a dusty corner only becomes dustier. He doesn't use his dish, does not work with it, does not live in daily

contact with it, but rather it is unknown and distant to him. At the end of his life he dies full of greed, hatred and delusion

2. The second dish is also dusty and stained with rust, but its new owner cleans it, uses it and cleans it again afterwards so that eventually it becomes free of stains and shiny. So too, someone's mind might be filthy but, in accordance with truth, he recognises his deficiency and makes it his task to remove what is wrong. He doesn't criticise others' defilements but takes the exhortation of the great ones seriously and scrutinises himself regularly. He meditates quite often and, persevering, rejects the unwholesome tendencies. Soon his mind becomes cleaner, tidier and lighter—the original shine of the brass dish is restored. He dies purer than he was born.

3. This dish is bought clean and without stains, but the owner doesn't use or clean it; instead he throws it into a dusty corner where it soon becomes dusty and stained. Thus someone is born as a pure one, close to the divine state he came from in his previous birth, without many worldly desires, free from ambition, full of inner happiness—a person of calm, *samādhi*. Yet in his mind he doesn't recognise what treasure he owns. He just enjoys the stillness, caring neither about the maintenance nor increase of his treasure. Hence the lovely, alluring world of sense objects—especially human beauty—will seduce him. "What's wrong with looking at the beautiful?" he thinks, or, "I may just as well take this pleasure along, too." Thus he deliberately watches the pretty, deceptive appearance of forms, he increases his longing for them (dust) and thereby diminishes his purity. When his desires are not fulfilled, he becomes angry or gets into a bad mood. Because of delusion, he now looks for more and more sensual happiness and so he dies full of dust and dirt. He did not use his dish nor clean it from the daily dust and dirt that fell onto it from outside. This is the great danger of dazzling appearances.

4. This dish is bought clean and without stains and here the new owner is again someone partially free of worldly desires. He has the same calmness of mind, but he knows this treasure and knows its value. Therefore, he will be concerned to maintain it and take care of it, wiping out the remaining rust stains as well

as preventing new stains from arising. Thus the clean dish becomes ever more clean, the brass shining and gleaming ever more brightly. This person will die purer than he was born, and reach complete purity.

52. The Dirty Cloth (MN 7)

When a dyer puts a dirty cloth full of stains into a solution of blue, yellow, red or brown dye, it can only become an impure, dirty colour, because the cloth itself was already dirty. When it dries, the stains still show through because the dirt has been dyed along with the cloth. Initially the cloth was stained and dirty in its original colour; now it is stained in its new, different colour. Similarly, a bad destiny can be expected if the mind is sullied. If the cloth were pure and bright in the first place, it will look also well dyed and pure in its new colour. Similarly, a good destiny can be expected if the mind is unsullied. One who has gained the best result of practice, the arahant, is called "one bathed with the inner bathing."

Explanation

The cloth: our mind and the emotions, or the heart with its qualities and abilities.

The stains: the tendencies of sensual greed, hatred and violence, expanded in the text of MN 7 into sixteen defilements of the mind. They sully the conscience, cloud the vision and prevent calm of mind and breakthroughs into wisdom.

The dye: the world, the environment, one's respective surroundings, the milieu. Even if someone changes the milieu, he always takes himself along. If an angry man has made himself unpopular and so moves to another city, his anger will soon emerge again. Even if an angry person escapes from this world by committing suicide, in the next life an angry infant will be born. The new dye of the outer experience cannot prevent the stains of the mind (desires) from showing themselves again.

The four colours: symbolically all the possibilities of external change, whether the denser (blue), the lighter (yellow), the more affective (red) or the mixed (brown). No matter how deep the colour, no matter how revolutionary the external impressions, the stains beneath the colour remain.

Cleaning: recognising the pollutions of the mind as enemies, evaluating them as negative, depriving them of their power, and rejecting them again and again until they are gone. In this way one takes care of the cleaning of the cloth, follows the instructions of the cleaner (the Buddha) instead of the instructions of the dyer (world).

Bathed with the inner bathing: the arahant with a completely clean and free mind without any stains because he has purified it first in inner battle and then in inner calm. Whatever meets him from an "outer bath"—the splashes and colourings of experiences—meets a pure mind (cloth), so that all dyes come into contact only with purity. Whatever he encounters, he is and remains pure.

53. The Five Hindrances
(Adaptation of MN 39.14; DN 2)

A man is given credit and he has to exert himself strenuously to repay the debt and interest. Then he becomes ill and cannot work. As it takes too long for him to make payments to his creditors, he is put into a debtor's prison until a guarantor can free him by making a payment for him. Because a guarantor does not come, he is eventually sold as a slave (to recover some of the money lent). Out of distress, he escapes into a wilderness where he is threatened by privation and robbers instead of creditors.

Explanation

1. *Credit* represents desires. By former virtuous activities someone has reached human rebirth with credit, that is, a certain amount of recognition of desire. As a human being, he should use this opportunity to diminish his desire in order to become independent. Yet, instead, he wants only to enjoy himself and so enters into debt (greed) in order to gratify his desires and has to earn more money accordingly. He takes more and more credit and makes himself more and more dependent upon creditors, with ever higher interest to pay.

2. *Illness* is hatred. The debtor becomes angrier and angrier with his creditors, who keep pressing him for payments. He is filled with hostility towards the many obstacles obstructing his greed. When he is angry and in a bad mood, his mind is sick and he is unable to work or enjoy anything. He stops earning and what he previously enjoyed proves disagreeable. He has no appetite but is eaten up by his anger and so becomes even sicker.

3. *Imprisonment* is sloth and torpor. Since he cannot achieve any real well-being, he gives up exerting himself. He does not want to know about working on himself, finds all self-education boring and dreary, and allows himself to languish in the stifling dullness and lassitude of worldly banality. Thus he is in prison, the debtor's tower, where he sits doing nothing, walled in by his lack of energy.

4. *Slavery* is unrest and displeasure. Occasionally he rouses himself and begins to make heroic exertions to do something to escape from his apathy. But then he overdoes it: The tyrant of his "I" demands ever new achievement, ever greater feelings of success, setting meditative records, and so he becomes ever more impatient and fidgety.

5. *The desert wilderness* is obsessive doubt. Because his restlessness does not lead to any sort of well-being, he runs away from the teaching and into occult border territory, into secret lore and the esoteric—in short, to the wilderness of sects and opinions. He runs from master to master, from book to book, always in doubt as to whether the teaching is right. This running becomes the purpose of his life and an end in itself: to run away from himself toward intellectual will-o'-the-wisps, where each and everything vacillates, causing uncertainty because no real well-being is achieved. The result is that he wastes his life and wins nothing on his own, losing his energy in the process. At the end of his life he has more debts (desires) than before. Having done nothing good, he sinks below the human level.

However, he who works on himself repays the debts to the outside and acquires internal possessions, that is, wholesome qualities. Because he owns something wholesome, he is cheerful and contented, and so disturbances drop off him. He is spiritually independent, thereby healthy and not susceptible to infections. He sees other attainable and meaningful goals, and he does not let himself get distracted by worldly ways but transcends the prison of sensuality. His inner goals are reached by letting go of the ego and its demands for admiration, and thus he does not fall into the obsessive neurosis of the 'I'-dictatorship, which impatiently demands achievement. Since he achieves more well-being this way, he becomes certain of the path to liberation without further questioning or searching. His restless doubt is pacified, he knows where safety is, he is close to the safe place, and he is staying on the edge of the village where robbers and predators do not dare to approach.

54. The Water Mirror (AN 5:193; SN 46:55)

1. A big pot has been filled with clear water, but because lac, turmeric, indigo and madder dyes have been added, one cannot see the reflection of one's face as it actually is. Likewise, if the mind (clear water) is irritated by sensual addiction, that is, pervaded and overcome by passion-coloured longing, and if one neither knows nor aspires to escape from this situation, then one understands neither one's own benefit nor that of another. Whatever wisdom and discourses one has memorized and rehearsed, even for a long time, one is unable to remember.

Water permeated by an impure mixture of colours is distorted in an iridescent manner. In the same way, sensual longing distorts things and leads to belief in nonexistent values while the precious things one has learned simply do not come to mind. However if one knows desire as both a hindrance and a pollution and aspires to escape from it, then that is already the first step to its fading away (*virāga*).

2. Water in a pot is heated over fire so that it boils. In this case, one also cannot use the water as a mirror because of the bubbles and steam. Likewise, instead of being lured by shimmering attraction, the mind is now strongly repelled and fired into anger, hatred, aversion, rejection and ill-will. This disturbance obstructs vision. The anger boiling within prevents any sober observation.

3. The water has been left untouched for a long time so that algae and water plants have grown there. It is entirely covered and overgrown so now there is no place one could use to see the

reflection of one's face. It is the same with the third of the five hindrances, the so-called 'sloth and torpor' or 'weary boredom with the wholesome.' Tiredness leads one to believe there is a mossy cushion there inviting one to sleep. Weariness represses and overgrows all positive impulses to pick oneself up, and so one has no interest in anything. Thus sloth and torpor cause one to remain within worldly banality.

4. Now the water is agitated by wind and stirred up. Because of the waves and turbulence one again can't see one's face properly. It is the same with restlessness and displeasure, excitement and impatience. The mountainous waves and tempests create excitement; one is engaged by the whirlwind of the 'I.' Nothing happens fast enough for impatience, which feels that all development is too slow. One is always feeling down in the valley and striving energetically upwards. "Let's go!" shouts excitement, while impatience cries, "Still not yet?!"

5. Finally, the pot with dirty, stale and polluted water is placed into darkness so one cannot even see that it is discoloured and impure. It is the same with obsessive doubt, the uncertainty concerning the secure, safe place. One is standing in darkness and believes that all one has to do is to illuminate the place artificially with flashes of thought in order to see one's reflection in the water. It doesn't even dawn on one that all one will get to see is dirty water, so one is doubly deceived.

If the pot of water is clear, serene, limpid and set in the light, then one can see the reflection of one's face as it actually is. Likewise, if the mind is free from the five hindrances, then one understands one's own benefit and that of another. And whatever wisdom and discourses one has memorized and rehearsed, even if they have not been recited for a long time, one can remember.

55. The Strangler Trees (SN 46:39)

From tiny seeds sprouting in nooks high up on large trees, enormous trees with great trunks can grow that eventually overgrow, bend, twist, split and strangle the host trees so that the latter suffocate and die.[37] What giant trees are these? They are the strangler figs: the assattha fig, the banyan fig, the parasitic fig, the

Similes of the Buddha

cluster fig, the hairy fig, and the kapitthana fig. Which trees do they overgrow? Hardwood trees, such as teak, satinwood, neem, ebony and diospyros.

Similarly, the hindrances can suffocate someone who has renounced the world and become a monk. His good intentions are suffocated by the hindrances, which bend, twist and split him.

Explanation

The five hindrances—those pollutions of the mind—start as very small thoughts and tendencies but when not checked and removed, they slowly grow larger, forming big solid trunks which overgrow the mind and paralyse wisdom.

Strangler fig trees, especially the banyan and parasitic fig, have large horizontal branches which stretch out in all directions and then put out air roots which grow down, sink into the ground then send up growths as new trees, sometimes forming whole groves. They symbolize the continually expanding, insatiable, entangling and overwhelming nature of the mental defilements. As is said in Suttanipāta:

---

37. Strangling fig trees, all of the Ficus family, are common in the tropics and their abundant figs are an important source of food for birds and animals. The tiny seeds of the strangling figs land on other trees through the droppings of birds and animals which have eaten the figs. If it has lands in a suitable place such as a little nook such as a fork or the hole left by a broken branch in which humus accumulates, then the seed will sprout. The young fig tree's roots will slowly grow down along the trunk. After some years, depending on the height of the host and the amount of moisture and food, the roots will eventually reach the ground. Now the fig tree has a steady supply of moisture and nutriment and will grow quickly. Its roots merge into trunks which completely encircle and enmesh the trunk of the host, which slowly suffocates, dies, rots away and serves as nutriment for the strangler fig. Strangler figs can also grow on walls and roofs of houses, and if left unchecked will split the walls and foundations, as can be seen at the temples of Angkor Wat in Cambodia. The popular *Ficus benjamina* grown indoors in the West is a strangler fig.

> Greed, hatred and delusion...
> They are born from the moisture of craving,
> originating within oneself, like the Banyan
> overgrowing the (host's) trunk. (Sn 273-74)

The seven factors of awakening (*bojjhaṅga*), however, are non-obstructions, non-stranglers of the mind. They oppose and remove the hindrances. Like a kind forester or gardener freeing the hardwood tree by cutting away the roots and trunks of the strangler, so the factors of awakening cut away the hindrances and free the mind. Just as the hardwood trees grow even more mighty if they are unobstructed, so the seven factors of awakening develop even more if the five hindrances have been removed.

56. The Obstructed Mountain Stream (AN 5:51)

In the mountains, there is a long, fast-flowing stream. If a man were to break the banks on both sides of the stream, thereby diverting the current so that it is divided and scattered, the stream can then neither travel far nor run fast carrying things along with it.

Similarly, a person who has not overcome the five hindrances can neither recognise his own good nor another's, and therefore he cannot realize clarity of knowledge and holiness.

Explanation

The long, fast, mountain stream which carries things along with it is the mind with its powers and abilities of faith, mindfulness, energy, calm and wisdom. The man who disperses the stream is wrong mindfulness. Thereby faith or confidence, the foundation of the powers, is weakened.

Sensual desire or worldly longing causes the unrestrained opening up of the senses. It breaks the banks of sense restraint and causes sensuality to overwhelm the mind. This sensual desire for worldly pleasures, for variety, which causes the mind to leave its own safe territory and venture into the realm of Māra, is the first and fundamental hindrance. It diverts faith and prevents it from flowing in the right direction, that is, towards liberation.

The division, diversion and dispersion of the current equates to aversion. Before, there had been one single direction toward liberation; now there are right and left factions and disintegration in the middle. This is the hindrance of hatred.

Since confidence is destroyed by greed and hatred, energy is lacking. The stream seeps into the plains, spreads out over the surface and doesn't flow far. This is sloth and torpor.

As the stream can no longer flow swiftly, it wastes its energy by turning in circles. Whirling around and filling holes and hollows indiscriminately, it represents restlessness and impatience, which run to and fro aimlessly instead of going into the depth of calm (*samādhi*) and then on to transcending the world.

Since such a flat and shallow stream cannot carry objects any more, it is not navigable by boats. One is quickly stranded somewhere and remains stuck. This is obsessive doubt, which doesn't produce any serviceable results but always causes the mind to run aground.

57. Similes for Sensual Desire (MN 54, Thī 490–509)

A group of seven similes is given in MN 54 to explain the danger of sensual desire. In addition to these seven similes, three more are added elsewhere (MN 22 = Pac 68 = CV 1.32; AN 5:76; and Thī 488–491), although these three additional similes are not explained in the texts. The first seven similes show sensual desire as an initially tempting, seductive image, while the latter three depict desire straightaway as evil, an evil which never really brings any well-being.

1. **Bare bones.** A hungry dog waiting near a butcher's shop is thrown a meatless bare bone. Because it is a bone and smells of the meat and blood formerly covering it, the dogs chews on it again and again with the expectation of getting something from it. Yet because it is completely bare, the more the dog chews the hungrier it becomes. The dog thinks he is very close to the

promised gratification, but like the goddess Fortuna standing on her rolling ball,[38] he never reaches what he longs for.

In the same way, sensual desire is unsatisfactory. One trusts in the objects of desire (bare bones), but the hope that satiation can be found there is deceptive and forever disappointing. Desire is insatiable, and by continuing to appreciate it (chewing), it is merely strengthened, i.e., one becomes more dissatisfied. Every gratification of greed is as unsatisfactory as the bare bone is for the dog, yet one lives in the illusion that there is something to be had in it.

If one were to snatch the bare bone away from the dog, objectively he would be relieved from a senseless source of restlessness, yet subjectively he would fly into a rage. It is from this subjective point of view that this second simile should be understood.

2. **Pieces of meat.** A bird of prey (vulture) has carried off a piece of meat, but other vultures attack it and try so hard to get it that the vulture lets go so as not to be injured. The realization of one's desires feels good at the time it is experienced. These moments of enjoyment are created by one's former virtuous acts. But even this meat on the bone (merit) is endangered because one has also created competitors with earlier acts (other vultures), who, as a multitude, are stronger and hence can snatch away the object of one's desire. These troublemakers may be envious family members, jealous neighbours, competitive colleagues, rivals, a dispossessing government or enemies in times of war. All belong to the human realm.

3. **Torches of straw.** Whoever carries a burning torch of straw against the wind is burned by the flames blown back by the wind towards him. Thus he is burned by the very thing he carries. This compares to the fiery plans we want to carry out against the wind of worldly circumstances. Things happen in other ways than we expect; there are setbacks, particularly of the kind which are our own fault. We overexert ourselves and

---

38. Fortuna is the Roman goddess of good luck, who holds the horn of plenty and a rudder. She stands on a rolling ball. The rudder denotes desire for wealth guiding the mind of men and the rolling ball the instability of fortune.

consume our energies in power struggles. We overeat and smoke and intoxicate ourselves, having a good time, wasting all physical energies in pleasures, and so we ruin the body, wear down the mind, and age prematurely. These days it is called "stress." In the past it was called "burning the candle at both ends."

4. **Glowing embers.** In the social arena, misuse of the fire of our energies is shown when we are inconsiderate toward others. We then make life hell for ourselves as well as others. The judge of the Realm of Death waits for us, and the wardens of hell drag us into the fire. The resistance of the man who is being dragged by the wardens of hell to a pit of glowing embers (MN 12) is of no use, for he must bear the consequences of the fire of his reckless passion. Violation of others summons the devils, even here on earth where justice drags us away from pleasure in front of the judge and into the hell of a punishment camp or prison. (This simile is common: DN 34.8; AN 8:28; AN 10:90; Sn 396; SN 35:244; SN 12:63).

5. **Dream image.** Desire is like a beautiful dream from which one awakens into profane reality—a shattered illusion which contains nothing of the dreamt splendour. We had imagined it to be so nice, but the dream is finished, and all of a sudden the world is empty, grey and dreary. Only melancholic memories remain. As Shakespeare put it so aptly in one of his sonnets, "Before, a joy proposed; behind a dream" (*Sonnet* 129): first the intoxication, then the sobering and disillusionment; first the dream, then the bitter awakening (Cf. Sn 807).

6. **Credit.** Someone borrows money, buys many precious things and displays them everywhere. Many envy his enjoyment of the riches. They, however, don't see how he has achieved it; they don't see that he lives on credit and that he is in deep debt. Similarly it is with objects of desire, which we have borrowed for a while through past virtue, but for which we have to pay interest. In order to maintain what we have, we must invest further virtue. Yet while we are enjoying ourselves, we want only to enjoy. Therefore, our credit is continually snatched away from us, and at the latest at death. There in the ghost realm the enjoyer stands with empty hands. Since he did not generate merit, he

does not reach heaven, nor even again the human state. His merit has expired and so his sham possessions are confiscated, and the poor soul sits there "where there is wailing and gnashing of teeth." (This simile also occurs above at Simile 53 and in J 494 and 540).

7. **Fruits of a tree.** A man has climbed a fruit tree and is eating the succulent fruit with pleasure. He only needs to seize the fruit and take it with both hands. He is literally 'on top.' Another man comes along, however, who cannot climb but who nonetheless wants to enjoy the same thing, so he fells the tree. Consequently, the first man falls down. Thus it happens that even when there are no vulture-like enemies, there are still overlapping spheres of interest. Without being aware of me, somebody else wants to have the same object of pleasure and takes the fruit from my mouth. Or he builds a superhighway in front of my house. Or he invents something that renders me unemployed. Or he seduces my spouse. Or he has my house pulled down. Or he has me ousted or killed. How often is the happiness of others, without any evil intent, possible only at my expense?

8. **Butcher's knife and block.** By enjoying desires, we are effectively putting our own head on Death's butcher's block; again and again we bleed to death as weaklings. Everyone who indulges his desires is like a vampire or leech sucking his own blood. On our long travels through saṃsāra we have spilled more blood being executed and slaughtered than there is water in the world's oceans.

9. **Spearheads.** Desire is like a constant drilling, disturbing our peace and penetrating like a spear head, a spike, a sting or an arrow tip. Constant stings act like a spur by which animals are urged on. "More, more!" say desires, as they continue to drill.

10. **Head of a snake.** Desire is like the venom of a poisonous snake. The serpent in Eden was only seductive, but here the snake is straightaway evil and dangerous, aiming its strike to cause us misery. Thus all sensual pleasure is deadly and should be avoided. In the Sutta Nipāta the Buddha says:

> Whoever avoids sensual pleasures,
> Like a snake's head with one's foot,
> That mindful one passes beyond
> this entanglement in the world. (Sn 768)

* * *

The likening of sensual desire to poison is also found in a simile in SN 12:66 and MN 46.19:

There is a bronze cup with a drink that looks, smells and tastes deliciously. A very thirsty and overheated man comes who wants to drink. He is warned that the drink is laced with poison and that it will kill him, but nevertheless he ignores the warning and keeps regarding the drink as pleasant, healthy and safe. Hurriedly and without consideration he drinks it all and as a result soon dies a painful death.

The thirsty, overheated man: someone affected by craving. *The delicious drink*: sense objects that appear beautiful, pleasant and safe. *The poison*: ignorance, eventually leading to death and birth. *The people who warn*: the Buddha and his noble disciples. *The ignoring of the warning*: conceit due to wrong view. The *regarding of the drink as pleasant and safe*: distorted perception. The *hurried, inconsiderate drinking*: the clinging to sensual pleasure (kāmupādāna).

58. The Leper (MN 75)

The body of a leper is covered with foul sores full of maggots and is slowly rotting away. To escape the maddening itch of the scabs he has already scratched open with his fingernails, he cauterises his body at a pit of glowing embers.

If this leper were eventually to be cured of his disease by the medicine prepared by a doctor, he would neither envy other lepers trying to alleviate their pain at the charcoal pit, nor would he long for a cure. For if he were healthy, the pit of glowing embers would not be a relief but suffering, and he would not be in need of a cure.

If the cured leper were grabbed by two strong men who dragged him violently to that pit of embers, would he not make all possible efforts to free himself and keep his body away from the pit? He certainly would, because the fire with its terrible burning is as painful to bear now as it was before. But when he was sick he was mad. What seemed painful to bear, he distortedly perceived as pleasant. His itching sores were much more unbearable than the heat of the fire which, by comparison, seemed to be relief.

When the leper cauterises his body at a pit, his open wounds become even more infected, and then the wounds itch, ooze and stench even more. Yet he still feels a certain kind of well-being, a certain pleasure in cauterising his open sores. This small pain compares well to the great pain of incessant itching. So he keeps going to the pit and the wounds become even worse.

Explanation

The leper: everyone with sensual desire.

Open wounds and sores: the vulnerability and sensitivity of the six sense inner sense bases caused by craving for sensual pleasures. (See Simile 44.)

The maggots: inner turmoil, dissatisfaction.

The itching: craving, looking outside for gratification.

Scratching scabs off with the nails: fanciful thoughts about indulging in sensual pleasures.

The pit of glowing embers: the outside world, Māra's territory, the five pleasure objects, otherwise used as a simile for hell.

Cauterising the body: indulging in sensual gratification, distortedly experiencing pain as happiness.

The doctor: the Buddha.

The cure: the enjoyment of higher happiness. The supreme well-being resulting from taking the medicine of calm and insight (*samādhi* and *vipassanā*).

The cured patient: the arahant. He doesn't envy the lepers, those who are affected by the disease of sensual desire. Enjoying a higher happiness, he can find no delight in their pleasures. He can renounce the common and vulgar, just as one reborn in heaven does not yearn for worldly pleasures.

The two strong men: unwholesome thoughts or advice of bad friends who try to suggest he should indulge in sensual pleasures or aspire for the higher, but impermanent, happiness of heaven.

To pull back one's body: to resist and get away from these bad influences.

To be mad: the impairment of the faculty of wisdom because of the distorted perception which causes suffering to be viewed as happiness.

Distorted perception: perceiving what is suffering as happiness, what is not-self as self. Beings take the gratification of desires to be true happiness; they can't see that sensual happiness is just another form of suffering—there is no lasting satisfaction in sensual pleasures. As the Buddha said:

> The unpleasant in the guise of the pleasant,
> he undear in the guise of the dear,
> pain in the guise of happiness,
> overcome the heedless one.(Ud 2.8)

Open wounds becoming more infected: when pursuing craving for sense pleasures, the wound of the inner sense bases become more painful, the itching more unbearable, i.e., the craving becomes stronger. After the gratification, the itchy craving for more scratching and cauterising increases.

Pleasure in scratching the sores: gratification of the desire which abates craving for the moment and provides a momentary pleasure. However, due to paying attention only to this tiny bit of well-being, one doesn't notice the worsening of the sores.

59. The Four Herds of Deer (MN 25)

A herd of deer in the forest is lured by bait put out by a deer-trapper and unwarily enjoys it, falling into intoxication and heedlessness. Thus this herd is completely given into the hands of the hunter and, with this power, he does what he wants with the deer.

So too can be a herd of people. Even if they are decent and religious, if they enjoy the worldly bait of the five sense objects as a matter of course, they cannot consequently escape the domain of Māra (Death) and Māra's entourage, his armies of sensual desire, dissatisfaction, gain, honour, uncertainty, etc. (Sn 3:2).

A second herd of deer, deterred by the miserable fate of the first herd, abstains from the bait, that unfortunate food, and withdraws instead deep into the forest. But in the dry season, due to a lack of adequate forage, emaciated, the herd returns to the hunter's food and suffers the same fate as the first group of deer.

The second herd of humans looks deeper and notices the deadly danger of sense enjoyment and withdraws into asceticism. However, by mere external cutting off and repression, this second herd creates a craving for compensation, and afterwards falls all the more for sensuality, even though it has already reached temporary feelings of liberation. Because it is still seeking well-being, when inner well-being ceases due to weaknesses of the body, from exhaustion, hunger and disease, etc. It throws itself onto the more easily obtainable sensual well-being.

A third herd of deer takes into consideration the fate of the other two herds and avoids the extremes of enjoyment and repression. It remains close to the place where the hunter put out the bait, but not too near and not too far. Here, it feeds without blind enjoyment and avoids intoxication and heedlessness, always withdrawing quickly into the forest when danger threatens. The hunter is unable to detect where the herd comes from and where it goes, so he constructs a large fence around the feeding place and the surrounding territory. Then he follows the herd and discovers its hiding place since it cannot go beyond the fence. Thus this herd also falls into his hands.

Similarly, the third herd of humans takes the necessities of life from the senses, but after each meal they return quickly into the realm of mental contemplation, delighting in the deeper insights and serenity of the absorptions (of *jhāna* and formlessness), creating a self-sufficient island for themselves. Such people continues to believe in the outside world, taking the prison of the sense world to be the whole, and remain within the limits of the fence of rational thinking, which takes its data constantly from the sense world. They believe that the problem lies in the relationship of 'I' to the world and get bogged down by that belief. Staying under the spell of the world they have constructed, clinging to their views, they cannot escape from it.

A fourth herd of deer takes the failure of the other three herds into account and looks for a place inaccessible to the hunter. Despite his fencing, the hunter cannot find the herd because the herd stays away from the bait and fence. So this fourth herd escapes him. These are the people who first penetrate the sense world as the realm of craving and therefore strive to overcome it, and secondly, also take the absorptions as transitional stages, so that, thirdly, they do not rest until the last mental fetter is dissolved and the safe place of Nibbāna is reached. They do not form self-views and world-views on emerging from the absorptions. Māra has no access to them. Nibbāna alone is the secure place, beyond the world, inaccessible to Māra. For someone who walks in that direction, the absorptions are a temporary safe place and a preliminary stage of final liberation.

A similar simile, as a triad, is given in MN 26.32–42. In the first instance the deer lies snared in the snare of sensual pleasure; in the second it lies unfettered on the snare due to wisely understanding the danger of it, and can flee if the hunter approaches; in the third instance it dwells outside the hunter's territory in the deep forest of jhāna.

Another similar simile is in DN 13.26–30. In the first case, a man stands on the bank of a river desiring to cross but his hands are bound behind him with a strong chain, so he is unable to swim. The bondage is his indulging in the five objects of sensual desire and knowing no way out. In the second case, the man is not chained but he lies down to sleep on the river bank covering his body and head. This means he outwardly no longer enjoys sensual desires (there is no chain), but inwardly he has not yet driven out the five hindrances, i.e., inner longing with its consequences. He indulges in the sleep of complacency. If he takes off the blanket of hindrances, and rises and swims across the river with right effort he will reach the farther bank and the safety of Nibbāna.

60. The Pieces of Wood (MN 36.17–19)

Before the Buddha attained enlightenment—i.e., after he had left his two teachers and when he was still searching for awakening—three similes occurred to him while having to rely completely on himself. These similes, occurring spontaneously, had not been heard by him before, and they determined his further way.

1. A wet, thoroughly soaked piece of wood is lying in water. A man with a fire-stick wants to use the piece of wet wood as the base stick on which to start a fire by friction. He rubs his fire-stick on the wet piece of wood (still in the water) but all his effort and struggle do not make fire and light, and he reaps only weariness and disappointment. It is the same with those spiritual seekers who, whether they are striving or not, will not be able to reach knowledge and enlightenment because they are not living physically withdrawn from sensual pleasures and because they have not eradicated their inner desire for sensual pleasures.

The piece of wood: the body.

Wet and thoroughly soaked: he is completely permeated inside with sensual addiction; all six senses are full of sensual desire.

Lying in the water: on the outside, he pursues sensual pleasures; he is lying in the water of sensuality.

The man with the fire-stick: the mind seeking freedom, spiritually striving people.

Making fire: creating the warm well-being of calm of mind.

Making light: achieving insight, breaking through into wisdom and enlightenment.

Generating friction by rubbing with the upper fire-stick: meditation.

Weariness and disappointment: when the physical and mental exertion of the meditator doesn't lead anywhere. Tired and disappointed he gives up.

2. A wet, soaked piece of wood is taken from the water and placed on dry land far from the water, but in this case too, the man cannot produce either light or fire because the wood is still wet. It is the same with those spiritual seekers who are striving and no longer indulge in sense pleasures outwardly, living ascetically (on dry land), yet whose inner desire and longing remains unchanged because they haven't driven out their inner sensual addiction. The Bodhisatta practised like that as an ascetic: he externally renounced gratification of sensual desire, but he hadn't driven it out of his body.

3. A piece of wood is completely dry, lying on land far from water. Light and fire can now easily be produced by the man. Similarly, those ascetics who have inwardly as well as outwardly renounced and driven out sensual addiction can attain calm and wisdom, with or without much meditation.

61. The Flies (AN 3:126)

A rotten piece of meat in the heat of summer gives off a stench of decay that attracts innumerable flies. So too, where a mind is corrupted by worldly longing there is also the stench of the carrion of hatred. Where the stench of hatred is, there also are the innumerable flies of evil and unwholesome thoughts.

Explanation

A longing mind is like the rotten piece of meat. The mind, as such, is pure (AN 1:6; cf. AN 3:100; MN 140.20), however, it is corrupted and made rotten by looking at superficially tempting sensual objects. But these objects of sense desire are empty, dependent upon transitory external conditions and not the independently and objectively existing good they appear to be. A monk who does not exercise restraint towards his senses, says the Buddha, spoils his mind, because he breeds passionate yearnings that destroy his independence. As a monk, he dies of inner putrefaction.

Where such longing for the world dominates, aversion and hatred arise to the same degree. He becomes angry, bitter, quarrelsome and unjust, and he nurtures hatred. Wherever he goes he kicks up a stink and nobody can stand him. To distract himself from the hunger of his longing, he is on the lookout for conflicts and squabbles so he can let out his aversion.

As a consequence of the defilements of greed and hatred, thousands of thoughts, considerations, plans and memories arise in such a monk. Pressured by his craving, thoughts incessantly buzz around him. He is persecuted by his thoughts as though they were annoying flies.

Since he cannot ward off these provocative thoughts and, as a monk, cannot fulfil them either, the repressed thoughts accumulate and mentally play out in his imagination. These are the flies, the spiteful spirits persecuting him wherever he is. Because he cannot stop his thoughts he becomes paranoid. The wholesome insight and loyalty to the Sangha, the monastic order, fight back and forth with unwholesome sensual longing. He wants to rid himself of such thoughts, wants to force himself into peace of mind, but that is impossible as long as he does not uproot their cause. Therefore, the Buddha here says:

> The corrupt monk, unguarded in eye and ear
> And unrestrained in the senses,
> As swarms of flies follow the stench of carrion,
> He is followed by thoughts of sense desire.

62. The Foolish Monkey (SN 47:7)

In the Himalayas, there are rugged, uneven areas where neither humans nor monkeys have access. There are other areas still too rugged for humans but just fine for monkeys. Finally, there are delightful, even areas where both monkeys and humans have access.

In an area of the third type, a hunter sets a pitch trap on a path monkeys take. Those monkeys who are not greedy avoid the trap when they see it. However, when a greedy, foolish monkey comes, he does not pass by the trap but instead grabs the trap with one hand, thus becoming stuck to the glue of the trap. In order to loosen his hand, he grabs hold of the trap with his other hand, which also becomes stuck. In order to get them both free, he uses first one foot and then the other, but becomes only more stuck. Finally, trying to free his hands and feet, he uses his mouth to help, but that becomes stuck too. Sticking fivefold to the trap, the hunter comes along who spears the monkey, taking both monkey and trap.

The same happens to a monk who goes into foreign territory, accessible to Māra (Death). This is the area of the five senses. Greedy for attractive shapes, words, perfumes, food and affectionate embraces, he is taken in by Māra. Letting himself be caught in one area, and noticing the fetter, the unwise monk changes over to another area and gets entangled there too, and so he sinks ever deeper into misery.

However, the monk who moves in his own safe territory, who pays attention to the four foundations of mindfulness, becomes free and independent. Identification with the body, feelings, mind and mental objects is gradually abandoned. These four observations and identifications move from the habitual, subject side of existence to the object side, from the 'inside' to the 'outside.' The 'I' then becomes the pure observer, which is finally also let go. The 'I'/'mine' or subject/object duality disappears when the subject is seen as dependently arisen on the object, impermanent, suffering and not-self (see SN 35:93).

This mindfulness turned inwards, towards oneself, is the correct attitude in the territory accessible to both monkeys (monks) and the hunter (Māra), namely the realm of the five senses.

The areas where only monkeys—but not Māra—can go are the eight absorptions in which Māra's eye is blinded (MN 25). Because the monkey has all of well-being inside himself, he does not peek at the outside.

Finally, what is the area where even the monkeys cannot go? If one takes the monkey as a simile for consciousness, then there are two areas outside its seven habitats or stations: the realm of unconscious beings and the realm of neither-perception-nor-non-perception (DN 15.33). Alternatively, this area could be Nibbāna.

63. The Beauty Queen (SN 47:20)

In a town, a dancing girl gives a performance. "The most beautiful girl in the country is here! The beauty queen is dancing!" So shout the people as they flock and crowd together *en masse*. That dancing girl unfolds all her dancer's charms and enchants everyone with her singing. More and more people come from everywhere to see and hear. There is a lot of pushing and shoving.

Among those flocking together there is a man who wants to live and not die, who seeks well-being and loathes pain. He is told: "Dear man, here is a bowl full to the rim with oil. You must carry it between the crowd and the girl. Following close behind you will be a man with a drawn sword. If you spill even one drop, he will chop off your head." Would that man neglect paying attention to the bowl? Would he turn his attention outward in a light-hearted mood? Certainly not.

Explanation

The beauty queen: alluring sensuality to be seen and heard, to entangle and captivate one.

The crowd: fellow people all striving after sensual gratification and thereby forming a stream.

The man: the reflective person who aspires to real rather than transitory well-being and therefore has to leave the crowd; he has go against the stream of the world.

The advisor: the Buddha.

The bowl full of oil: mindfulness directed to the body, the contemplation of the true, non-beautiful nature of the body (*asubha*), which goes against the stream of sensuality the crowd of humanity follows.

The swordsman with the drawn sword: the threat of death for one who indulges in sensuality.

Spilling drops: inattention to oneself; approving sensual desires and following them externally without heed, whereby one enters the realm of death.

The man will try hard to get as quickly as possible out of the crowd that is dragging him along and endangering him, and he will do so without himself pushing anybody (anger). He will watch the bowl (seeing the true, non-beautiful nature of the body) with such one-pointed attention that he will have no time to look at the girl (sense pleasure). He must not sit down wearily (sloth and torpor) because the crowd would overrun him. Yet he also must not hasten excitedly ahead (restlessness) because he might spill the oil. Doubt concerning the precariousness is removed by the swordsman; without looking, the man knows that he is right behind him. The situation thus demands overcoming the five hindrances and thereby passing beyond the crowd of sensuality to the safety of Nibbāna.

64. Seed of the Bitter Gourd (AN 10:104)

If one plants the seed of a bitter gourd into moist soil and it sprouts, everything that the bitter gourd plant assimilates while growing, be it earth or water, gets a bitter, pungent taste. Why? Because the seed is bitter.

In the same way when a wrong view dominates in the mind, anything one undertakes and carries out—actions, words and thoughts—towards the outside, as well as anything one cherishes inside—intentions, aspirations, inclinations, activities—all will lead to what is unwanted, undesired, unpleasant—in short to misery and misfortune. Why so? Because the view is evil.

Explanation

Seed (or germ): the view, the model, the template according to which everything, good and evil, is directed in the person.

The bitter gourd seed: the seed of wrong view in which all latent bitterness or evil is contained. As examples of its opposite, right view, the Buddha mentions seeds of rice, sugar cane and grapes.

Moist soil: the human mind which is so affected by ignorance and craving that it is capable of accepting all sorts of wrong views.

Earth and water: nutriments of the seed corresponding to those of the person who needs to the nourishment of material (solid) and mental (liquid) nutriments.

Growing: just as the gourd gradually develops a stem, leaves, flowers, fruit and seeds, so the person also develops the wrong Eightfold Path. All activity toward the inside or outside unfolds and develops according to the template of the view: it sets the Path.

Bitter, pungent taste: All human striving, all activity directed towards well-being leads, when based on wrong view, to unpleasantness, to suffering, i.e., to the opposite of what is ultimately desired. One's external actions upset other people, making things forbidding, with the result that one's mind becomes confused, the body overstrained and the mind darkened. No matter how much one meditates, matters only get worse. (Cf. the simile of the small lump of salt put in a small vessel with fresh water in AN 3:99.)

65. The Hare Imitating the Bathing Elephant (AN 10:99)

A mighty elephant comes to a great pond into which he steps to take a playful bath, splashing his ears and back. After he has had a drink, enjoyed and refreshed himself, he leaves the pond and goes wherever he likes. A hare watching thinks to itself: "Who is this elephant? I shall go and do what he did. What he can do, I can do, too!" In haste, without further consideration, the hare jumps into the pond, where it can only go down and drown, or jump back out horrified. Why? Because such a small being cannot find any footing in the depth.

In the same way, whoever has not reached the maturity of *samādhi* but wants to live in solitude in the forest will either go mad or run away horrified.

Explanation

The great pond is the profound solitude and silence of the deep forest, or the depth of the ocean of the mind.

The elephant is someone who has acquired strong powers by mentally developing himself through meditation.

The stepping into the pond is the taking up of solitary life in the silent woods, or, at a higher stage, the experience of the solitude of profound calm of mind, *samādhi*.

The playful splashing bath is the delight of well-being resulting from purification of mind.

Drinking is permeation of the body therewith.

The going away as one likes is leaving the forest and returning into the world mentally purified and no more affected by external things, or alternatively, it could be using *samādhi* for wisdom breakthroughs, formlessness or exercises in *satipaṭṭhāna*.

The small hare is the immature meditator who still needs the support of good friends and a supportive environment in order to progress.

His comparing himself with the elephant is his own ignorance, his conceit and his impatience.

Hastily jumping into the pond stands for the immature, wilful and premature attempt of going into deep solitude in search of peace of mind.

Drowning is madness, while the *jumping out* is being repelled from the solitary life, and perhaps even of the religious life and possibly from all meditation, due to the need for sensual stimulation. (See the Meghiya Sutta at Ud 4.1, MN 4 and Dhp 344.)

The Buddha then gives three images for stages in the inner maturity of the person.

1. Just as a baby amuses himself by playing with his own excrement—a useless pleasure—so the sensual human plays with his own and other excrement-filled bodies.

2. Just as the growing child plays with all kinds of toys and games of movement and skill, so the virtuous play with the world by making merit.

3. Just as the adult enjoys himself with his five senses, so one mature in meditation enjoys absorptions in ever finer forms, even up to the extinction of the mental taints.

66. Three Inscriptions (AN 3:130)

If one chisels an inscription or drawing into stone, wind and rain will not soon erase it, and it will remain visible for a long time. In the same way there can be a human who becomes angry often and easily, who becomes excited over the least thing and, because he cannot easily forget, the anger remains with him for a long time. Anger is chiselled deeply into his mind, being clearly engraved, easily readable. Over and over again he comes back to it.

If one scribbles something into sand, it soon disappears, be it through wind, rain, time or other people. It doesn't last long; it is obliterated or covered over, becomes unreadable and disappears completely. In the same way a person can fly into anger often and easily, but his anger doesn't stick to him, so he calms down and softens quickly, regretting his vehemence and being ready for reconciliation.

Finally, if one tries to write or draw into water, it disappears immediately, remaining not even for an instant. In the same way there can be a human who, even if he is confronted roughly, with hostility and unjustly, does not become angry but remains conciliatory, friendly and mild. (Compare the sutta on the four snakes in AN 4:110).

67. The Sore, Lightning Strike and Diamond (AN 3:25)

If someone even slightly touches a festering sore with a piece of wood or glass, the sore will burst open, secreting pus. Similarly, a person who is filled with the venom of anger will be offended even if one says something innocuous. If it doesn't agree with him, he becomes angry, irascible, cross, raving or furious. His mind is like a sore. Spitting venom, he explodes in rage. He is interested in nothing but venting his aggressions onto others; he has no thought for anything else (compare the loathsome person, etc., in AN 3:27).

Just as in the middle of a dark night one can see things very clearly for a moment when there is a lightning flash, just so a noble person can discern and see the Four Noble Truths for a brief moment; lightning-like they become evident to him, like a "flash of inspiration." His mind will perceive a flash of understanding, lighting up the Four Noble Truths again and again. This is his fire; this interests him. He has no mind for quarrels and anger.

When one owns a diamond, one can cut the hardest things, even rock or iron, without it being affected. Similarly someone who in this lifetime attains liberation has a mind like a diamond. It penetrates all things but is itself invulnerable and cannot be affected. He always sees things correctly, whereas the angry one never sees correctly, and the one with occasional flash-like inspirations sees things only sometimes.

68. Shedding Old Skin (Sn 1–5)

1. He who can curb his anger
   as soon as it arises,
   as a timely antidote will check
   snake's venom that so quickly spreads,

—such a monk gives up the here and the beyond,
just as a serpent sheds its worn-out skin.

2. He who entirely cuts off his lust
as entering a pond one uproots lotus plants,
—such a monk gives up the here and the beyond,
just as a serpent sheds its worn-out skin.

3. He who entirely cuts off his craving
by drying up its fierce and rapid flow,
—such a monk gives up the here and the beyond,
just as a serpent sheds its worn-out skin.

4. He who entirely blots out conceit
as the flood demolishes a fragile bamboo bridge,
—such a monk gives up the here and the beyond,
just as a serpent sheds its worn-out skin.

5. He who does not find core or substance
in any of the realms of being,
like flowers that are vainly sought
in fig trees that bear none,
—such a monk gives up the here and the beyond,
just as a serpent sheds its worn-out skin.[39]

In these first five verses of the Sutta-Nipāta, similes are given for five qualities the disciple overcomes.

Anger is compared to the poison of a snake diffusing throughout the body of one who has been bitten. Overcoming anger is compared to a medicinal herb which, when made into a balm, soothes the bite and cleans the blood. The antidote to active anger is the attitude of bearing up, patient acceptance.

Greed—contrary to poisonous anger—is compared to a beautiful flower, a lotus in a lake, toward which one feels drawn. But this must be torn out with stem and root in order not to suffer from its transitoriness.

Craving, appearing in the form of greed and hatred towards the objects of the six senses, is compared to a swiftly-flowing

---

39. Translation by Nyanaponika Thera, *The Worn Out Skin*, Wheel Publication No. 241, BPS, Kandy.

river: Over and over again new and alluring objects come to us with craving chasing after them, so that we have no time for reflection. This current of craving must first be stopped, then dried up completely until its extinction.

Conceit is compared to a fragile bridge of bamboo built across a stream. Thus the conceit 'I am' rises above reality and builds a bridge from the feeble material of deluded thoughts. This footbridge exists only as long as there has been no penetration into its weakness; once penetrated, it is swept away with the power of right view, like the bamboo bridge by a mighty flood.

Delusion is here described as the impossible view that there is a fixed core in becoming, an 'I'—this is like the searching in vain for a blossom in a strangler fig tree.[40] Whoever knows that no flower of self can be found in the fig tree of existence considers everything as coreless, insubstantial, and not-self.

In the following twelve verses (Sn 6–17), greed, hatred and delusion are described again under different aspects. Each of the 17 verses makes a comparison with a snake—just as a snake sheds its old skin, leaving behind that which was connected to it for a long time, so the disciple leaves behind him, strips off, pulls himself out of this or the other world, which was connected to him for so long.

69. Conquering the Citadel (MN 22; AN 5:71–72)

An arahant possesses five characteristics that can be compared to five aspects of conquering a fortified town inhabited by robbers.

1. Since he has entirely overcome ignorance, has altogether abandoned wrong views and personality view, he is to that extent a barricade breaker. He has removed the palisades and outer fortifications of wrong views in himself. The barrier of ignorance has been shattered.

---

40. The flowering fig is a popular simile in Indian literature to denote something which is absent or impossible. The ancient Indians did not know that figs have flowers inside the small hollow fruits. Tiny wasps bore into the fruits to get to the flowers and thus pollinate them.

2. Since the arahant has overcome renewed becoming and the creating of birth cycles, he has to that extent filled up the moat of saṃsāra with its crocodiles and whirlpools, so that his forces can gain access into the city.

3. Since the arahant has uprooted the pillar of craving, he has to that extent pulled out the supporting palisades, corner posts and pillars of the town. Even though the palisades of personality view put up the most resistance, he has uprooted, torn out and destroyed this fortification.

4. Since the arahant has forever eradicated the five lower fetters and can never return to the sense world, he has to that extent removed the bar of the door leading to the centre of the fortress.

5. And since the arahant has also eradicated the five higher fetters—mentioned here synecdochically as the conceit "I am"—therefore he has also conquered the centre of the fortress, which must strike the flag. The conceit "I am" is the flag, the emblem, the identity—and it must capitulate unconditionally so that Nibbāna is realized.

The arahant has won the state of imperturbability, has snatched the citadel town away from Māra to become its lord, a lord over the mind.

70. The Charnel Ground (AN 5:249)

Just as an ancient Indian charnel ground is filthy—filthiness being its chief characteristic, being a place where rotting corpses are eaten by maggots and scavengers such as crows, vultures and jackals—just so is a person whose chief characteristic is that he is filthy in actions, words and thoughts. He acts in unclean, unwholesome ways due to having an impure attitude of mind.

Just as the filthy charnel ground is also evil-smelling, having a repulsive stench, so too a bad reputation is spread about a filthy man. He is loathed everywhere; his deeds stink to high heaven.

Just as the charnel ground with its stench of decay is dangerous because of the risk of being attacked by wild animals, demons, and the risk of infection and spread of disease, and is thus to be avoided if possible, so also good people avoid a filthy one because they do not want to be attacked and infected.

Likewise in AN 3:27: Just as a snake smeared with excrement soils whatever it touches, one with a bad reputation smears everyone who has anything to do with him.

Just as the charnel ground is the habitat of wild demons and bloodthirsty evil spirits attracted by the filth, so the filthy one tends to live with those who come together as equals in a society of equally filthy ones.

Just as the charnel ground is a place of moaning, many beings sadly bewailing that they have to leave their loved ones there, so also good people moan when they see 'filthy' members of the Sangha: "Oh, how miserable that we have to live with such people!"

Part 6

WHOLESOME SKILLS

71. The Divided River (SN 48:43)

A mighty river flows towards the east, slopes towards the east and is directed towards the east. Along its course, the river meets an obstacle and flows around it so that the obstacle becomes an island. The river is the same before the island and after the island, i.e., to the east and in the west of it, it flows along placidly, lightly and evenly. But on both sides of the island—i.e., north and south of it—the river is turbulent and foaming. There, it shows its potential power to overcome or get around the hindrance and continue on its way to the east as quickly as possible. This power comes from its descent, its ability to return to and follow again its original direction.

Explanation

The five faculties of faith, energy, mindfulness, calm and wisdom are comparable to the placidly flowing river. They are the river leading to liberation mentioned in SN 55:38 in Simile 31. Just like the Ganges river flows in the easterly direction, so the faculties flow in the direction of Nibbāna. Thus it is said that the monk on the Noble Eightfold Path is bent and directed toward Nibbāna, just as the Ganges and four other Indian rivers are bent toward the east (SN 45:91–97) and toward the ocean (SN 45:97–102) respectively. Also, it is said that a monk who develops the Noble Eightfold Path tends toward seclusion like the Ganges towards the east. As one cannot change the Ganges' direction towards the west by digging, similarly one could not move a monk who much develops the Noble Eightfold Path to give up his monkhood and become a layman again (SN 45:160).

However, the same faculties can also be viewed from the perspective of the closely related five powers. In this case, "power" is the capacity to overcome obstacles, to succeed against the obstructions put up by craving. The powers are the manifestation of the faculties, their test, their application in practice. That is why it is said in AN 5:15 that the five powers can be observed in meditative training, that is, faith can be seen in the four factors of stream-entry, energy in the four right efforts, mindfulness in the four foundations of mindfulness, calm in the four jhānas and wisdom in the four Noble Truths. In the context of this simile, just as the potential strength of the river is revealed when its current flows around an island, so the potential powers of the striving noble disciple are revealed when meeting with inner and outer temptations and resistances. The stronger the focus of the faculties, the stronger the fighting powers. And the more the powers are trained and strengthened, the more powerful becomes the current of wholesome faculties.

72. The Mighty Ocean of the Dhamma (Ud 5.5; AN 8:19–20)

Just as the mighty ocean has eight qualities in which beings delight, so the Teaching and Discipline (Dhamma-vinaya) have eight qualities in which monks delight again and again.

Just as the ocean tends downward gradually and becomes deeper without an abrupt slope, so in the Teaching and Discipline, training, practice and progress are gradual, and there is no sudden realization of arahantship. There are always the three stages of virtue, calm and wisdom.

Just as the ocean is stable and does not overflow its shores, so monks on the training path do not transgress the training rules, especially the four main rules which lead to expulsion from the order, even for the sake of their lives.

Just as the ocean does not tolerate corpses but throws them onto dry land, so a corrupt monk who transgresses any of the four main rules is quickly removed from the Sangha. He is as if dead; he has excluded himself from the Sangha.

Just as great rivers flowing into the mighty ocean thereby lose their former names and lineage, so members of the Sangha henceforth lose their caste and all other former differences, having become alike as monks of the Buddha.

No matter how many rivers flow into the ocean nor how much rain falls into it, the water of the ocean does not become less or more. So also, no matter how many monks attain the element of Nibbāna-with-no-residue when they pass away, the Nibbāna element becomes neither less nor more but remains always the same in vastness.

Just as the ocean has only one flavour, that of salt, so the Teaching only has one flavour, that of freedom, i.e., the entering into Nibbāna and the giving up of all suffering arising out of craving and ignorance.

Just as the ocean contains a multitude of treasures—pearl, crystal, lapis lazuli, conch, quartz, blood coral, gold and silver, rubies and cats' eyes—so also the Teaching contains a multitude of treasures on the way to freedom, namely the four foundations of mindfulness, the four right efforts, the four bases of power, the five faculties, the five powers, the seven factors of awakening, and the Noble Eightfold Path.

Just as mighty beings live in the ocean—various kinds of giant squids, sharks and whales, as well as asuras, nāgas and gandhabbas—so in the Teaching too there are mighty beings—the stream-enterer, the once-returner, the non-returner, the arahant. Just as in the ocean there are beings of different sizes, so too on the way from the path to the fruit there are different degrees of strength among the four stages of liberation.

73. The Four Noble Truths (SN 56:31–40)

Just as the leaves on a large tree are far more numerous than the few leaves which one can hold with one hand, so too, all that Buddhas discover is far more numerous than the truth they teach in the form of the Four Noble Truths. Why is this? Because only these Four Noble Truths are wholesome and lead to liberation; all the various other things they discover are like the empty rustling of leaves. (SN 56:31)

Just as leaves of an acacia, cedar or myrobalan are too small for scooping water, whereas the leaves of the lotus, kino and māluva creeper are suitable and large enough, so also one who has not understood the Four Noble Truths cannot end suffering, but one who does understand them is able to do so. Just as small leaves are unsuitable to drink water from and to quench one's thirst, without the Four Noble Truths one is unable to quench the thirst of craving for existence. Furthermore, just as small leaves cannot provide a cool breeze if used as fan, without the Four Noble Truths one cannot get the gentle cool of Nibbāna as opposed to the heat of the passions. (SN 56:32)

Just as a stick thrown repeatedly into the air will fall sometimes onto one end, sometimes onto its side, and sometimes onto its other end, so beings hindered by ignorance and fettered by craving tumble about in transitory existence. They are thrown into the coarse world of the senses (the one end) by their coarse craving, into the middle Brahmā world (the side), or into the realm of formlessness (the other end). Yet they always come back to the coarse sense world if they do not understand the Four Noble Truths and thereby put an end to suffering. (SN 56:33; similar in SN 15:9.)

Just as someone whose hair or turban is on fire must rouse himself, must put forth great willpower and effort, zeal and energy, mindfulness and clear comprehension in order to escape from a fiery death, so too must one who wants to rescue himself from the suffering of old age, sickness and death, put forth those powers for the understanding of the Four Noble Truths. Just as the person whose hair or turban is on fire, the clearer he sees his peril, the more he exerts himself, so too the more clearly one sees suffering, the more one will put forth effort. (SN 56:34; also in AN 4:93; AN 8:74.)

A man's life-energy lasts about hundred years. If someone were to make him an offer that he would understand the Four Noble Truths at the end of his 100 years on the condition that he accepts 100 strikes with a spear three times every day, he should accept the offer. Why? Because in this saṃsāra everyone has already been struck by spears and axes, has been pestered, tormented and tortured for such a tremendously long time.

Anybody who realize the Four Noble Truths after receiving daily 300 spear strikes in this life would realize them easily and happily. The Buddha adds that the breakthrough to understanding the Four Noble Truths is accompanied by happiness and joy. (SN 56:35; also SN 12:63; MN 129)

A man has made all the wood in India into sticks to use them to spear all the water animals in the ocean. But it is not even possible for him to spear all the large and middle-sized animals, let alone all the small animals. Likewise without full understanding of the Four Truths it might be possible for someone to reduce gross, superficial and visible suffering but not the finer, hidden and underlying suffering of impermanence. However, whoever understands the Four Noble Truths becomes also freed from fine and hidden impermanence and suffering. (SN 56:36)

Just as the reddish glow of early morning is the harbinger and announcement that sunrise will follow inevitably within a short time, so right view is the harbinger and announcement of the Four Noble Truths, and will be followed inevitably by the realization of these truths. (SN 56:37; AN 10:121; SN 45:49)

Just as the world is dark and grim as long as the sun and moon do not shine, so the world is spiritually dark and grim as long as there is no Accomplished One to teach the Four Noble Truths. (SN 56:38)

Just as a tuft of cotton wool because of its lightness is blown around by the wind—eastward by the west wind, westward by the east wind, southward by the north wind and northward by the south wind—so too the worldling hastens aimlessly from guru to guru, from opinion to opinion. Sceptically, he looks up to one teacher today and up to another tomorrow, asking himself, "I wonder whether he is accomplished and knowing?" But whoever has thoroughly understood the Four Noble Truths no longer goes from guru to guru. He is not driven to eastern and then western opinions, not to northern and not to southern views. Instead his mind is like an Indra Pillar, an iron pillar fixed deeply in the ground, which doesn't sway or waver, tremble or quiver however many swirling winds storm about it from all directions. (SN 56:39; cf. Sn 231, Dhp 95, Th 663, DN 29.26.)

Just as a mighty stone pillar sunk halfway into the ground would not be moved by any amount of wind and weather, storm or rain, so too, no matter how many clever hair-splitters, mental acrobats and masters come from all four directions, the one who has deeply penetrated the Four Noble Truths cannot be shaken or thrown over in the least. (SN 56:40)

74. The Noble Eightfold Path (SN 45:149–160)

1. As all strenuous activities depend on and are supported by the earth, and just as all plant growth depends on the earth and expands supported by it, so too the Noble Eightfold Path depends on and is supported by virtuous, wholesome states. (SN 45:149–50; cf. SN 46:143–144, SN 49:23–25)

2. As all *nāgas* grow up and become strong supported by the Himalayas to travel via creeks, streams and rivers to the ocean, so the Noble Eightfold Path is developed supported by virtue (SN 45:151. This simile of the streams is used differently in SN 46:1; SN 49:23; SN 55:38; SN 12:23; AN 3:93.)

3. As a tree inclined towards the east will fall to the east when cut down, just so a monk who develops the Noble Eightfold Path is inclining towards Nibbāna. (SN 45:152; cf. SN 53:22)

4. As a pot knocked over lets all the water run out with none of it flowing back in, just so a monk on the Noble Eightfold Path lets all unwholesome things run out and does not take them back in. (SN 45:153; see also AN 11:14; AN 3:30)

5. As only a rightly directed spike of barley is sharp enough to pierce the skin of hand or foot and draw blood, just so only through a rightly directed view, through a rightly directed development of the Noble Eightfold Path, is it possible to pierce through the veil of ignorance, win true knowledge and realize Nibbāna. (SN 45:154; see also AN 1:5; SN 45:9)

6. As different winds blow through the sky—winds of the four directions, with and without dust, cool and hot, gentle and violent, just so in the mental sky of the Noble Eightfold Path, the treasures of liberation develop—four foundations of mindfulness, the four right efforts, the four bases of power, the five faculties, the five powers, the seven factors of awakening. (SN 45:155; cf. SN 36:12–13)

7. Just as the clouds of swirling dust in the last month of the hot season disappear when large rain-clouds pour down rain, so too through the Noble Eightfold Path do all unwholesome things disappear. (SN 45:156; see also SN 54:9; AN 6:60)

8. Just as a strong wind scatters and drives away even great rain-clouds, so the Noble Eightfold Path destroys even strong evil and unwholesome things. (SN 45:157)

9. Just as people from all four directions and from all four castes come and go in a guesthouse, so wholesome things move into the mind of one who trains on the Noble Eightfold Path and unwholesome things move out. (SN 45:157; see also SN 36:14)

10. Just as a crowd of people would only reap fatigue if they were to try to divert the eastward course of the Ganges to the west, so also kings, ministers, relatives and friends of a monk would only reap fatigue if they were to try to persuade a monk who cultivates the Noble Eightfold Path to relinquish the training and return to lay life. (SN 45:160; cf. SN 35:244; SN 52:8)

The simile of the boat in SN 45:158 is also in SN 22:101; see Simile 45.

75. Highest Diligence
(SN 45:139–148; AN 10:15; SN 22:102)

Just as among all beings with two, four or more feet, whether percipient, non-percipient or without perception or neither-percipient-nor-non-percipient, the Buddha is considered the highest among them, just so all wholesome states have diligence (*appamāda*) as their foundation and starting point, diligence is declared the highest, first and best of them all. For if a monk is diligent, it can be expected that he will train in and maintain the Noble Eightfold Path. (SN 45:139; AN 10:15)

Just as among all footprints of earthly beings, that of the elephant is foremost in size, just so diligence... is the best. (SN 45:140; AN 10:15; see also MN 27 & 28)

Just as all rafters in a gabled house run and incline towards the gable, are directed and meet there, the gable being considered the main point, the highest part, just so diligence... is the best. SN 45:141; AN 10:15; see also SN 46:7; SN 46:7; SN 22:102)

Just as among all root scents the black orris[41] is the best, among all heartwood scents the red sandalwood, and among all flower scents the jasmine is the best and highest fragrance, just so diligence... is the best. (SN 45:142–144; AN 10:15; SN 22:102)

Just as all lesser kings follow the emperor, who is considered the highest of monarchs, just so diligence... is the best. (SN 45:145; AN 10:15; SN 22:102)

Just as the light from all stars together amounts to not a sixteenth of the brightness of moonlight, just so diligence... is the best. (SN 45:146; AN 10:15; SN 22:102)

Just as the sun in a clear and cloudless autumn sky dispels all darkness and radiates, beams and shines, just so diligence... is the best. (SN 45:147; SN 22:102; AN 10:15; see also It 27; SN 2:29; MN 46; AN 3:92)

Just as all rivers in India run towards the ocean, and as the ocean is the greatest water among them..., just so diligence... is the best. (AN 10:15)

Just as of all cloth, Benares silk is the best and is considered the highest... just so diligence... is the best. (SN 45:148; AN 10:15)

Just as when cutting a cluster of mangos at the stem, all the fruits hanging at that stem come along... just so diligence... is the best. (SN 22:102)

76. The Three Fields and Water Pots (SN 42:7)

A farmer has one good field, one mediocre field, and one bad field which is rocky and salty.

When he sows seed, he will first sow it into the good field and then into the mediocre one. Perhaps he will also sow a little left-over seed into the bad field from which he expects a yield no better than cattle fodder.

Monks and nuns who enter the Sangha with faith and commitment are like the good field. To them the Buddha shows the Teaching most thoroughly and extensively—the Dhamma which is good in the beginning, in the middle, and at the end.

---

41. Orris is the root of some species of iris. Once important in western herbal medicine, it is now used mainly in perfumes.

Why is that? Because they take refuge in him and produce the highest yield of fruits of practice—stream-enterers, once-returners, non-returners, and arahants.

Laymen and laywomen are like the mediocre field. They are the second group to be shown the Teaching, though not quite as extensively. Why? Although they don't have the same degree of commitment as monks and nuns, they have also taken refuge in him and produce some fruits of practice.

Other ascetics and priests are like the bad field producing a little fodder. Why is that? Although they follow wrong doctrines (the rocks and salt in the soil), if they only understand a single sentence of the Teaching it will be for their long-lasting happiness and might eventually produce a few fruits of practice.

Consider the man who has three clay water pots. One of them is made of thick clay and has a protective inner coating; nor does it have cracks. Consequently water does not seep out and evaporate. The second pot also has no cracks but it does let a little water slowly seep through and evaporate because it has thin areas and no inner coating. The third has both cracks and thin areas that let water seep through quickly. When the man wants to store water, he first uses the good pot, then the second pot; the third he uses for no more than the immediate purpose of washing dishes.

Monks and nuns are like the first pot, laymen and laywomen like the second, and members of other sects like the third.

Members of the Sangha have no cracks, which is to say their minds are without gaps insofar as they solidly take refuge in the Buddha, the Dhamma and the Sangha. Nothing seeps away from them; they retain good states, develop more, and eventually can become arahants.

Lay followers also do not have cracks, and they also can practice the Teaching to some extent and become stream-enterers. Yet some water evaporates gradually through the sides because they don't have the same thick clay shell of good friends and good conditions for practice as exists within the Sangha. Also they don't have the inner protective coating of virtue as high as monks and nuns. Their minds are more distracted and drawn out by the conditions of lay life, like the water slowly seeping out from the pot. They cannot go beyond the stage of non-returner to become arahants, just as the second pot cannot remain full.

Devotees of other teachings are full of cracks. Almost everything of the Buddha's Teaching that enters their mind quickly leaks out again through the cracks of wrong view and the thin clay of lack of virtue and other supportive conditions.

Compare also field and seed (SN 55:25), seeds and five plants (SN 22:54; see Simile 24), spoiled seed (AN 6:62) and seed and kamma (AN 3:33). The mind is also compared to a water pot in AN 3:30, here in relation to its ability to listen to the Dhamma and remember it.

77. The Sticky Resin and the Dam (AN 4:178)

There is a monk who attains calm liberation of the mind (i.e., one or all of the four formless states), but on considering the cessation of personality (*sakkāya-nirodha*), his mind doesn't launch towards it, does not gain confidence in it, settle down and resolve on it. He holds on to his absorptions like a man who grabs hold of a branch with resin-coated fingers and now his hands are stuck to it.[42]

The branch symbolises the absorptions, which are not yet heartwood but are only adjacent to the heartwood. The hand sticking to the branch symbolizes the mind sticking to the peace, happiness, stability and apparent security of the absorptions. Only when the monk's mind gains confidence in the thought of the cessation of personality or self-view (*sakkāya-diṭṭhi*) can he win supramundane right view, i.e., stream-entry.

---

42. See SN 22:90 where it is said that Venerable Channa's mind, despite reflecting on the impermanent and not-self nature of the aggregates, "does not launch towards, gain confidence in ... the stilling of all formations ... Nibbāna. Instead, agitation and clinging arise, and the mind turns back, thinking 'But what will happen to my self?'" Channa's mind became fearful of letting go of "his self" and turned back to the clinging to what it falsely conceived as being a more secure state. Compare SN 35:136/Suttanipāta verses 764–771.

When after attaining stream-entry he again generates calm liberation of the mind, his main concern is to destroy the remaining ignorance. Again, he initially might have neither inclination nor satisfaction to do so. His mind is like a reservoir, where water (wholesome things beginning with stream-entry) has accumulated for several years. If one were to block the inflows (i.e., not hearing encouraging teachings on the elimination of ignorance) and then leaves the outflow open (by enjoying wholesome things after developing absorption without developing further insight, using up the harvest of previous good kamma) and, thirdly, no rain comes from outside (i.e., to persist in the striving for liberation), then the dam of the reservoir will not break. That means the monk will not break through the barricade of ignorance and reach Nibbāna. If, however, the inflows are opened, the outflows blocked, and rain falls (i.e., he hears more of the teaching, overcomes the lower fetters such as sensual desire, and he persists in breaking through ignorance by destroying the conceit 'I am' by perceiving impermanence, suffering and not-self), then the dam can break. Then the mass of obstructing ignorance can be broken up and swept away under the pressure of the power of wholesome qualities.

78. The Merchant (AN 3:20)

A merchant with three qualities soon attains wealth and an abundance of money.

He possesses keen insight into his profession. He calculates exactly, "When this merchandise is bought for this much and sold for that much, there will be so much capital and so much profit."

He is clever. He precisely understands profitable buying and selling of his goods.

He has a firm support. Rich citizens know his keen insight and industriousness, know that he makes a lot of money and that, apart from the expenses of keeping his family, he has money left over for interest payments so they willingly extend him credit and enjoy lending him money at good interest rates.

Likewise, a monk who has three qualities soon attains wealth and an abundance of spiritual property.

Wholesome Skills

1. He has keen insight into the profession of an ascetic. He knows precisely that what he buys in the world is only suffering and that it comes at a high price (i.e., the First Noble Truth: suffering); secondly, he knows that he can only sell at a loss and that he will suffer deficiencies because of his loss-making business (the Second Noble Truth: craving as origin of suffering); and thirdly, he understands that he can only make profit with his capital (the Third Noble Truth: cessation of suffering) if it is meaningfully invested in a way that it will result in more and more gain (the Fourth Noble Truth: way to cessation). In short, he sees that in saṃsāra he will always go bankrupt sooner or later because one always tends to overdo, whereas on the path to independent well-being of freedom from craving (Nibbāna), profit only ever increases.

2. He is clever. Diligently he tries to overcome evil qualities and to cultivate good ones with iron determination. Tireless in the wholesome, he doesn't buy unprofitably (whatever increases neediness and dependence), and he rejects all untrustworthy offers. He buys only real and immaculate products that bring honest profit (whatever increases independence).

3. He has firm support from well-tested, experienced monks, who know the laws of existence, the discipline, and the methods of practice. From time to time, he goes to them to ask about theory and practice. They explain those things to him, disclosing what is unclear to him, removing all his doubts. The experienced monks notice that he is sincere, that he asks honestly. They notice also that they do not waste their time and wisdom with him, but rather that he will use what they say profitably, so they open the treasure chambers of their minds (lend money), and he leaves contentedly, realizing for himself what they have experienced.

The monk who left home with confidence attains with keen insight (right view) and cleverness (right effort) and with firm support, i.e., with right intention and mindfulness. Soon wealth (calm of mind) and abundance (wisdom and liberation) are obtained.

79. The Bamboo Pole Balancing Act (SN 47:19)

A master acrobat lets his young female disciple climb onto a high bamboo pole which he balances on his chest. He says to her, "Protect me and I shall protect of you. Thus shall we, guarding and protecting each other, show our tricks, get a good wage and come down safely." But the disciple replied, "No, master, we shall not do that. Instead, you protect yourself and I protect myself. So shall we, guarding and protecting ourselves, show our tricks, get a good wage and come down safely. That's the way we'll do it."

The Buddha approves of the method of the acrobat's disciple. The master acrobat has to be told that by protecting himself first, by carefully paying attention to what he needs to do himself—holding the bamboo pole firmly, positioning it in such a way that the pupil can jump and climb up, and watching the pole continuously so that he does not lose control over it—he protects the disciple by not letting her fall down. He also protects himself because if he lets the disciple fall, he too may stumble and fall, as well as injuring or killing her for which he would be punished and lose his profession. The disciple likewise protects herself by keeping her attention on keeping herself standing or sitting carefully balanced and without making sudden, jerky movements; otherwise she might fall down or make the master acrobat lose control over the pole and thus cause her fall, which would mean severe injury or death. If the master primarily pays attention to the pupil, then he would not pay enough attention to his own tasks. The same applies to the pupil, who would fall down if she watched the master and paid no attention to her own balance. Thus through each primarily paying attention to themselves, the acrobats protect each other.

The balancing act of the two acrobats, still carried out by gypsies in India, is an image for self-development through the practice of the four foundations of mindfulness and the Noble Eightfold Path, leading to true, stable mental balance. Only when working together in the proper way, by paying right attention to ourselves first, by keeping our own mental balance, can we attain true well-being. One cannot start by demanding another that he should only pay attention to you. On the contrary, he first has to pay right attention to himself, guard his own mind and gain spiritual balance himself, and after that, take care of others through encouragement and teaching.

A similar sentiment is expressed by the Buddha in the Sallekha Sutta: "That one who is himself stuck in the mire should pull out another who is stuck in the mire is impossible; that one who is himself not stuck in the mire should pull out another who is stuck in the mire is possible. That one who is himself untamed, undisciplined, unextinguished, should tame ... another is impossible. That one who is himself tamed ... should tame ... another is possible." (MN 8.16) See also Dhp 166: "One should not neglect one's own welfare for the sake of another's, having well understood one's own welfare, one should be intent on one's own real welfare." (There is wordplay here: *sadattha* can mean "the real/good welfare/goal" as well as "one's own welfare/goal.")

The taking care of oneself is called "establishment of mindfulness," *satipaṭṭhāna* by the Buddha, although the term is not used here in the specific sense of the "foundation of mindfulness" but more generally as in MN 137. The Buddha teaches by way of this simile that *sati* begins inside, but at the same time has an effect on the outside.

So how does one guarding and paying attention to oneself guard others? The Buddha says, "By practice, development and frequent repetition," namely by training in *sati*. While by considering and remembering the teaching, one protects oneself against the hindrances to liberation, and at the same time one also protects others from one's own acquisitiveness and one's own aggression and violence. Even someone who just keeps the rules of virtue prevents an immeasurable amount of misfortune, which in the course of a long time he would have inflicted on others. Furthermore, one gives a good example by one's conduct, inspiring others to follow a good example, or at least show restraint out of respect. [43]

"Protecting oneself, one protects others" is explained in Jātaka story 76 in the instance of a monk travelling with a caravan. When they camped for the night, he practised walking meditation throughout the night. Robbers intending to rob the caravan thought he was a watchman and didn't dare to attack.

How is it that in paying attention to others, one guards oneself? The Buddha says: "By patience, non-violence, loving kindness, and empathy." When one directs *sati* towards the mind of others, one trains oneself in loving understanding, and when others request something, one takes an interest. By this consideration for others, one diminishes one's own desires and protects oneself from their evil consequences, from darkness, remorse, fault-finding and bad rebirth. So it is that by increasingly focusing on 'others' with loving kindness, one reduces the 'I,' thereby diminishing the split or barrier between 'I' and 'other.' And if one develops complete all-embracing loving-kindness and combines it with insight into the conditioned nature of this state (see MN 52), the 'I' is permanently dissolved.

80. Seven Jewels (SN 46:42)

Just as with the arising of a wheel-turning emperor (*cakkavatti*: lit. "wheel-turner") in the world, his seven jewels arise; so too, with the appearance of a Perfectly Awakened One in the world, the seven awakening factors arise as well.

1. For the emperor, a wheel jewel arises, the steering-wheel of world-rulership to guide the moral order of humanity. It runs ahead of him, conquering the world, turning everything to the best outcome. Then it stands at his head to crown him. In the

---

43. One can also take into account the balancing of the teacher/pupil relation expressed in the simile. To start practising, one needs a teacher or spiritual guide but if a pupil becomes overly dependent upon the teacher's example and encouragement and is not able to practise independently, then this will eventually lead to stagnation and deterioration in his practice. The pupil should also not become angry when the teacher challenges him and requests him to do difficult things. Likewise if the teacher pays too much attention to the pupil, not enabling the pupil to practise independently, or scolding and challenging him too much, then the pupil will not progress. There is also an imbalance when the pupil does not practise what the teacher teaches him, and when the teacher does not practise himself what he teaches the pupil and not setting the right example. (See MN 122.)

same way, the awakening factor of mindfulness bestows rulership over oneself, turns back the steering-wheel towards the inside, thereby turning everything to the best outcome.

2. The emperor also possesses an elephant jewel, the best white state-elephant, which can lift him high above the crowd and can trample all his enemies. In the same way, the awakening factor of wise investigation of the laws of nature lifts one beyond the world and tramples all false perceptions of permanence below it; it effects the final discrimination between what is wholesome and unwholesome, high and low.

3. As his second animal, the emperor possesses a horse jewel which takes him with lightning speed wherever he wants to go. In the same way, the awakening factor of energy carries one with the speed of thought to the bliss of calm and insight. It quickly and powerfully overcomes the pollutions and hindrances, just as a horse overcomes distances in space.

4. The emperor also has a gem jewel, a self-luminous diamond, bright as daylight even at night. In the same way, the awakening of rapture produces self-luminosity, radiant bliss existing independently from external light.

5. The emperor possesses the woman jewel, the ideal companion, the duty-conscious consort, who is a faithful companion and refuge, the soul of the palace, the manager of his estate. In the same way, the monk in the awakening of tranquillity has the refuge of being at home, the harmony of mind remaining faithful to him, inseparable even in turmoil.

6. The second person among the emperor's jewels is the treasurer jewel, the ideal minister of finance, who oversees monetary needs so that borrowing is unnecessary. The monk who has the awakening factor of calm of mind similarly has a treasure. It is the greatest of possessions and makes him independent of the world, without borrowing from it.

7. The third person among the emperor's jewels is the chancellor jewel, the ideal advisor. In the same way, the monk who has the awakening factor of equanimity has the surest authority, one suggesting the best course without being partial.

81. Six Causes for Falling Back (AN 6:60)

1. Since a cow likes to eat young seedlings, she tramples down rice fields. To stop this misbehaviour and keep her calm and quiet, she is tied up with a rope or shut in a shed. Would it be correct if someone were to say that this cow will no longer trample the fields? Certainly not. The cow could break the rope or escape from the shed and wander into the field again.

In the same way, there is a monk who, as long as he is with the Buddha or with a congenial monk, is completely gentle, deferential and calm. Their example and presence inspire and restrain him. But separated from them and freely left to his own devices, he is drawn to the great variety of spiritual and worldly people in society. Being unrestrained and chatty his sense-addiction increases, so he gives up his monkhood and wanders uncontrolled in the world like a straying cow.

2. A big rain cloud bursts and turns the dust at a crossroads into mud, but not for ever, since wind and sun will quickly dry up the moisture. People and cattle will then walk over the place and new dust will arise.

In the same way there is a monk who, secluded from desire and unwholesome states, wins the first *jhāna*, which is accompanied by consideration and contemplation, with rapture and bliss born of seclusion. Nevertheless, like the first monk, he later falls again under the spell of the variety of society. The blissful serenity of the first *jhāna* is like the cloudburst calming and binding the dust of the world for a short time so that his perception of the world is covered over. But the world's diversions emerge again, and instead of perception of unity the monk experiences again the perception of variety of humans and animals, winds and rain, the so-called 'world.' This experience again erases the world-transcending absorption, covering it over again so that it becomes ineffective, and so the monk fall back again into worldliness. The dust is there again.

3. Near a village or town, there is a large pond filled to its rim with water from heavy rain clouds. Thus, shells, gravel and stones on the bottom of the pond become invisible. But humans and animals will drink from that pond and the sun and wind of the hot Indian summer will dry up the water, and so the bottom

will become visible again.

In the same way, there is a monk who, after passing beyond thought and contemplation (*vitakka-vicāra*), wins perfect contentment and unification of mind in the solitude-born serene bliss, the blessing of the second *jhāna*. This time the rain (*jhāna*) penetrates not only the superficial dust but fills the entire depth of the pond so that the chaotic muddy gravel on the bottom is hidden, and there is a uniform surface to the water (smoothed, calm mind). However he also falls for the world again. But it takes longer this time before the perception 'world' returns, that is, until the water evaporates. The seasons have to change before the ground becomes visible again.

4. One who has eaten his fill of excellent food will be satisfied and have no interest in lesser foods, but only for as long as the nourishing juices of that food are still in his body. In the same way, a monk wins the well-being of equanimity beyond happiness in the body, the blessing of the third *jhāna*. Here, the well-being doesn't fall from the sky onto the earth (rain), but the nourishing juice (*oja*) suffuses the whole body, thereby making it immune to all lesser nutriment. However when that nourishing juice is consumed and fades away, then the monk again starts liking the taste of the worldly nutriments, falling again for the bait of the world.

5. In a mountain valley, there is a large pond, protected from winds and free of waves. But it cannot stay like this forever, for at some time clouds and winds from the four directions will cause rain and waves.

In the same way a monk wins the perfect, purified equanimity of the fourth *jhāna*, beyond pleasure and pain. This time the pond (the mind) is not near a village but remote in the mountains where it is difficult for humans to reach. Normally the pond is free from waves and smooth as glass, representing the unworldly, perfected equanimity of the highest *jhāna*. However he also falls back again. At some time—perhaps it may take years—winds and clouds arrive again from outside, i.e., excitement, movement and unrest reach the mind. The water (mind) is ruffled into waves by the eight worldly winds, and it comes to know ups and downs again, and pleasure and pain instead of equanimity.

6. A king with his fourfold army (elephants, horses, vehicles and soldiers) is on a long march and makes camp for one night in a forest thicket. Because of the noise of the elephants, the horses, the vehicles and the soldiers, as well as of the racket of kettle drums and trumpets, the chirping of crickets is wholly inaudible. Yet when the army moves on, one hears their chirping again.

In the same way, a monk who strives for liberation attains the four formless attainments by not paying attention to signs of form. That is, he goes beyond the fourth jhāna of the form sphere. Like the chirping of crickets, the fine craving for forms and signs become inaudible through the overwhelming experience of the four formless spheres, the fourfold army. Yet this craving returns when the monk emerges from the formless attainments, and like the others he too falls back. A monk who has experienced the formless attainments but has not gone beyond them by developing deep insight into their impermanent nature can still fall back.

82. The Twelve States of Consciousness (DN 2; MN 77)

1. Just as a skilful bath attendant sprinkles bath powder into a metal basin, mixes it gradually with water, and kneads it until it forms a ball which doesn't ooze or drip, so a monk makes the rapture and pleasure born of the first jhāna completely drench, fill and pervade his body.

Here the *basin* is the mind; the *bath powder* is the body purified by virtue; water is the pleasure or well-being of the seclusion of absorption. The *ball of bath powder* is the living experience of the first jhāna. The pleasure from rapture born of solitude is used to completely drench and saturate the body in order to drive out all vestiges of sensuality. *No oozing or dripping* is to use nothing of the pleasure for worldly purposes; the rapture does not go out into the external world but remains contentedly within the confines of the body.

2. Just like a lake with no inflow from north, south, east or west; with no clouds forming above it or rain falling into it, but

fed by a spring on the bottom of the lake, would be exclusively and completely drenched, filled and pervaded by the cool spring water welling up, in the same way a monk experiences the rapture and pleasure born of the concentration of the second jhāna completely pervading his body.

The lake stands for body and mind. The *spring* is the pleasure of the concentration of the second jhāna, which no longer needs any skilful thinking but wells up on its own. Having *no inflowing streams* is the absence of all sensual inflow; the mind is one-pointed and unified and no input from the senses can penetrate. *No clouds and rain* is the absence of thought and contemplation (*vitakka-vicāra*). The spring of pleasure, rapture born of concentration, is totally used for the purpose of pervading the mind-made body (lake) so that all vestiges of subtle thinking and wanting are driven out.

3. Just as in a lotus pond some flowers grow and develop underwater, remaining completely beneath the surface, taking nourishment only from the depths of the pond so that their blossoms and roots are entirely drenched by cool water from the roots to the tips of the flowers, in the same way a monk experiences the pleasure born of the absence of rapture of the third jhāna completely pervading his body.

The *lotus flowers* are the even more refined mind-made body. The *cool water* of the pond is the pleasure or happiness of the third absorption. *Remaining underwater* means no longer protruding into rapture. The *self-nourishment* of the flowers in the pond symbolises the pleasure detached from rapture, existing in and of itself. The *pervasion* of the flowers by cool water is the driving out of the vestiges of mental rapture.

4. Just as a man sits covered from head to toe by a white cloth completely covering his body so that no part of him is exposed, in the same way a monk experiences the pure bright mind of the fourth jhāna completely pervading his body.

Here the *man* is the body. The *cloth* is the uniform, even surface of the equanimous happiness of the fourth jhāna; *white* symbolises the purity and brightness of mind in this state. *Being completely covered* means the complete exclusion of pleasure and pain by equanimity, which is neither-pain-nor-pleasure.

Moreover, the last vestiges of physical activity are silenced by the pure bright mind as the breathing temporarily ceases in the fourth *jhāna* (see DN 33.3.2, AN 10:72, SN 6.15 v. 611). The monk uses equanimity to pacify the finest physical *saṅkhāra* without remainder and thereby silences the body completely.

The mind is at its purest and brightest in the fourth jhāna and therefore malleable and workable. The mind can now be directed towards developing the higher knowledges such as the divine eye, and, more importantly, to develop insight and wisdom leading to arahantship. (Cf. MN 140.20 and AN 3:10 = Simile 49.)

5. Just as a beautiful, well-cut and transparent beryl gem through which a coloured thread—blue, yellow, red, white, or brown—is strung, and a man takes it into his hand and examines it, noticing both the beauty of the beryl gem and the coloured string going through it, in the same way the monk discerns, "This body of flesh is made up of the four elements, procreated by parents, maintained by nutriment, subject to decay and to complete fading away, and this is my consciousness tied and bound to it."

The *gem* is the flesh-body. Its *having been worked into facets* is the purification through the four *jhānas* which have polished away all the multifaceted mental defilements so that it is now beautiful, limpid and transparent. The *coloured thread* running through it is the capacity of awareness and discernment, the stream of consciousness. Its *colours* (the four primary colours plus brown) are the purity of consciousness, its splendid colour. Clarity of insight discriminates the transient body from the continuity of mind, the stream of consciousness, that continues after death.[44] Stream-entry, the first of the wisdom breakthroughs, is thus described.

6. A man pulls the inner stalk out of the outer sheet of a reed, or a sword from its scabbard, or a snake out of its sheath of

---

44. In DN 28.7 a monk, after contemplating the parts of the body, discerns the uninterrupted stream of consciousness, and whether it is established in this world and the next or not. In MN 140.19 it is said that just purified, bright consciousness remains after contemplating the four elements in the body.

worn-out skin.[45] Each time he knows there are two things, one of which comes out of the other. In the same way, a monk pulls another body—the mental or fine-material body (stalk, sword, snake) out of the flesh body (reed, scabbard, sheath). The mental body, though mentally created, still has form and is endowed with all sense faculties, lacking nothing.

All the three examples describe a close connection or entanglement. The inner stalk of the reed has grown inside the outer stalk and is completely enclosed by it. The sword is sheathed in a cover especially made for it. The slough, the old skin of the snake, completely covers it until it is cast off. Thus these similes show the close connection between the mental or fine-material body and the body of flesh, as well as the capacity to step out of the body through psychic power.

7. Just as a skilful potter can produce all the pots he wants from well-prepared clay, or a skilful ivory-worker can produce all the ivory works of art he wants from well-prepared ivory, or a goldsmith can produce all desired gold articles from well-prepared gold, so the monk can wield psychic powers in many ways.

These three crafts describe progressive stages of sophistication, the materials becoming firmer and the works therefore more durable. The most fragile is clay, ivory is somewhat more durable, and the most valuable is gold. In the same way, the monk can produce whatever bodies and figures he likes from a well-worked mind (clay, ivory, gold). The mind produces everything that he desires. He can let appear a thousand bodies, walk through walls or fly through air (clay); he can touch enormous celestial bodies with his hand (ivory); or he can even take the body of flesh to the Brahmā realm (gold).

8. Just as a man travelling down a long road who heard the sounds of kettledrums, drums, conches, trumpets and other horns would immediately know, "Those are sounds of kettledrums,

---

45. *Ahi-karaṇḍa* can also be interpreted as a bamboo wicker-basket of the kind a snake-charmer uses, but the other two similes indicate two things which are in very close proximity. A snake and its skin therefore makes more sense. Cf. *ahi-kosa*, "snake-slough" in Sanskrit where *kosa* can mean "slough/sheath" as well as "box/casket."

drums, conches, trumpets and cymbals," so a monk with a heavenly ear, purified and reaching beyond human limits can hear both heavenly and human sounds far and near.

Here the *long road* is the endlessness of the transitory world of *saṃsāra* in which one wanders around, wondering and questioning. The five instruments describe the five sounds of the beings in the five realms of existence: hell (kettledrums), animal (drums), ghost (conches), human (trumpets) and god (cymbals). Whether beings are near or far, on, above or below the earth, in every case he knows what kind of being is speaking, understands their voice and can also speak to them. (In MN 77 this simile is limited to the trumpet and blowing it oneself; at AN 4:191 there is a similar simile as in DN 2).

9. Just as a young, attractive man or woman looking at the image of his or her own face in a clean, bright mirror or reflected in a clear water surface would know if there were a spot or not on it, even so a monk can know the mind of another being with his mind—whether or not it is polluted by defilements or whether or not this or that power or burden is dominant (as in MN 10).

The young person here is the monk with psychic powers wishing to know the mind of others. The mirror or clear water is the monk's own pure mind, his sensitivity. His 'own' face in the simile is the image of the 'other' being reflected in his own pure mind, the projection of one's own capacity to discern. Having a spot on the face or not means the mind's impurity or purity; in particular, he can know whether another has attained stream-entry or arahantship or has attained a state of calmness of mind.

10. Just as when a man goes from his village to another, then to another and from there back to his own village and can then recollect exactly how and where on his visits he stood, sat, spoke or remained silent, so too, the monk can remember his past lives.

At first he can remember one of them, then another one, a further one and then numerous other ones until he returns in his mind to this present life. He knows in each case where he was born, what his name was, what his caste and livelihood were, what kinds of pleasure and pain he experienced, and what the end of that life and the subsequent life were like.

11. Just as a sharp-eyed man standing on the top of a tower in the market place would observe three kinds of behaviour in the people below—entering houses and leaving them again; or wandering around on the streets; or sitting in the centre of the market—so too, a monk can see beings disappear and re-appear according to their dark or light actions.

The *marketplace* here means existence, or intermediate existence (*antarābhava;* see Simile 48). *The tower* is surmounting wisdom. See the simile of standing on a mountain and looking down in MN 125.9; MN 26.20; Dhp 28. The *three modes of behaviour* refers to the three levels of existence—the worlds of sensuality, form, and non-form. The people entering and leaving houses are those who put on gross or fine material bodies, and settle down in them. The people who walk along the streets and continue wandering farther are the pure Brahmā beings. They exist with a fine mental body. The third group of people who just sit still without wandering around are the formless beings who dwell in sublime equanimity. The monk sees former, present and later existences of beings, changing according to their merits. In MN 77 the simile is shortened to include only passing to and from two houses. At Simile 48 there is an interpretation of these similes as denoting the *antarābhava*, the in-between-existence state.

12. If there were in a mountain valley a clear, transparent lake and sharp-eyed man standing at the shore who could see shells, sand and pebbles and shoals of fish swimming and resting in the clear water, even so a monk, having developed the fourth jhāna, directs his purified, unshakeable and malleable mind to the destruction of the taints (*āsava*). Reflecting upon the taints as they truly are, and having fully liberated his mind in this way, he knows that his work is finished and that there will be no more rebirth.

The *mountain* stands for the higher perspective. The *lake* is existence. Transparency means that the whole of existence is completely clear to the observer. *Standing at the shore* means the observer stands outside of existence; having reached the farther shore, he is an onlooker at the whole of existence. The *shells* of the inner sense bases enclose the bodies of living beings. *Sand*

and pebbles represent the knitting of fine and coarse forms, the outer bases. *Shoals of fish* are the conditional relationships among feelings, perception and formations. *Swimming fish* stand for movement and change (the sense world) and *resting fish* for non-movement (the immovability of the form and formless worlds). Having paid attention to the conditioned nature of the taints, seeing them as they truly are in accordance with the four Noble Truths, *the sharp eyed man*, the monk who develops deep insight, detaches himself entirely from them and becomes an arahant.

83. The Cowherd (MN 33; AN 11:18 & 23)

Since everyone who aspires to purify his mind must watch over his mind as much as a herdsman watches over his herd, the Buddha frequently uses the image of a cowherd in similes (MN 33–34; MN 19.12). In the Greater Discourse on the Cowherd (MN 33) he addresses the monks as follows.

"When a cowherd possesses eleven qualities, monks, he is capable of caring for and protecting a herd of cattle. What eleven? They are when a cowherd has knowledge of physical form, is skilled in understanding their characteristics, removes flies' eggs, dresses wounds, smokes out the sheds, knows where the fording place is, where the drinking-place is, and the best path for cows; he is skilled in the pastures, he does not milk dry but leaves some milk in the udders, and pays special attention to those bulls who are fathers and leaders of the herd.

"In the same way, a monk with the eleven same qualities could come to growth, maturity and fulfilment in this teaching and discipline."

Explanation

According to the Buddha, the cowherd as well as a monk would be successful with eleven positive qualities. The similarity of both the cowherd and the monk is that they have to observe and to take into consideration certain qualities and circumstances if they want to reach their goal. The goal of the cowherd is to feed the cattle well and to bring them to growth and maturity because he lives depending on them. This is his livelihood, his occupation on which his well-being depends. The monk, on the other hand, has chosen the overcoming of all suffering and the attainment of final well-being as his occupation. This is his goal.

To understand the eleven similes it is essential to keep the starting point in mind. Here the Buddha does not start as usual with mental states, which he then explains with the help of similes taken from normal life, but instead he starts here with a concrete image, the cowherd. In the sequence of tasks relating to the cowherd, he describes three things. The first and most important is the attitude of the cowherd to the herd: knowing the body and its characteristics, removing flies' eggs, dressing wounds. Secondly he has to know five things about the cattle's environment—smoking out sheds, the ford, watering place, path and pasture. Thirdly he must watch himself with respect to two things—milking the cows and attending to the bulls.

The Buddha also follows this sequence when he refers to the spiritual qualities of the monk. These eleven things do not comprise a line of development—they don't have the character of a path—but rather are entirely dependent on the sequence of the cowherd's qualities.[46] The only system underlying the eleven qualities is that they are all things which have to be developed.

1. The herdsman must know the physique of his cattle. He must be able to discriminate them, he must know how many animals he has, which are his and which his neighbour's. He should know the age of his animals, and other relevant facts. In short, he should be completely familiar with their physical form.

In like manner the monk must know the nature of the body, namely the four elements and whatever form spatially exists derived from them. He must know that this is all that there is to form: there is no materiality as such behind it, no original substance, and no world as such. Further, form changes continuously: there is no permanent foothold in it; it is always appearing and passing away between birth and death. This is the wisdom of the monk concerning the first of the five aggregates.

---

46. This is the same with the 32 marks on the body of the Buddha (e.g. DN 30), with respect to which 20 spiritual qualities are randomly presented, because they only follow a sensory succession from foot to head.

2. The herdsman must be knowledgeable with respect to characteristics. He must know the character of his animals and their peculiarities: One cow tends to run away, another eats the neighbour's crops, one must be hit hard to get up, one likes to graze near the marsh, two animals don't like each other, and so on.

In like manner the monk must discern correctly what actions characterize both foolish and wise people (see MN 129). Form is only a tool of the psyche; it is actions that indicate the nature of the psyche. He can see in himself and in others how actions reveal character. By penetrating forms, he becomes aware of the psyche.

3. The herdsman should remove flies' eggs. When flies lay eggs on wounds of the cattle, he has to know this and to remove them to protect his animals from the torment of crawling maggots in the wound.

In like manner, the monk should remove evil thoughts so they do not torment him and do not arouse him to do evil. This is effort; specifically, the second of the four right efforts, namely removing thoughts of desire, hatred and violence, are cited here.

4. The herdsman must dress the wounds when his animals have hurt themselves so as to and help them heal and keep flies out. He has to be able to apply medical herbs and bandages.

In like manner the monk must guard the sense doors, his inner vulnerability. The definition of the first right effort—restraint of the senses—is given here.[47]

5. The herdsman must be able to light a fire and make smoke to drive mosquitoes and gnats away. This is the first of the five things of the environment that he has to master.

In like manner, the monk should be able to ignite others by instruction and to be able to articulate his convictions. Whoever makes the teaching the basis of his life can also transmit something of it to others, be it little or much, more or less skilfully. He who on the contrary does not talk at all about the teaching, not even to those close to him, lives a split existence and is unable to progress. Where there is energy, one can light a fire to drive away

---

[47]. The placing of the second right effort before the first demonstrates that there is no sequence to the similes here.

numerous wrong views and deluded opinions (mosquitoes and gnats). How could anyone who consents to wrong views grow in the teaching? This quality also belongs to energy: It is the external side of right view which expresses itself here and provides answers to the questions of others.

6. The herdsman must know where the ford is when he drives his cattle across a river. In the rainy season, every stream becomes a river so that one must know exactly the depth and fordability of the water to prevent the animals drowning or being carried away (see also the image in SN 1:1).

In a like manner the monk should know how to safely ford the river of saṃsāra. From time to time, the monk should visit senior monks to ask his questions and so dissolve the doubts that obscure his view of the further shore of Nibbāna and the way to get there.[48] Only when learning from others about the goal and the way to it can the monk discern the ford to the further shore, to Nibbāna. In MN 43.14 it is said that when right view is assisted by the five factors of virtue, learning, discussion, serenity and insight it will result in liberation.

There is another simile of a cowherd crossing the ford at the Shorter Discourse on the Cowherd in MN 34. Here the simile applies to teachers who guide their disciples in the wrong or right way: A foolish cattle herdsman, not examining the near shore and the far shore, drives his herd all together across the river at a place where there is no ford and therefore his herd perishes midstream. The wise cattle herdsman, examining well the near shore and the far shore, drives his herd across according to strength and age, first the older strong bulls and finally the young calves, and only at a place where there is a ford. Likewise, the Buddha safely guides his herd of noble disciples, the arahants first and the Dhamma- and faith-followers last across the stream of saṃsāra to the further shore of Nibbāna.

7. The herdsman must know the watering places where his cattle can drink.

In like manner, the monk must know the mental spring, the watering-place refreshing him spiritually when he feels parched.

---

48. If there were a sequence to the similes here, then this quality should come first since right view comes first.

This is the inspiration and gladness that comes with the Teaching of the Buddha, the higher feeling of happiness, the bliss of understanding the Truth that arises out of right view. This is the last of the seven qualities of the mind which complete stream-entry in MN 48.13.

8. The herdsman must know the way to the pastures—the small, difficult tracks through rice fields, forests, swamps and over mountains.

In like manner, the monk must know the Noble Eightfold Path, that is, the wisdom concerning the fourth Noble Truth. The Noble Eightfold Path is the method to obtain permanent calm of mind.

9. The herdsman must know the quality of the pasture, the usefulness of grasses and herbage, shady places and so forth.

The monk in like manner must know a spiritual pasturage or his feeding place, namely the foundations of mindfulness by which he nourishes himself and which make him develop as a child is nourished and grows through food. (See SN 47:6 & 7, where the four foundations of mindfulness are said to be the ancestral domain and resort.)

10. The herdsman should leave some milk in the udder.

The monk must know moderation in accepting gifts from generous laypeople. If he does not know moderation, asking more and more, then the laypeople will lose faith and stop giving; his source of requisites will then dry up. More importantly, he should not over-milk so that calves, the weaker ones, also can live. He should not be an exploiter but be considerate towards others as a necessary character trait. This belongs to virtue, proper conduct, and again, it is also effort.

11. The herdsman should respect the bulls, taking their welfare into consideration. He has to work with them, not against them.

In like manner, the monk should honour elders in the Sangha, the experienced fathers of the Teaching. He should treat them with love and give importance to what they say. He should honour them, serving them with actions, words and thoughts. This is also a quality that belongs to the sphere of virtue, to proper conduct and obedience. As in MN 48, it is one of the qualities that is a prerequisite for attainment of stream-entry.

In looking over these eleven qualities, it may be noticed that faith is missing. This is because faith is presupposed as the impetus for monkhood, as stated in the gradual training (*anupubbasikkhā*; DN 2, etc.).

Instead, energy is amply present. Two qualities relate to energetic effort for the acquisition of right view (making smoke and knowing the ford), two qualities represent virtue (not milking dry and honouring elders), and two belong to the four great exertions (removing flies' eggs and dressing wounds).

Mindfulness and calmness of mind are mentioned once each (pasture and watering place). Wisdom is considered insofar as two qualities concern the aggregates, namely body (form) and the mind (characteristics), that is, the first of the Four Noble Truths. A further quality (path) represents the Fourth Noble Truth.

Thus the qualities are not mixed together in an arbitrary way, but instead encompass the five wholesome qualities or faculties.

In AN 11:23 only the negative qualities of this simile are mentioned. Here it is said instead that a monk with these bad qualities is be incapable of training in the contemplation of impermanence, suffering and not-self with regard to the six sense bases and the states arising dependent upon them.

84. The Mice (AN 4:107)

There are four kinds of mice: the mouse that digs a hole but does not live in it; one that lives in a hole but has not dug it; one that neither has dug a hole nor lives in a hole; and one that digs a hole and also lives in it.

Likewise in the world can be found four kinds of persons. The one who digs holes but does not live in them has theoretically acquired the Teaching, with thorough effort, and in studying it over and over, he has learned much of it by rote. In short, he views the Teaching theoretically, scientifically and objectively, not as a compelling, subjective and personal way of living. He has dug and dug, has excavated a deep spiritual hole and has made a dwelling place and refuge but it is one that only others can use and find spiritual security in it. He himself cannot live in it because he has not understood the Four Noble Truths. His tragedy is that he is useful to others but not to himself. He is like the mouse digging a hole for other mice.

The person who lives in a hole that he hasn't dug himself is one who has not studied the theory of the teaching in depth but he is one who uses the work of another and strictly applies it to himself. He may have heard only little, yet that little he comprehends. He understands the essentials, the Four Noble Truths, so it can be said that he lives in the dwelling of the Teaching without having built it himself.

The person who neither digs a hole nor lives in one is the ordinary worldling who lives far from the Truth, who neither aspires to inner spiritual security nor realizes it. Without the protection of a hole, he lives in the open and is exposed to many dangers, like a mouse without a hole; it may get caught by a cat!

The person who digs a hole and also lives in it is the one who deeply investigates and studies the teaching and also lives accordingly. He digs himself a sanctuary and then lives in it secure and at ease.

For a corresponding simile of clouds that thunder and rain, see AN 4:101–102.

85. The Palm Stump

The simile of the palm stump is one that appears very frequently. It occurs in the Pali Canon no less than 64 times, referring to various unwholesome states that are to be overcome. The most detailed form of this simile is seen in MN 36.47 (= MN 49, MN 68, MN 105.2,3). It is as follows.

Just as a palm tree whose crown has been cut off is incapable of further growth, so too the Tathāgata has abandoned the taints (*āsavā*) that defile, generate future birth, ripen in suffering and lead to future birth, ageing and death, has made them like a palm-stump, done away with them, so that they can't rearise in the future, has cut them off at the root, made them like a palm tree stump.

In Thī 478, the Buddha has abandoned sensual desire and made it "like a palm-stump." In all the other texts, the simile is mostly aimed at the description of the arahant who has overcome all taints.

The basic message of the simile thereby always refers to something unwholesome which is abandoned, destroyed, eradicated, exterminated, uprooted, dissolved, and annihilated.

The Structure of the Simile

The palmyra palm tree, also called sugar palm tree (*Borassus flabellifer*), is a large fan-palm with huge leaves used for making fans and writing paper. It fruits are eaten and the sap of its inflorescence is used to make sugar. The stately trees often dominate agricultural landscapes in India and the rest of Asia. It has three parts: a root, a trunk and a crown. The root is invisible underground; the trunk is long, leafless and fibrous; and the crown is located high up at the top, with fronds, blossoms and fruits. If the crown is cut off, then the palm tree is reduced to the trunk and roots. The trunk and roots of palm trees are incapable of further growth and soon die, because they don't receive energy from the crown anymore.

When the branches and trunk of other trees have been cut, the roots and stump quickly produce new shoots with leaves, making further life possible. But this is not the case with a palm tree: it just dies, which is why the simile refers specifically to a palm tree.

The crown of the palm tree is the ignorant mind with its wrong way of viewing, its wrong way of perceiving reality in the five aggregates (*khandhas*), and its fundamentally wrong valuing, which sustains the trunk and roots of the tree (the taints). If the aggregates are no longer valued and affirmed (if the crown is removed) and if therefore right view is perfected so that nothing transient is grasped any more, then the last and subtlest taints die off because they are no longer powered by the energy of valuing. The roots and stump cannot survive, because they are no longer provided with energy from the top and don't have the potential to generate new shoots.

The aggregates of the arahants may still exist for some time but free of the taints and grasping, just like the stump or trunk of the palm tree remains upright for a while until it eventually decays, breaks down, or is blown down by stormy winds. The Buddha says:

Just as, monks when cutting a cluster of mangos at the stem, all the fruits hanging at that stem come along, so the body of the Tathāgata stands with the conduit of existence cut off—as long as his body will stand, so gods and humans will see him, but with the disintegration of the body at the end of life, gods and humans will not see him anymore. (DN 1, end. Cf. SN 22:102).

Further he says: "[Purified states] are my pathway and my domain, yet I do not identify with them." (MN 47.13).

There is another point to add regarding the simile of the palm stump. While one usually has to dig laboriously to remove a tree's roots after felling in order to prevent it from regenerating, this is not necessary in case of a palm tree: One can leave it to its own transience. Likewise, one who is freed of the taints does not need to annihilate his body—he leaves it to its transience in just the same way.

Thus the arahant says:

> I do not rejoice in death,
> I do not rejoice in life,
> But I await my time,
> Mindful and clearly aware.[49]

Different ways the simile is employed

From the viewpoint of the psyche, the taints are cut off at the root (*ucchinna-mūla*), yet from the view point of the palm-tree, it is removal of the crown that cuts off the sap-stream, but in effect both are the same because the excision applies to both the existential taints and the biological taints. It is fitting that both cannot regenerate and grow anymore.

The simile of the palm tree is used according to the view point in another way as well. The living palm tree stands for prosperous life, yet the dead palm-tree stump is a positive image, standing for liberation from the illusive saṃsāric life. The dried up palm-tree stump without crown is the image of

---

49. Th 196=607=655=686, cf. 1002 "... but I await my time, like a worker his wages."

unmasked saṃsāra, which has entirely lost its enticing appearance. The arahant stands outside saṃsāra, beyond the khandhas, in the dimension of freedom from death. In this way, the palm-tree symbolizes mortality.

The image of the dead palm tree is so impressive as a negative that it is used sometimes for worldly loss. For example, it is used to indicate that one's children die without heirs as the punishment for reviling noble monks. Here the inability of the palm tree to regenerate is equal in meaning to barrenness (SN 3:1 and J 530, verse.)

However, the complete opposite image is presented in the Vinaya. Here a simile is given for each of the four offences leading to permanent expulsion from the Sangha (*pārājika*), and the simile for untrue claims to have realized superhuman qualities is that of a decapitated palm tree. The living palm tree thus stands for the higher right virtue of the monk, while the dead palm-tree represents the monk who is dead for the Sangha.[50] (Mv VI.78 = Pār IV.3)

What gets destroyed?

The negative state that becomes annihilated in the simile of the palm stump is described in quite different ways in various passages in the texts. Listing these descriptions gives, so to speak, a catalogue of all that is overcome by an arahant. They can be divided into two main groups, namely the taints as such and the results or effects of the taints.

1. The taints as such

1a) Given as main terms are:
 - most frequently, craving, hatred and delusion (*rāga, dosa,*

---

50. A monk who has committed this offence automatically falls away from his status as a *bhikkhu*, one who has received the full acceptance in the Order, is undertaking the training rules as laid down in the Code of Discipline (*Pātimokkha*), and can participate in legal acts of the order such as the Uposatha observance. Although the offender can't be a full monk anymore in this life, this does not mean that he can associate with monks anymore, and he can remain a novice or layman living in a monastery.

Similes of the Buddha

moha) (MN 43, MN 55, MN 140, AN 3:63, 69, 72, AN 10:20, DN 33.3.3.5, DN 34.2.3.7);
- five times, as the taints (*āsavā*) (MN 36.47, MN 49, MN 68, AN 4:36+195);
- as further aspects of the taints, the 5 hindrances (SN 54:12), and variously, desire, lust, delight, craving, whatever engagement and clinging, mental standpoints, adherences and underlying tendencies (*cetasā-adhiṭṭhāna-abhinivesanusayā*) (SN 22:3, SN 22:112/SN 23:10).

1b) Given as special taints are:
- the 'I-belief' (*asmi-māna*) (MN 22.35/AN 5:71–72, AN 4:38 and AN 4:200);
- sense pleasures (*kāma*) (SN 35:104, and Thī 478/480);
- taste (*rasa*) and enjoyment (*bhoga*), which the Buddha overcame (AN 8:11);
- doubt (*kaṅkhā*) (Nidd I 109, Kathāvatthu 102);
- affection or needy love (*pema*) (AN 4:200); and
- the most refined fetter, namely the fetter of the base of neither perception nor non-perception (MN 105).

2. The Results of the Taints

2a) Craving, the manifest side of greed and hatred (MN 22.33/AN 5:71–72; MN 73, SN 35:103, AN 4:254).

In its perceptual aspect, craving corresponds to ignorance (*avijjā*), as mentioned too in MN 22.31 and AN 5:71–72. Craving is also mentioned in the enumeration in SN 22:112/SN 23:10.

2b) Grasping, the manifestation of the taints in mental activities or formations (*saṅkhārā*) which are directed towards the transient.

It is the grasping of kamma arising out of greed, hatred and delusion (AN 3:33); or it is wrong conduct in deeds, speech and thoughts (AN 8:11–12/Pār I.1/Mv VI.31). It is the grasping of the affectionate clinging (*upayūpādānā*) (SN 22:3, SN 22:112/SN 23:10), or, the grasping of wrong views (MN 72.20, SN 12:35–36. It is the attributions of clinging or the acquisitions (*upadhi*) (MN 140.27).

2c) Lastly, the cycle of rebirths (MN 22.32), and future birth and renewed existence (AN 8:22/Pār I.1/Mv VI.31).

It is inevitable that the above summary appears quite dry. This can only be avoided by reading the quoted passages oneself. Then it becomes evident from the context how the Buddha uses the simile and why. By seeing it in different contexts, the decapitated palm tree confirms again and again the profound statement:

> Know that ignorance is the head, and that knowledge fells the head,
> When conjoined with faith, mindfulness, calm, desire, and energy. (Sn 1026)

INDEX OF SIMILES IN THE SUTTAS

This is an index of the similes and metaphors that appear in the suttas. Only the imagery that illustrates points of Dhamma is included here; imagery that serves primarily a literary or narrative function is not included (e.g., Ambapālī's description of her long-lost youthful beauty). The subject of each image is given in parenthesis (). The tilde (~) stands for the head-word in a given entry.

John Bullitt

A

Acrobats (watching after oneself/others) SN 47:19
Ancient city (awakening) SN 12:65
Animals bound together by a rope (lack of mindfulness) SN 35:206
Archer: (brevity of life; heedfulness) SN 20:6; archer's apprentice (jhāna) AN 9:36: See also Arrow, Fletcher.
Arrow: (dukkha) Sn 3:8; poisoned (speculative views) MN 63, (craving) MN 105, (contagiousness of evil) It 76; person shot with two ~ (physical and mental pain) SN 36:6; in the heart (sensuality) Sn 4:15; piercing a horsehair (subtlety of Dhamma) SN 56:45; Th 1:26; removed (greed) SN 1:5; shot into the night (bad people) Dhp 304; straightened by a fletcher (see Fletcher). See also Doctor, Fletcher.

B

Bamboo: destroyed by its own fruit (evil) Dhp 164, It 50; spreading (solitude in the wilderness) Sn 1:3
Bath-man or bath-man's apprentice (rapture of 1st jhāna) DN 2, DN 11, DN 12, MN 39, MN 119, AN 5:28
Bandits (external sense media) SN 35:197
Barley reaper (defilements) Mil II.1:8
Beast of burden (persistence) Sn 1:4
Beauty queen (mindfulness) SN 47:20

Bee gathering nectar (sage) Dhp 49

Bird: escaping from net (rarity of heavenly birth) Dhp 174; leaving no track (arahant) Dhp 92; sighting shore (seeking the Buddha; meaning of Tathāgata) DN 11, AN 6:54; spattered with dirt (mindfulness) SN 9:1; with wings as its only burden (contentment) DN 2, DN 11

Blindness (ignorance) MN 75

Blind men: row of (ignorance) MN 95; and the elephant (ignorance) Ud 6.4

Blind sea-turtle poking his head up through a yoke (rarity of human birth) MN 129, SN 56:48

Boat being bailed out (defilements) Dhp 369

Bog (sensuality) Sn 4:15

Boil, festering (the body) 9:15

Boiling the River Ganges (speech) MN 21

Bones: chain or heap (sensuality) MN 54, AN 5:76; mountain (length of saṃsāra) It 24

Bottomless chasm (painful feeling) SN 36:4

Boulder thrown into lake (kamma) SN 42:6

Bowl of poison (passion) Thī 14

Branch, man grasping a (self-view) AN 4:178

Bubble on water (appropriate attention) SN 22:95

Bull: born into a herd of cattle (arahant) AN 5:179; yoked to a load (endurance) Th 14:2: See also Cow.

Burning ghee or oil (meditation on the fire property) Ud 8.9, Ud 8.10

Burning grass or leaves (not-self) SN 35:101

Burning refuge (dukkha) Sn 3:8

Butcher or butcher's apprentice: (meditation on the four properties) DN 22, MN 119; (trance of non-breathing) MN 36: See also Bull, Cow.

Butcher of goats (kamma) AN 3:99

Butter from water(wrong view) MN 126

C

Calf not seeing its mother (change & alteration) SN 22:80: See also Cow.

Carpenter: (wearing down the effluents) SN 22:101; (self-control)

Dhp 80, Dhp 145; (applied thought) Mil II.3:13
Cart wheel (suffering) Dhp 1
Catching arrows (brevity of life; heedfulness) SN 20:6
Cave (the body; sensuality) Sn 4:2
Cesspool difficult to clean (impurities) Sn 2:6
Chaff: (corrupt person) Sn 1:5, Sn 2:6; (dead body) SN 35:69; (others' faults) Dhp 252
Chariot: (anger) Dhp 222; (the body) Dhp 151; (concentration) AN 5:28; (mindfulness) MN 119; (world) Dhp 171
Chariots, relay (stages of insight) MN 24
Charioteer (sense-restraint) Dhp 94
Cheater (others' errors) Dhp 252
Children playing with sand castles (aggregates) SN 23:2
City of bones (the body) Dhp 150
City superintendent at a crossroads (consciousness) Mil II.3:12
Cleansing of the body with scouring balls and bath powder (cleansing the mind) AN 3:70
Cleansing of the head with paste and clay (cleansing the mind) AN 3:70
Cliff, frightful (fear of birth, ageing, and death) SN 56:42
Cloth: person covered with white (4th jhāna) DN 2, DN 11, DN 12, MN 39, AN 5:28; soiled (conceit) SN 22:89; to be dyed (defiled and undefiled mind) MN 7, Ud 5.3
Cock's feather in fire (unattractiveness) AN 7:46
Conch-trumpet blower (sublime attitudes) SN 42:8
Constellations (heedfulness) AN 10:15
Cotton tuft (rapture) Th 1:104
Couple eating their child (purpose of food) SN 12:63
Cow: butchered (meditation on the four properties) DN 22, MN 119; flayed (contact) SN 12:63; led to slaughter (inevitability of death) AN 7:70, Sn 3:8; milked dry (lack of moderation) MN 33, AN 11:18; producing milk, curds, butter, ghee, etc. (practice for oneself and others) AN 4:95; roaming in the mountains (mastery of jhāna) AN 9:35; skinned (sensuality) MN 146; that runs away (fool) SN 11:5; udder (brief time) SN 20:4: See also Bull, Butcher.
Cowherd: competent (skilfulness) MN 33, AN 11:18; counting another's cattle (heedlessness) Dhp 19; driving cattle (ageing

and death) Dhp 135; incompetent (unskilfulness) MN 33, AN 11:18; mindful of his cows (skilfulness) MN 19; prodding and poking his cows (skilfulness) MN 19; reflecting on the places his cattle have wandered (uposatha) AN 3:70: See also Bull, Cow.

Crafts, Trades, and Professions. See Archer, Bath-man, Butcher, Carpenter, Charioteer, Cowherd, Doctor, Elephant tamer, Fletcher, Goldsmith, Horse-trainer, Irrigator, Ivory carver, King, Magician, Potter, Silversmith, Trader, Turner, Warrior, Weigher.

Creeper pod (future dangers) MN 45

Crooked chariot wheels (faults) AN 3:15

Cymbals striking together (contact) Mil II.3:8

D

Darkness, intergalactic (fear of birth, ageing, and death) SN 56:46

Debt (conviction) AN 6:45

Deer that wanders in the wilderness (solitude) Sn 1:3

Dewdrop on tip of grass blade (brevity of life) AN 7:70

Digging in earth (speech) MN 21

Dirt-washer (purifying the mind) AN 3:100 (i-x)

Doctor (the Buddha) MN 63, MN 105: See also Arrow.

Dog: chasing swine (gratitude) SN 7:14; gnawing on a chain of bones (sensuality) MN 54; tied to a post (self-view) SN 22:99, SN 22:100:

Donkey that thinks it's a cow (insincerity with regard to the Dhamma) AN 3:81

Drawing pictures in space (speech) MN 21

Dream, waking from: (sensuality) MN 54; (death) Sn 4:6

Drinking water (subduing hatred): from a clear pool AN 5:162; from a dirty pool AN 5:162; from a puddle in a hoof-print AN 5:162

Drum peg (listening to Dhamma) SN 20:7

Dry piece of wood (mindfulness) MN 119

Dung beetle (pride) SN 17:5

Dust: on a fingertip (dukkha) SN 13:1, (rarity of human birth) SN 20:2; thrown into wind (evil) Dhp 125

Dusty road (household life) DN 2, DN 11, DN 12, MN 36, MN 125

E

Earth (arahant) Dhp 95

Elephant: and the blind men (ignorance) Ud 6.4; footprint (four noble truths) MN 28, (heedfulness) SN 3:17, AN 10:15; in battle (patient endurance) Dhp 320, Th 3:8; in battle (sensual passion) AN 5:139, (sense-restraint) AN 5:140; in rut (self-control) Dhp 324, Dhp 326; in the wild (mature companion) Sn 1:3; relieves an itch (solitude in the wilderness) AN 9:40; renouncing its herd (solitude in the wilderness) Sn 1:3; snared (attachments) MN 66; stuck in mud (heedfulness) Dhp 327; tameable (factors for exertion) MN 90; tamed (self-training) Dhp 322

Elephant-tamer (renunciation) MN 125

Embers in a pit (passion) Thī 14

Empty water pot (mindfulness) MN 119

Executioner: five (aggregates) SN 35:197; sixth (passion/delight) SN 35:197

Eyes, man opening and closing his (faculties) MN 152

F

False path in the forest (wrong eightfold path) MN 19

Farmer's urgent duties (self-training) AN 3:91

Field: neglecting one's own (teaching Dhamma) DN 12; spoiled by weeds (passion) Dhp 356

Fire: (clinging) SN 12:52, SN 35:28, SN 44:9; (heedfulness) Dhp 31; (passion) Dhp 251; (discernment) Th 1:3; fire's destination (Nibbāna) Ud 8.10; fire not returning (solitude in the wilderness) Sn 1:3; hidden in ashes (unskilful action) Dhp 71

Fire-stick (sensuality) MN 36; (feeling) SN 48:39

Firebrand with excrement: (practicing Dhamma for no one's benefit) AN 4:95; (failing to practice Dhamma) SN 22:80, It 91

Fish: caught in net (solitude in the wilderness) Sn 1:3, (sensuality) Th 4:8; caught in trap (sensuality) Ud 7.4; caught on a hook (six senses) SN 35:189; in dried-up puddle (self-view) Sn 4:2, SN 5:10; flip-flapping on dry land (unsteady mind) Dhp 34; rising through the water (recognizing a wise person) AN 4:192; rotten and wrapped in grass (associating with fools) It 76; struggling in water (quarrelling) Sn 4:15

Index of Similes in the Suttas

Fisherman (Māra) SN 35:189

Flame: overthrown by wind (arahant) Sn 5:6; passed from one lamp to another (rebirth) Mil III.5:5; unbinding of (Nibbāna) Thī 5:10;

Fletcher straightening an arrow: (exertion) MN 101; (training the mind) Dhp 33, Th 1:29; (restraint) Dhp 145, Dhp 80: See also Arrow.

Flies' eggs (sensuality) MN 33, AN 11:18

Flood (craving, sensuality, becoming, ignorance) SN 1:1, SN 45:171; (greed) Sn 4:15; sweeping away a sleeping village (death) Dhp 47, Dhp 286: See also River, Ocean.

Flower: blossom (speech) Dhp 51; heap (skilfulness) Dhp 53; scent (integrity) Dhp 54: See also Lotus.

Flower-arranger (Dhamma follower) Dhp 44

Foam (the body/form) SN 22:95, Dhp 46

Fords (asking questions) MN 33, AN 11:18

Forest: (desire) Dhp 283; (Dhamma) Sn 2:1

Fort (mind) Dhp 40

Fragrances (heedfulness): flower AN 10:15; root AN 10:15; wood AN 10:15

Frontier fortress: (the body) SN 35:204; (seven skilful qualities) AN 7:63; (liberation is not for everyone) AN 10:95; (guarding oneself) Dhp 315, Th 14:1; foundation post (conviction) AN 7:63; moat (shame) AN 7:63; encircling road (concern) AN 7:63; weapons (learning) AN 7:63; army (persistence) AN 7:63; gate-keeper (mindfulness) AN 7:63; ramparts (discernment) AN 7:63; stores of grass (1st jhāna) AN 7:63; stores of rice (2nd jhāna) AN 7:63; stores of sesame (3rd jhāna) AN 7:63; stores of tonics (4th jhāna) AN 7:63

Fruit, ripe (death) Sn 3:8

Full moon (discernment) Thī 1:3: See Moon.

Full water pot (mindfulness) MN 119

Fumigation (teaching Dhamma) MN 33, AN 11:18

G

Gem with coloured thread inside (clear seeing) DN 2, DN 11, DN 12

Gift of food (good will) SN 20:4

Goat butcher (kamma) AN 3:99
Gold: coins raining (sensuality) Dhp 186; disappearance of (disappearance of Dhamma) SN 16:13; ingot (discernment and virtue) Dhp 229; mountain (sensuality) SN 4:20; ornament (arahant) AN 4:28
Goldsmith: purifying gold (purifying the mind) AN 3:100 (i-x), AN 3:100 (xi-xv); crafting any kind of article (supernormal powers) DN 2, DN 11
Gong (applied and sustained thought) Mil II.3:14
Gourds in autumn (bones) Dhp 149
Grass: with sharp blades (wrong practice) Dhp 311; wild grass after rain (dukkha) Dhp 335
Green reed cut down (foolish person) SN 1:10
Ground far from the sky (foolish person) SN 5:10
Guest house (feelings in the body) SN 36:14
Guest refusing the host's food (insulting behaviour) SN 7:2

H

Handful of leaves (Dhamma) SN 56:31
Hands clapping (contact) Mil II.3:8
Hawk attacking quail (mindfulness) SN 47:6
Head of snake (sensuality) Sn 4:1
Head on fire: See Turban on fire
Head sliced open with sword (pain) MN 36
Hell, saved from (Dhamma) DN 12
Hen covering her eggs (virtue, etc.) MN 53, SN 22:101
Herd of cattle (arahant) AN 3:57
Herons wasting away (falling short of celibacy) Dhp 155
Himalayas (good people) Dhp 304
Hog, fat and lazy (foolish person) Dhp 325
Honey ball (flavour of Dhamma) MN 18
Hooks (six senses): SN 35:189
Horse: awakened by the whip (conscience) SN 1:18; deprived of fodder (father of fools) SN 7:14; fast (wise person) Dhp 29; stallion (self-training) Dhp 94, Dhp 144, Dhp 380; stirred by a goad-stick (trainable person) AN 4:113; tamed (self-tamed person) Dhp 322; thoroughbred (arahant) Th 2:27, Thī 5:10; thoroughbred (jhāna) AN 11:10; thoroughbred (qualities of a

Index of Similes in the Suttas

consummate monk) AN 3:94, AN 8:13; unbroken colt (jhāna) AN 11:10
Horse-trainer (trainable person) AN 4:111
House: built from the bottom up (four noble truths) SN 56:44; fireproof (mindfulness/awareness) SN 35:202; flammable (mindfulness/awareness) SN 35:202; on fire (the body) SN 1:41; with poor roof (unguarded mind) AN 3:105.

I

Illness, man recovering from (hindrances) DN 2, DN 11, DN 12, MN 39
Incense wrapped in leaf (associating with people of integrity) It 76
Indra's pillar (arahant) Dhp 95
Inscription in rock or water (anger) AN 3:130
Insects falling into flame (ignorance) Ud 6.9
Iron ball aflame, eating or swallowing an: (restraint) Dhp 307, It 48, It 91; (sensuality) Dhp 371
Irrigator (self-control) Dhp 80, Dhp 145
Island (refuge in Dhamma) DN 16, DN 26, SN 22:43, SN 47:13, Dhp 25, Dhp 236, Dhp 238, Sn 5:10
Ivory carver or his assistant (supernormal powers) DN 2, DN 11

J

Jackal (the perils of fame) SN 17:8
Jail, person thrown in (kamma) AN 3:99
Jar: filled with water (right concentration) AN 5:28; filled with ghee or oil (virtue) SN 42:6, SN 55:21; made of clay (the body) Dhp 40

K

King: hearing a lute (not-self) SN 35:205; renouncing kingdom (solitude in the wilderness) Sn 1:3, Dhp 329; seeing no danger after victory (virtue) DN 2, DN 11:

L

Lake: deep and calm (wise people) Dhp 82; dried-up (virtue) Dhp 155; free of mud (arahant) Dhp 95; person stranded in the middle (clinging) Sn 5:10; spring-fed (jhāna) DN 2, DN 11, DN

Similes of the Buddha

12, MN 39, MN 119, AN 5:28; unruffled by wind (arahant) It 92:
Lamp: going out (detachment) SN 54:8; in a dark house (insight) Mil II.1:14; passing its flame to another (rebirth) Mil III.5:5; in the dark (stock exclamation of appreciation of the Dhamma)— see Putting upright what had been overturned
Leaf, yellowed (ageing) Dhp 235
Leaky boat (pain) Sn 4:1
Leaves: blown from a tree (unwholesome states) Th 17:2; handful of (Dhamma) SN 56:31
Leper covered with sores (sensuality) MN 75
Lily/lotus crushed in hand (self-view) Dhp 285
Limb falling from tree (Nibbāna) SN 47:13
Linchpin in a moving cart (generosity and kindness) AN 4:32
Lion: in the wild (solitude in the wilderness) Sn 1:3, Sn 3:1; unstartled by sounds (wise person) Sn 1:3, Sn 1:12
Line drawn on water (brevity of life) AN 7:70
Loan, man taking out a (hindrances) DN 2, DN 11, DN 12, MN 39
Log in a stream (path of practice) SN 35:200: See also Stream.
Lost caravan leader (virtue) Sn IV.13
Lotus: crushed in the hand (self-view) Dhp 285; pond (jhāna) DN 2, DN 11, DN 12, MN 39, MN 119, AN 5:28; pond (the world) MN 26; rising above the water (Tathāgata) AN 10:81; scent of (self-view) SN 22:89; unsmeared by water (solitude in the wilderness) Sn 1:3, Sn 1:12; unsmeared by water (sensuality) Sn 4:9: See also Flower, Water on a lotus.
Lute, disassembled (not-self) SN 35:205

M

Magic show (the body) Thī 14
Magician (consciousness) SN 22:95
Man: burning different kinds of wood (persistence and exertion) MN 90; carrying burning grass torch (sensuality) MN 54; pursuing a woman (unworthy teacher) DN 12; repaid by king (feeling) Mil II.3:9; returning home after long absence (kamma) Dhp 219; seeking heartwood (seeking the Buddha) MN 18, MN 138; seeking heartwood (appropriate attention) SN 22:95; seeking heartwood (not-self) SN 35:193; with borrowed goods (sensuality) MN 54;

Index of Similes in the Suttas

Man & woman in love (desire)": MN 101
Meat thrown into a fire (brevity of life) AN 7:70
Merchant with caravan (avoiding evil) Dhp 123
Middle of the sea (stillness of mind) Sn 4:14
Milk: (evil deed) Dhp 71; from a cow (self-view) DN 9; from a cow's horn (wrong view) MN 126: See also Cow.
Mirage: (the body) Dhp 46, Thī 14; (perception) SN 22:95
Mire, person stuck in the (ignorance) MN 8
Mirror of the Dhamma (stream-entry) DN 16
Money (uposatha observance) AN 10:46
Monkey: caught in tar trap (mindfulness) SN 47:7; in forest (heedlessness) Dhp 334; swinging from branch to branch (untrained in Dhamma; inconstancy of mind) SN 12:61, Sn 4:4
Moon: (arahant) Dhp 413; (good will) It 27 (a), (b); (heedfulness) AN 10:15; (jhāna) Dhp 387; full (arahant) Thī 1:3; set free from a cloud (heedfulness, skilfulness) Dhp 172, Dhp 382, It 74; waning (unvirtuous person) DN 31, SN 5:10; waxing (virtuous person) DN 31;
Morning star (good will) It 27
Mother risking life for child (good will) Sn 1:8
Mountain: of gold (sensuality) SN 4:20; of solid rock (arahant) Ud 3.4, Th 14:1 of solid rock (imperturbability) AN 6:55; of solid rock (restraint) Dhp 7;
Mountains crushing in from all directions (brevity of life) SN 3:25
Mules, tamed (self-tamed person) Dhp 322
Muñja grass (resolve and determination) Sn 3:2
Mural painted on wall (the body) Thī 14
Murderer with sword: (disenchantment) AN 6:103; (heedfulness) AN 7:46
Mustard seed: (passion) Dhp 407; (sensuality) Dhp 401: (Note: the famous parable in which the Buddha instructs a grieving Kisā Gotamī to fetch a mustard seed from the first household she can find that has never known death is found in the Commentaries to Thī 10:1 (Thī-a X.1) and Dhp 114.)

N

Noise from a soft cat-skin bag (speech) MN 21

O

Ocean: an abode for mighty creatures (Dhamma-vinaya) Ud 5.5; crossing over the (arahant) SN 35:187, It 69; slope of ~ floor (progress of Dhamma practice) Ud 5.5; greatness of (stream-entry) SN 13:8; intolerance to dead bodies (unvirtuous person) Ud 5.5; many treasures of (37 wings to awakening) Ud 5.5; middle of ~ is calm (stillness of mind) Sn 4:14; polluted by a pot of poison (abuse towards the Tathāgata) It 89; salty taste of (release) Ud 5.5; stability of (restraint of the Vinaya) Ud 5.5; steady level of (Nibbāna) Ud 5.5: See also Flood.
Oil from gravel (wrong view) MN 126
Oil lamp: depends on wick and fuel (feeling) SN 36:7; flickering of (six senses) MN 146
Ornament of gold (arahant) AN 4:28
Ox: (suffering) Dhp 1; (person who doesn't listen) Dhp 152; eating corn (sensuality) SN 35:205; joined by a single yoke (sense-bases and their objects) SN 35:191

P

Painting of a woman or man: (not-self) SN 22:100; (nutriment) SN 12:64
Palm leaf dropping away (aversion): It 88
Palm tree: with top cut off (awakening) MN 105; uprooted (awakening) MN 49, SN 22:3, SN 41:7, SN 44:1:
Pastures (mindfulness) MN 33, AN 11:18
Path, man showing the (Tathāgata) SN 22:84
Peacock (jhāna) Sn 1:12
Peg in drum (listening to Dhamma) SN 20:7
Person looking down from a rocky crag (wise person) It 38
Person reflecting on another (higher knowledges) AN 5:28
Person riding a small wooden plank in the great ocean (laziness) It 78
Pillar at a bathing ford (wise person) Sn 1:12
Pit of embers: (intellectual intention) SN 12:63; (sensuality) MN 54, Thī 14
Plough (discernment) Sn 1:4: See also Yokes.
Poison (evil deeds) Dhp 123
Poison, man drinking: (restraint) MN 105; (volition) Mil II.3:11

Polished shell (life as a bhikkhu) DN 2, DN 11, DN 12, MN 36, MN 125, Ud 5.6
Pond (integrity): delightful, SN 3:19; haunted, SN 3:19
Pool of water: clear or muddy (mind) AN 1:45-46; in a mountain glen (arahant) DN 2, DN 11, DN 12, MN 39
Poor person: (fetters) MN 66; (speech) AN 10:24
Pot: flattened metal (Nibbāna) Dhp 134; of pickled greens (passion) Thī 1:1; smashed by stone (delusion) Sn 3:2
Potter or potter's apprentice (supernormal powers) DN 2, DN 11, DN 12
Potter's clay vessels (inevitability of death) Sn 3:8
Princes of wattle-and-daub towns (heedfulness) AN 10:15
Prison, man released from (hindrances) DN 2, DN 11, DN 12, MN 39
Propagation of plants (aggregates) SN 22:54

Q

Quail snared by a rotten creeper (attachments) MN 66

R

Rabbit caught in snare (fetters) Dhp 342
Raft (eightfold path): MN 22, SN 35:197, Sn 1:2
Rafters of house: (defilements) Dhp 153; (heedfulness) AN 10:15
Rag, saving the good part of a (subduing hatred) AN 5:162
Rain: (austerity) Sn 1:4; entering hut (passion) Dhp 13; from a cloud (generosity) It 75; from a thunderhead (discernment) AN 4:102; sent by devas (brevity of life) AN 7:70; stilling a cloud of dust (silencing one's thoughts) It 87, Th 15:1
Rams butting heads (contact) Mil II.3:8
Reeds or rushes: destroyed by their own fruit (defilements) SN 3:23; drawn from their sheaths (supernormal powers) DN 2, DN 11, DN 12; matted (craving) AN 4:199:
Reflection of one's face in mirror (mind-reading) DN 2, DN 11 DN 12; ("I am" with possessiveness) SN 22:83
Reservoir with four inlets and outlets (virtuous conduct) AN 8:54
Rhinoceros horn (solitude in the wilderness) Sn 1:3
Rich person (speech) AN 10:24
Riddle tree (purity of vision) SN 35:204

Ridge-pole of house (ignorance) Dhp 153
River: (craving) Dhp 251, It 109; flow down to the sea (heedfulness) AN 10:15; carrying everything with it (brevity of life) AN 7:70; swift current (hunger) Sn 4:15, (hindrances) AN 5:51; gives up its name upon reaching the sea (going-forth) Ud 5.5; person swept away by a (not-self) SN 22:93: See also Flood.
Road: (eightfold path) MN 33, AN 11:18; dangerous (evil deeds) Dhp 123
Rock: broken in two (sphere of nothingness) MN 105; in wind (wise person) Dhp 81
Roots, medicinal (craving) Dhp 337
Rubbish pile with lotus (Buddha) Dhp 58
Rust eating iron (evil deeds) Dhp 240

S

Sack full of grains (the body) DN 22, MN 119
Salt: in water (evil deed) AN 3:99; taste of ocean (Dhamma) Ud 5.5
Sand castles (aggregates) SN 23:2
Saw used by an attacking bandit (patient endurance) MN 21, MN 28
Seed: (conviction) Sn 1:4; bitter (wrong view) AN 10:104; capable of sprouting (kamma) AN 3:33; mustard ~ (sensuality) Dhp 401; mustard ~ (passion) Dhp 407; rotting in a field: SN 5:10; sweet: AN 10:104: See also Mustard seed.
Seedling not watered (change & alteration) SN 22:80:
Seizure (anger) Dhp 251
Servant murdering his master (not-self) SN 22:85
Shack, flammable (mindfulness/awareness) SN 35:202: See also House.
Shadow that never leaves (kamma) SN 3:4, SN 3:20, Dhp 1
Sheaf of barley thrashed repeatedly (foolish person) SN 35:207
Sheaves of reeds (dependent co-arising) SN 12:67
Ship left ashore over winter (fetters) SN 22:101
Shore: far (Nibbāna) SN 35:197; far (external sense media) SN 35:200; near (self-view) SN 35:197; near (internal sense media) SN 35:200: See also Stream.
Shot with arrow (craving) Sn 2:10, Sn 4:1; (present kamma) MN 101

Index of Similes in the Suttas

Shuttle (wise person) Sn 1:12
Silversmith (purifying the mind) Dhp 239, Sn 4:16
Sick man, taking pity on a (hatred) AN 5:162
Slavery, man freed from (hindrances) DN 2, DN 11 DN 12, MN 39
Snake: giving one's hand to a poisonous ~ (sense-restraint) MN 105; pulled from its slough (mind-made body) DN 2, DN 11; shedding its skin (defilements) Sn 1:1; water-snake bites man (wrong grasp of Dhamma) MN 22
Snapping one's fingers (equanimity) MN 152
Snare (delusion) Dhp 251
Sore, festering (lack of sense restraint) AN 3:25
Sound of drums (clairaudience) DN 2, DN 11, DN 12
Soup tasted by ladle (wise person and fool) Dhp 64
Space gathered under the term "house" (form) MN 28
Spear (good-will) SN 20:5
Spider snared in its own web (passion) Dhp 347
Spitting (equanimity) MN 152
Spring-fed lake: See Lake.
Staircase build at a crossroads (wrong view) DN 9
Stallion. See Horse.
Stick thrown up into the air (rebirth) SN 15:9
Stone ball thrown into wet clay (mindfulness) MN 119
Storekeeper (perception) Mil II.3:10
Storm cloud (evil) Th 14:1
Stream: sinking in the middle of (passion) SN 35:200; snared by a whirlpool (sensuality) SN 35:200; washed up on high ground of (conceit) SN 35:200; See also Shore.
String, ball of (craving) AN 4:199; thrown against a door (mindfulness) MN 119; unwinding to its end (end of suffering) DN 2
Strong man: nourished on royal food (foolish person) Sn 4:8; extending his arm (appearance/disappearance of devas) DN 20, SN 6:1, SN 6:2; extending his arm (equanimity) MN 152;
Suckling calf going to its mother (desire) Dhp 284, Ud 7.4: See also Cow.
Sun: dispelling the dark (absence of delusion) It 88; filling the sky (heedfulness) AN 10:15; filling the sky (awakening) Ud 1.3; speed of (death) SN 20:6

Similes of the Buddha

Sunlight: (merit) It 27; (virtue/concentration/discernment) It 59; not landing on ground (consciousness) SN 12:64
Surgeon: see Doctor
Swans: flying (enlightened ones) Dhp 175; taking off from a lake (mindful ones) Dhp 91:
Swift pair of messengers (*samatha-vipassanā*) SN 35:204
Sword drawn from its scabbard (mind-made body) DN 2, DN 11, DN 12

T

Tall building in central square (passing away and re-appearance of beings) DN 2, DN 11, DN 12, MN 39
Tangle: SN 7:6
Tangled skein (craving) AN 4:199
Tank filled with water (supernormal powers) AN 5:28
Tendon in fire (perception of the unattractive) AN 7:46
Thief shot with spears (consciousness) SN 12:63
Thoroughbred. See Horse.
Thundercloud: (conviction) SN 3:24; (discernment) AN 4:102
Tortoise evading a jackal (sense-restraint) SN 35:199
Track of ox (kamma) Dhp 1
Trades. See Crafts and Trades.
Trader watching over a fine steed (self-training) Dhp 380
Trail in space (arahant) Dhp 254
Travel: from village to village (recollection of past lives) DN 2, DN 11, DN 12, MN 39; in desolate country (hindrances) DN 2, DN 11, DN 12, MN 39
Treasure, doorways leading to (doors to the Deathless) MN 52, AN 11:17
Tree: changing (inconstancy) MN 146; gold (the body) Thī 14; growing back after having been cut (craving) Dhp 338; growing on mountain (craving) AN 3:48; haven for birds (conviction) AN 5:38; killed by vine (vice) Dhp 162, (three unskilful roots) AN 3:69; leaning to the east (virtue) SN 55:22; overcome by wind (restraint) Dhp 7; pliant (the mind) AN 1:47; shedding its leaves (solitude in the wilderness) Sn 1:3 (a, b); with delicious fruit (sensuality) MN 54; with roots cut (aggregates) Thī 5:8

Index of Similes in the Suttas

Tuning a stringed instrument (right effort) AN 6:55
Turban or head on fire, person with (aroused persistence) AN 6:20 (a, b), AN 10:51, Th 1:39
Turban tightening around one's head (pain) MN 36
Turner or turner's apprentice (mindfulness) DN 22
Turtle lanced by harpoon (the perils of fame) SN 17:3
Tusker: see Elephant.

U

Putting upright what had been overturned (stock exclamation of appreciation of the Dhamma) DN 2, DN 12, DN 16, DN 31, MN 4, MN 41, MN 57, MN 58, MN 72, MN 75, MN 107, MN 135, SN 3:1, SN 7:2, SN 7:6, SN 7:14, SN 7:17, SN 12:48, SN 35:127, SN 42:2, SN 42:3, SN 42:6, SN 42:8, SN 42:9, SN 51:15, AN 3:65, AN 3:72, AN 4:111, AN 4:184, AN 10:176, AN 10:177, Ud 5.3

V

Village: empty (internal sense media) SN 35:197; leaving one's (jhāna) MN 105
Vine: creeping (craving) Dhp 334; killing a tree (vice) Dhp 162
Vipers (elements) SN 35:197
Vomit, person eating his or her own (fetters) MN 105
Vulture forced to drop his prey (sensuality) MN 54

W

Warrior: (celibacy) AN 5:75, AN 5:76; (Buddha) Dhp 387; untrained (hindrances) SN 3:24, (worthy monk) AN 4:181
Waste-water pool (ignorance) AN 4:178
Water: container filled to brim (mindfulness) MN 119 (a, b); drawn from a pond (stream-entry) SN 13:2; drops in a hot pan (mindfulness) MN 66, SN 35:203, (equanimity) MN 152; filling a jar (evil) Dhp 121; person sinking in (factors of awakening) AN 7:15; ripples (preoccupations) Sn 4:15; rolling off a lotus leaf (equanimity) MN 152, (dukkha) Sn 4:6, Dhp 336, (sensuality) Dhp 401, (greed) It 88;
Weigher holding a scale (virtuous conduct) AN 8:54

Well in desert (Nibbāna) SN 12:68
Wet piece of wood (mindfulness) MN 119
Wheels: four (prosperity) AN 4:31; of cart (kamma) Dhp 1
Wild deer: (arahant) Ud 2.10, (sensuality) MN 26
Wind: blowing across the sky (feeling) SN 36:12; blowing cotton fluff (dukkha) Sn 3:8; blowing leaves from a tree (awakening) Th 17:2; coming out of bellows (exertion) MN 36; overcoming a tree (restraint) Dhp 7; unsnared by a net (solitude in the wilderness) Sn 1:3, (wise person) Sn 1:12
Winnowing (faults of others) Dhp 252
Woman meeting her father-in-law (urgency) MN 28
Wood scrap (the body) Dhp 41
Wounded man wandering in jungle (restraint) SN 35:206
Wounds, dressing (restraint) MN 33, AN 11:18

XYZ

Yellow leaf: (ageing) Dhp 235; turning green (imperturbable) MN 105
Yokes: (sense-bases and their objects) SN 35:191, (rarity of human birth) SN 56:48, (sensuality, becoming, etc.) AN 4:10, (discernment) Sn 1:4

ABBREVIATIONS

References are to the editions and translations of the Pali Text Society (PTS), except for the translations of the Dīgha, Majjhima and Saṃyutta Nikāya, where the reference system as given in the translations published by Wisdom Publications has been followed.

AN   Aṅguttara Nikāya (section/book and discourse number)
Bv   Buddhavaṃsa (PTS page number)
Cv   Cullavagga (PTS page number)
Dhp   Dhammapada (verse number)
DN   Dīgha Nikāya (discourse and paragraph number of *Long Discourses of the Buddha*))
It   Itivuttaka (section/book and discourse number)
J   Jātaka (Jātaka story number)
Mil   Milindapañhā (PTS page number)
MN   Majjhima Nikāya (discourse number and paragraph number of *Middle Length Discourses of the Buddha*))
Mv   Mahāvagga (PTS page number)
Nidd   Mahāniddesa (PTS page number)
Pāc   Pācittiya-pāḷi (Vinaya-piṭaka rule and rule section number)
Pār   Pārājika-pāḷi (Vinaya-piṭaka rule and rule section number)
Pv   Petavatthu (PTS page number)
Sn   Sutta Nipāta (verse number)
SN   Saṃyutta Nikāya (section/book and discourse number of *Connected Discourses of the Buddha*)
Th   Theragāthā (verse number)
Thī   Therīgāthā (verse number)
Ud   Udāna (chapter and discourse number)

SELECT BIBLIOGRAPHY

Long Discourses of the Buddha, Maurice Walshe, Boston, 1995.

Middle Length Discourses of the Buddha, Bhikkhu Ñāṇamoli and Bhikkhu Bodhi, Boston, 2005

Numerical Discourses of the Buddha, Bhikkhu Ñāṇaponika and Bhikkhu Bodhi, Walnut Creek, 1999.

The Life of the Buddha, Bhikkhu Ñāṇamoli, Kandy, 2006.

Udāna and Itivuttaka, J. D. Ireland, Kandy, 2007.

Related Interest

GREAT DISCIPLES OF THE BUDDHA
Their Lives, Their Works, Their Legacy
by Nyanaponika Thera and Hellmuth Hecker.

A masterly compilation of twenty-four life-stories of the closest and most eminent of the Buddha's personal disciples. The profiles, set against the colourful social and cultural background of ancient India, bring to life legendary names such as Sāriputta and Moggallāna, Ānanda and Mahākassapa, and many more, enabling us to participate in their great breakthroughs, achievements, and activities in spreading the Dharma.

BP 417, 411 pp.

PEACE IN THE BUDDHA'S DISCOURSES
A Compilation and Discussion by Dennis Candy
The Buddha's discourses as recorded in the Pali Canon contain many references to the value of *santi*, or peace, at both the personal and social levels. The most significant of these references have been carefully selected and brought together into this single volume to help those who are interested gain an understanding of the full range and depth of what the Buddha taught about this important subject.

BP 424S, 142 pp.

COLLECTED WHEEL PUBLICATIONS
Various Authors
Each volume contains fifteen retypeset numbers of the renowned Wheel Publication series, dealing with various aspects of the Buddha's Teaching such as Buddhist philosopy, psychology, ethics, history, etc., as well as translations from Buddhist scriptures. The authors are Ven. Nyanaponika, Francis Story, Ven. Bodhi, etc..

Prices according to latest catalogue (http://www.bps.lk)

The Buddhist Publication Society

The BPS is an approved charity dedicated to making known the Teaching of the Buddha, which has a vital message for all people.

Founded in 1958, the BPS has published a wide variety of books and booklets covering a great range of topics. Its publications include accurate annotated translations of the Buddha's discourses, standard reference works, as well as original contemporary expositions of Buddhist thought and practice. These works present Buddhism as it truly is—a dynamic force which has influenced receptive minds for the past 2500 years and is still as relevant today as it was when it first arose.

For more information about the BPS and our publications, please visit our website, or write an e-mail or letter to:

The Administrative Secretary
Buddhist Publication Society
P.O. Box 61
54 Sangharaja Mawatha
Kandy • Sri Lanka

E-mail: bps@sltnet.lk
web site: http://www.bps.lk

Tel: 0094 81 223 7283 • Fax: 0094 81 222 3679